The American Ezra Pound

Richard Avedon's portrait of Ezra Pound. Rutherford, New Jersey, June 30, 1958.

The American

Ezra
Pound

Wendy Stallard Flory

Yale University Press   New Haven and London

Published with the assistance of the Frederick W. Hilles Publication Fund of Yale University.

Acknowledgments for permission to publish material in this book appear after the index.

Designed by James J. Johnson and set in Kennerly Roman type. Printed in the United States of America by Murray Printing Co., Westford, Massachusetts.

Library of Congress Cataloging-in-Publication Data

Flory, Wendy Stallard.
  The American Ezra Pound / Wendy Stallard Flory.
    p. cm.
  Bibliography: p.
  Includes index.
  ISBN 0–300–04236–1 (alk. paper)
  1. Pound, Ezra, 1885–1972—Biography—Psychology. 2. Poets, American—20th century—Biography. I. Title.
PS3531.082Z6288 1989
811'.52—dc19
[B]   88–27528
                                       CIP

10 9 8 7 6 5 4 3 2 1

For

David Allan Flory
Quentin Michael Flory
Graham Stallard Flory

Contents

Acknowledgments

My greatest indebtedness is acknowledged in my dedication. For their willingness to share with me their personal knowledge of Pound, I would like to thank Olga Rudge, Mary de Rachewiltz, Omar Pound, James Laughlin, Marcella Spann Booth, Lotte Frumi, and Father Aloysius Vath. For their interest in and support of my work, and for their most helpful suggestions for improvement, I particularly thank A. Walton Litz, Louis Martz, Daniel Hoffman, Sacvan Bercovitch, and M. L. Rosenthal. I am continually grateful to my earliest mentor in Pound studies, Eric Mottram, who introduced me to the study of American literature in such a galvanizing way that it became my permanent vocation and who has surely done more to interest British university students in American literature than any other professor in Britain. James Generoso has provided me with a wealth of information on Social Credit from his own researches and from his interviews with Social Creditors, as has David Anderson from his interviews with several of Pound's Italian acquaintances of the 1930s.

I have learned a great deal from discussions with George Kearns, Emily Wallace, Richard Reid, Christine Froula, James Wilhelm, Terri Brint Joseph, Timothy Materer, Patricia Willis, John Walsh, Ian Bell, Walter Baumann, Marianne Korn, and Alan Filreis and, together with all other Poundians, owe a unique debt of gratitude to Carroll Terrell for creating and tirelessly maintaining so far-reaching a network of communication for the sharing of information on Pound's writings and for promoting discussion and exchange of ideas on Poundian issues.

For their intellectual provocations and for their support and friendship I thank my colleagues at the University of Pennsylvania: Robert Lucid, David DeLaura, Robert Regan, Peter Conn, Paul Fussell, Wendy Steiner, Vicki Mahaffey, Elaine Scarry, Marjorie Levinson, Edward Irving, Alice Kelley, John Richetti, Jerre Mangione, and Jacqueline Wade.

For their generous hospitality during my research for and writing of this book, I thank Mary de Rachewiltz of Castle Brunnenberg, Tirolo; Peter F. Vecchio of Hoboken and Long Beach Island, New Jersey; and Ian Morrison of San Jose, California.

Also, and most particularly, my thanks to Peter G. Vecchio.

My research was supported by a fellowship from the National Endowment for the Humanities, a travel grant from the American Council of Learned Societies, and a summer research fellowship and publication expenses grant from the Research Foundation of the University of Pennsylvania. My thanks to Donald Gallup, David Schoonover, Patricia Willis, and Steven Jones at the Beinecke Rare Book and Manuscript Library, Yale University; Neda Westlake and Daniel Traister of Special Collections, Van Pelt Library, University of Pennsylvania; John Logan of the Department of Rare Books and Special Collections of the Firestone Library of Princeton University; and Evelyn Greenberg and Barry Lipinski of the Alexander Library, Rutgers University.

It has been a pleasure to work with Ellen Graham, my editor, Alexander Metro, my copy editor, and with Mark Loewenstern, my much-appreciated research assistant.

Abbreviations

WORKS BY POUND

The Cantos   *The Cantos of Ezra Pound,* 10th printing. New York: New Directions, 1987. All quotations from *The Cantos* are from this volume and are identified by canto number/page number.

C   Ezra Pound, *Confucius: The Great Digest, The Unwobbling Pivot, The Analects* (New York: New Directions, 1969).

EPS   Ezra Pound, *Ezra Pound Speaking: Radio Speeches of World War II,* ed. Leonard W. Doob (Westport, Conn.: Greenwood Press, 1978).

GK   Ezra Pound, *Guide to Kulchur* (New York: New Directions, 1970).

I   Ezra Pound, *Indiscretions,* in *Pavannes and Divagations* (New York: New Directions, 1974).

P/L   *Pound/Lewis: The Letters of Ezra Pound and Wyndham Lewis,* ed. Timothy Materer (New York: New Directions, 1985.)

SP   Ezra Pound, *Selected Prose: 1909–1965* (New York: New Directions, 1973).

T   Ezra Pound, *Translations* (New York: New Directions, 1963).

UNPUBLISHED POUND MANUSCRIPTS.

EPA   Ezra Pound Archive, Beinecke Rare Book and Manuscript Library, Yale University.

The American Ezra Pound

Introduction

For many people the primary impediment to approaching Pound's poetry unequivocally is not the difficulty of the verse, significant a consideration as this is, but the confusion, mistrust, or anger that they feel about the attitudes and behavior of the poet. The purpose of this study is to remove as much confusion as possible by examining and describing in detail the poet's motives, goals, attitudes, and changing states of mind. While this is in itself a complicated undertaking, given the highly idiosyncratic nature of Pound's behavior and the complexity of his motivations, elucidation of the complexity is only part of the challenge confronting the critic who takes on this task. In many cases readers will not be able to be receptive to any such elucidation until a considerable number of preconceived notions and ready-made generalizations about Pound can be held in abeyance.

To address what is most problematic about the case of Pound is necessarily to address the problem of antisemitism and collaboration in the context of World War II, and it quickly becomes clear that the same tendencies to avoid discussion or to settle for impressionistic and unanalytical commentary which have characterized so much thinking in the case of Pound, have also marked to a surprising degree thinking about the whole subject of wartime collaboration. Since some consideration of collaboration in general is necessary to provide, not just a context, but also a theoretical and conceptual basis for discussion of Pound's case, I have provided in an Afterword a brief overview of the way in which, after a long postponement,

1

issues of collaborationist accountability are now increasingly being addressed and in a way that is very likely to make possible more open discussion of Pound's wartime behavior.

For the writer who wishes to replace the caricatured, widely held notion of Pound with a more accurate portrait, the first task is to attempt to overcome the general resistance to any reconsideration of his case. For many people the case of Ezra Pound is closed and should remain closed. They know that while the United States was at war with Italy, Pound made broadcasts over Rome Radio in which he condemned Roosevelt and Churchill, accused them of having started the war, and frequently fell into antisemitic rantings. They also know that, although indicted for treason, he did not stand trial, on the grounds that he was mentally incompetent to consult with counsel. On the face of it, it is hard to think of a case in which a reexamination would seem less likely to lead to any mitigation of our sense of the guilt of the accused than that of an individual who, when the United States was at war with Italy, attacked President Roosevelt over Italian radio and broadcast accusations of Jewish conspiracies at the time of the Holocaust. Outrage is clearly the most appropriate initial response to his wartime behavior. It may even seem that to go beyond outrage to further analysis of his case is unnecessary, if not unjustified. Yet much can be learned from such an analysis, and not only about Pound.

A study concerned, as this one is, with understanding Pound's states of mind and motives as fully as possible must necessarily make a rigorous examination of the three most vexed issues of his case, his apparent un- or antiAmerican position, his antisemitism, and the finding of insanity. Although all three issues are highly complex and closely interrelated, the matter of his alleged unAmericanness is the easiest to address. As the following study will show in detail, there is such overwhelming evidence of his thoroughgoing, determined, and consistent Americanness of aims and priorities as an artist and as a reformer that the evidence can largely be left to speak for itself.

Most problematic, even preemptively so, is the matter of Pound's antisemitism. His work cannot be addressed in any unqualified way until this issue is examined in full, and it is a far more troubling and complex matter to investigate than the allegations of treasonous intent. Further, it is likely to be far more of a consideration for those whose outrage at Pound makes it impossible to take him seriously as a poet. Since the antisemitism of the radio broadcasts has kept so many potential readers from engaging with Pound's poetry in an unequivocal way or even at all, a thorough investigation of the issue might seem something of a priority, yet until now this issue has not generally been approached in a spirit of open-minded inquiry, free from reliance upon predetermined conclusions and polemical agendas. In fact, the desire that Pound's poetry be more widely and more unequivocally read is not in itself sufficient incentive to undertake a study of this kind. One must also have a strong interest in the larger issues of the case: those issues of moral accountability raised by antisemitism in general, and by the role of the collaborator and the collaborator-by-default in all aspects of the Nazi ascendancy and most particularly the Holocaust.

The lack of systematic and discriminating analysis of these issues has meant that no real distinction is made in the minds of many people between Pound and the worst of the war criminals. Indicted at the same time as they, he continues to be thought of as essentially one of them. Yet the anomaly of this becomes clear from an examination of the evidence against him. The other members of this group stood accused, for the most part, of perpetrating undeniable crimes against humanity. They had been instrumental in brutalization and murder, often of great numbers of people. Pound in his broadcasts had expressed pernicious views, but there was no evidence, nor even any suggestion, that what he had said was responsible for any action of any kind having been taken against even one individual. He had been included in this first group of highly visible war criminals not, as in their case, because of the brutal nature and lethal consequences of his actions but because of the bizarrely public nature of what, upon close examination, turn out to be highly eccentric and idiosyncratic activities.

An adequate understanding of the issue of Pound's insanity and of the connection between this and his antisemitism is only possible if the completely independent, unilateral nature of his reformist program is taken into account. A comparison of Pound's case with that of a war criminal such as Adolf Eichmann reveals not only the appropriateness of drawing a clear distinction between their cases but also, as chapter 4 shows, can help us to refine our general understanding of distinct kinds of psychological strategies for evading the responsibility of conscious moral choice. This comparison makes it possible to identify the principle which determined that Pound's broadcasts would have no destructive effect upon anyone other than himself. Eichmann's case shows what lethal consequences result when the individual chooses to renounce personal responsibility for moral choice and voluntarily delegates that responsiblity to others; Pound's case, how individuals who will not delegate this responsibilty and persist in acting on their own authority can be safeguarded against complicity in criminal acts against others.

Impressionistic generalization is not the only reason for the distorted nature of commonly held notions of Pound. Often one stage of his career or writing from one period is focused upon disproportionately and taken as the key to understanding the whole. Even when several of the poet's different sides are considered, it is often with little attention to their interrelatedness so that only a piecemeal sense of the poet and his literary achievement results. For example, the difficulty of much of *The Cantos* often means that readers focus primarily on the poetry of his early, more "aesthetic" period. Although the aestheticism and flamboyant bohemianism of his London years was only a passing phase brought decisively to an end by the First World War, Pound is commonly thought of as an élitist aesthete who sold his American birthright out of a servile admiration of the past greatness of European culture.

Even when the tenacity of his post-World War I commitment to economic reform is conceded, a common recourse is to see this interest of his as separate from his poetic concerns; to think of Pound the brilliant Imagist, Pound the credit-crank, and Pound the hate-filled radio broadcaster as though they were essentially separate identities. We see a typical instance of this in a book reviewer's claim: "For professional Poundians, of course, everything the master produced—whether it was gibberish on economics, foul-mouthed ravings on politics or sound guidance on the aesthetics of poetry—is taken for pure gold."[1] Another main task of this study will be to show the coterminousness of Pound the poet, Pound the economic theorist, and Pound the radio broadcaster; to show how far his economic views were from "gibberish"; to explain the nature of his antisemitism and the reasons for his moral collapse in the 1930s; and to show how, throughout his career, his aims were highly moralistic and characteristically American.

In his 1909 essay "What I Feel about Walt Whitman," Pound shows how important it is to him not just to be a technically accomplished poet but also to have, and to be able to convey, a "message" and, more specifically, the essential "American message." He writes, "I see [Whitman] as America's poet. . . . The vital part of my message, taken from the sap and fibre of America, is the same as his. . . . It is a great thing . . . to know . . . 'His message is my message. We will see that men hear it.'" As if to provide a corrective to all those critics who have insisted—and continue to insist—on claiming that Pound the writer was, and wanted to be, an adoptive European, he writes of Whitman, in this same essay: "Personally, I might be very glad to conceal my relationship to my spiritual father and brag about my more congenial ancestry—Dante, Shakespeare, Theocritus, Villon, but the descent is a bit difficult to establish. And, to be frank, Whitman is to my fatherland . . . what Dante is to Italy. . . . Like Dante he wrote in the 'vulgar tongue,' in a new metric. The first great man to write in the language of his people" (*SP* 145–46).

To understand the real nature of Pound's poetry and the spirit in which he was writing, it is necessary to appreciate how thoroughly its genesis lies in nineteenth-century American ways of thinking and seeing, the hallmark of which is moral earnestness. For this reason, chapter 1 focuses upon the ways in which Pound was exposed to this heritage of strenuous moralism in the course of his childhood through the influence of his schooling, his parents' church activities and missionary work, and the example of his paternal grandfather's exploits as frontier entrepreneur and politician.

An indispensable guide to this tradition is Sacvan Bercovitch's *The American Jeremiad,* which shows how the jeremiad of the Puritans, which castigated so that it might hasten the inevitable progress of American society toward its predestined ideal state, established ways of thinking which far outlasted the influence of the Puritan church and decisively shaped middle-class thinking about American society. In the final chapter of his book, Bercovitch briefly considers the persistence of the jeremiac mind-set in Emerson, Thoreau, Melville, Hawthorne, and Whitman and, although he does not look for evidence of it in later writers, the soundness of his thesis is strikingly borne out by the remarkable extent to which the characteristics of the American jeremiah are to be found in Ezra Pound (and by the way in which his attitudes and aims are almost bound to be misunderstood unless they are seen to be in this tradition).

That the international perspective of the American expatriate writers of the early twentieth century need not be thought of as in any way "un-American" can be seen as not paradoxical, but completely understandable in the light of Bercovitch's observations about the universalist and timeless significance that "America" held for its millenarianist jeremiahs. "Of all symbols of identity," he writes, only *America* has united nationality and universality, civic and spiritual selfhood, secular and redemptive history, the country's past and paradise to be, in a single synthetic ideal."[2]

Pound's and Eliot's motives for their exhaustive research into what they consider to be the greatest achievements of European arts and letters are explained by Whitman's observation:

The real interest of this people of ours in the theology, history, poetry, politics and personal models of the past (the British islands, for instance, and indeed all the past), is not necessarily to mold ourselves or our literature upon them, but to attain fuller, more definite comparisons, warnings, and insight into ourselves, our own present, and our own far grander, different, future history, religion social customs, etc. We see that almost everything that has been written, sung, or stated, of old, with reference to humanity under the feudal and oriental institutes, religions and for other lands, needs to be rewritten, resung, restated, in terms consistent with the institution of these States, and to come in range and obedient uniformity with them.[3]

Pound always proceeds on the assumption that American literary culture will eventually become vital and self-confident enough to supersede that of Europe. Like a true American jeremiah, he constantly reminds his readers how far they have fallen from the standards set by the Founding Fathers, how many obstacles stand in the way of the writer who is determined to produce work that is both excellent and specifically American, and, consequently, how much dedication and energy will be necessary if the obstacles are to be overcome. We find this theme both early in his career when the prospects for success seemed good and also later, when all signs were discouraging.

The sweep of his thought that reaches easily from America to Confucian China, to Provence of the Troubadours, to Tuscany of the Grand Dukes Leopold and Ferdinand, or to the Italy of Mussolini is a property of the same vision that projects forward from an idealized American past, when the country's leaders were men of heroic and noble stature, to a future America that will not be cheapened by mercantilism. In Pound's thought, the examples of Jefferson and Adams play the same monitory role that the exemplary leaders of the New England churches play for their Puritan descendants, who are constantly exhorted by their ministers not to betray the ideals of the Founding Fathers. The millenarianist spirit of the Puritans, the "dream of a society in which the fact could be made one with the ideal" (*AJ*, 29), was the inescapable legacy of Emerson, Whitman, James, Eliot, Williams, and Pound, and to a surprising degree they seem to share the same sense of mission and to be instinctively guided by the same moral imperatives.

In a comment that is as revealing about his own sense of literary mission as it is about that of his older compatriot and fellow exile, Eliot writes of the romanticism of Henry James that it "issues . . . from the imperative insistence of an ideal which tormented him. He was possessed by the vision of an ideal society; he *saw* (not fancied) the relations between the members of such a society. And no one, in the end, has ever been more aware—or with more benignity, or less bitterness—of the disparity between possibility and fact."[4]

The most marked differences among the legatees of this vision of the ideal society spring from the different ways in which the temperaments of the various writers lead them to react to this inevitable "disparity between possibility and fact." Eliot, who praises James for his benignity and lack of bitterness in the face of this disparity, was himself able (as we see in *Four Quartets*) to overcome his youthful tendency to bitterness. But perhaps the greatest trial for the writer in the jeremiac tradition is the strain of finally having to face the inevitability of this disparity, and it is not always possible for writers to attain the equanimity of Eliot and James. Bercovitch writes of the difficulty that this posed for Emerson in words that could equally well be applied to Pound: "No one made larger claims for the individual than Emerson did, no one more virulently denounced corruption in America, and no one more passionately upheld the metaphysics of the American sys' tem. . . . America for him symbolized a state of soul, a mode of civic and moral identity, a progressive view of history, and a distinct but flexible concept of elect nationhood. Above all, 'America' wed the ideals of individualism, community, and continuing revolution" (*AJ*, 183). The way in which "Emerson's vision of the country tottered uncertainly between misanthropy and chauvinism, shrill condemnation and critical acclaim" is identified by Bercovitch as "part of a national ritual mode."

The great challenge for American jeremiahs is in the need to come to terms with the inevitable failure of the ideal civic and cultural order to materialize, and their idealism can leave them particularly vulnerable to disillusionment and even despair. As Bercovitch puts it, "The symbol of America magnified the culture into a cosmic totality: hence the euphoria of its adherents. But the same process of magnification carried a dangerous correlative: if American failed, then the cosmos itself—the laws of man, nature and history, the very basis of heroism, insights and hope—had failed as well" (*AJ*, 190). Some writers, in the face of disillusionment, are unable to maintain their optimism and lapse into what Bercovitch calls the "anti' jeremiad: the denunciation of all ideals, sacred and secular, on the grounds that America is a lie" (*AJ*, 191). Pound, even at his most embattled and in the face of his greatest discouragement, would never accept this as a valid position and was impatient with a writer like Henry Adams, whose views Bercovitch sees as archetypally anti-jeremiac. Throughout the Rome Radio broadcasts, Pound portrays Adams as ineffectual and insufficiently coura' geous, the "weak and pindling . . . Henry [who] was not the man that his elder brother Brooks was" (*EPS*, 93). Pound's problem, in fact, was the opposite of Henry Adams's. Where Adams was too ready to take the pessimistic view, to succumb to what Eliot, who knew about it from personal experience, called "the Boston doubt,"[5] Pound clung to his optimism in a way that was finally very self-destructive.

Pound's recourse is closer to that of the "colleagues and heirs" of John

Cotton and John Winthrop, who, when they "came to feel that history had betrayed them . . . clung all the more tenaciously to their dream." Bercovitch notes how, for the writer who refuses "to abandon the national covenant," it is often the case that "his identification with America as it ought to be impels [him] to withdraw from what is America" (*AJ*, 29). What Bercovitch says of Cotton Mather at work on the *Magnalia Christi Americana* applies at least in part to Pound at work on *Guide to Kulchur*. For both, "the more tenaciously they uphold the ideal, the more they seem to be talking to themselves (and for themselves)," and "the rhetoric that bent history, theology, and sociology to that single [jeremiac] purpose—is ultimately forced back into the 'monument' of the individual mind and will'" (*AJ*, 86, 87, 89).

By the time he was making the radio broadcasts, Pound had withdrawn very far from his own present and into an alternate reality of his own making, but rather than pondering his dream in the privacy of his study, he was trying with great vehemence to din it into the ears of the world. The Puritan jeremiah knew that his audience was thoroughly familiar with the doctrine he was preaching and convinced of the validity of the Scriptures, which were the sum of his theory and the ground of his authority. Pound, however, could tell himself that his audience had failed to act upon his economic counsel, not because they were "stiffnecked," but because they did not yet fully understand his theories.

This was why he continued his propaganda for fiscal reform even after the war had begun and even after America entered the war. His sole aim was to dispel the ignorance about what he believed to be the eonomic causes of war, and this is why he kept up the frantic pace of his writing—of letters, articles, and tracts—and why he strove for the greatest possible public exposure through the radio broadcasts. He broadcast on Rome Radio but would willingly have broadcast over any microphone that he was given access to because he believed that what he was propounding were truths that would apply in any country of the world. He always reiterated his fundamental belief that the real enemy was ignorance. In a notebook which he had with him at the time of his admission to St. Elizabeths he had written: "Not United States the aggressor but ALL nations inveigled, against will of the people—this is—their people—by a process NOT understood even by most of the leaders—perhaps NONE of the chiefs understood it. No need to oppose evil, conscious evil inention, even of [Sir Anthony] Eden—but ignorance—abysmal ignorance."[6]

Pound's very imperfect grasp of his surrounding reality in the 1930s and 1940s was the consequence of his temperament as well as of his jeremiac sense of mission. He was particularly deficient in the introspective and reflective impulse that is a prerequisite for any discerning insight into those destructive forces in the psyche which are the source of social evil and injustice. His view of human nature was one-sided: he chose to concentrate on its positive, creative, and life-affirming side and to leave out of consideration, as far as possible, its darker side. His sense of evil was too generalized to be reliable and his preference was to be expansive and optimistic, to affirm the positive and, if this was not possible, to affirm the authenticity of what he felt and to count on the assimilation of discordant forces. His writings on religion, for example, show his impatience with religious practices which are anything other than wholly celebratory. Such temperamental tendencies are particularly likely to intensify those distortions of perception which are a common feature of jeremiac vision.

A writer in the jeremiac tradition is likely to be only imperfectly aware of "things as they are" for at least two reasons. For such a writer the norm is considered to be progress toward the ideal and away from the imperfect present. His preoccupation with the utopian future makes him selective about what he sees in the present and encourages him to concentrate unduly either on those shortcomings which seem most directly responsible for hindering reform or on positive developments which seem to be signs that there is some progress toward the ideal. In addition, the jeremiac writer will be tempted to close his eyes as far as possible to what is most discouraging in the present—to all those things which are evidence of how many obstacles lie in the way of reform. Often the most characteristic aspects of human behavior in the present will be among the most necessary to discount: the perennial tendency to subordinate larger questions of the good of society to concern for personal comfort and gain, the predictability of apathy, self-interest, greed, and shortsightedness. To pay too close attention to these is to run a serious risk of becoming discouraged. Even in those instances when special attention is paid to actions and attitudes which are destructive, there is the danger that they will be misrepresented if what is only the result of obtuseness is interpreted as deliberately obstructive. It is hard for the reformer to resist the temptation to portray those who are part of the current system as guilty of premediated sabotage when their only motive is lack of interest. We see this tendency in most social protest writers: in Pound's "Hell Cantos"[7] as in Ginsberg's *Howl* and, although it is rhetorically dramatic, it is so at the cost of misrepresenting what is usually a rather undramatic reality.

We see this tendency writ large in Pound's feelings about war and the prospect of war. Since the norm ought to be progress toward the ideal, even

the present with its delays and apathy is a falling away and a disappoint-
ment. From this perspective war is not just the tragedy of pointless
death—although it is certainly that—but a devastating reversal of the
whole process of aspiration toward the ideal, a flouting and discrediting of
the whole utopian enterprise. It represents a double tragedy—the tragedy of
the war itself with all its brutality and suffering, and the tragedy of the loss
of the vision with the depressing concomitant of this—the conclusion that
the perfectability of human society is a chimera.

The "one thing needful" for an efficient jeremiah or for an efficient
social protester of any kind is an understanding of the real nature of moral
corruption and of the way in which social abuses are the result of inevitable
weaknesses of human nature, particularly of pride, greed, and selfishness. It
was not that Pound was incapable of understanding this or even that he
resisted acknowledging it, but that, because of his temperament, he did not
turn his attention to it. He himself was unselfish and un-self-regarding to an
unusual degree and seems to have proceeded on the assumption—one which
he left unexamined—that most people were essentially like himself; that is,
more likely to be generous than selfish, to be kind and to believe the best of
others. Temperamentally inclined more to the intuitive than the reflective,
and to acting on impulse more than with deliberation, he must have felt
considerably confirmed in these tendencies by the surprising degree to which
his intuitive judgment in literary matters had proved reliable early in his
career. Yet to be an almost infallible judge of poetic effectiveness was no
guarantee of reliable judgment on political matters, and after the social
devastation of World War I, Pound believed that he had no alternative but
to make himself an expert on economic reform.

Whitman, who was like Pound in his preference for affirmation, also
had to adjust to the devastating spectacle of war and its disruption of
society, but by working directly with individual casualties of the war, he
could both feel that he was making a tangible contribution and see the war
not in general terms as a "national tragedy" but in intimate and specific
terms as the sum of such individual, personal tragedies as he was witnessing
at first hand. In Pound's case there was no counterpart to this opportunity
for direct participation in either of the world wars. In the Great War, he had
suffered a personal loss with the death of his friend, the young French
sculptor Henri Gaudier-Brzeska, but the war, so close in distance, was so far
from anything that had ever been a part of his own experience that it must
have seemed to be taking place in some alien and almost fabulous alternate
reality into which Gaudier simply disappeared. During World War II,
Pound wanted to see this alternate reality at first hand. When he learned of

the German discovery of the mass graves of Polish officers in the Katyń Forest and of the Polish government's request, on April 17, 1943, that the International Committee of the Red Cross send a team of investigators, he applied for a permit to accompany this commission as a neutral observer. He even considered trying to go there alone if his request were not approved. (As it happened, not only would his request be denied but the Soviet Union would prevent the investigation altogether.)

His impulse to go to Katyń was a positive one, and it is easy to imagine that the sight of a mass grave of murdered soldiers would have made war real to him in a way that it had never been before and would have anchored him in the Europe of 1943 as it really was, rather than allowing him to retreat further and further from reality into the drastically edited and theoretical and propaganda-distorted alternate version of a Europe in which Mussolini hated war and Hitler was primarily committed to social justice through sound economics. The corpses at Katyń might well have made the human capacity for evil more real to Pound and more to be reckoned with in his calculations of the prospects for success of his efforts at reform.

Hawthorne's meditation in "Earth's Holocaust" on the real source of social evil serves as a salutory warning to the over-optimistic social reformer with an insight that seems particularly prophetic of Pound's case:

How sad a truth, if true it were, that man's agelong endeavor for perfection had served only to render him the mockery of the evil principle, from the fatal circumstance of an error at the very root of the matter! The heart, the heart—there was the little yet boundless sphere wherein existed the original wrong of which the crime and misery of this outward world were merely types. Purify that inward sphere, and the many shapes of evil that haunt the outward, and which now seem almost our only realities, will turn to shadowy phantoms and vanish of their own accord; but if we go no deeper than the intellect, and strive, with merely that feeble instrument, to discern and rectify what is wrong, our whole accomplishment will be a dream."[8]

Pound's anticipated "just society" would, in fact, prove no more than a dream, and his private circumstances a nightmare.

Eliot, who devoted as much attention as Hawthorne to anatomizing the perverse and self-destructive drives of the human psyche, saw very clearly Pound's failure to concern himself with these, as he shows by his comments on Pound in *After Strange Gods*. To believe that "by tolerance, benevo-lence, inoffensiveness and a redistribution or increase of purchasing power, combined with a devotion on the part of an elite, to Art, the world will be good as anyone could require"[9] is to leave out of consideration what Eliot, writing in the Puritan tradition, follows Hawthorne in calling "Original Sin" and so essentially to do away with "the idea of intense moral struggle."

Since Pound chose not to consider the connection between social abuses and the general human predisposition toward pride, greed, and selfishness, his vision of social evil easily became a melodramatic one in which the participants had become—as Eliot had said would be the case with the characters delineated by writers who lacked a sense of "intense moral struggle"—"less and less real . . . more and more vaporous" (p. 42). Pound's villains, even when they have proper names, are not individuals but types and often caricatured types at that.

One might want to argue that in his "Hell Cantos" Pound had deliberately limited himself to presenting a vision of social evil and had no intention of offering any comprehensive presentation of evil in general, and yet the limitations of this vision of Hell come to seem in fact symptomatic of limitations in his vision of evil in general when we realize that he did not address elsewhere the considerations that he had passed over here. Eliot is justified in claiming that "Mr. Pound's Hell, for all its horrors, is a perfectly comfortable one for the modern mind to contemplate, and disturbing to no one's complacency: it is a Hell for the *other people,* the people we read about in the newspapers, not for oneself and one's friends" (43).

He is also right to be mistrustful of the validity of the insights into evil of the architect of this kind of a hell. A proper understanding of the problem of evil inevitably involves a recognition that one is personally implicated in this problem. It is not possible to understand evil without seeing that its roots lie in weaknesses of human nature that all people share. It is not possible to understand these weaknesses adequately without having studied their operation in one's own nature. A person as averse to introspection as Pound is likely to have a very inadequate insight into the complexities of human notivation and particularly into the deviousness and perversity of the operation of ulterior motives. The fact that he was not at all a devious person by nature only aggravated his tendency to be unaware of deviousness and deception in others. It also meant that he was not armed against the possibility of temptation to self-deception.

An American Childhood and the Ideal of Public Service

1

"This is my war all right, I have been in it for 20 years. My Grandad was in it before me."

(*EPS*, 120)

On January 24, 1946, in St. Elizabeths, for the benefit of the psychiatrist whose job it was to compile a "Family History" for patient #58,102, Pound spoke of the influence on him of his family background. He explained how the influences of two very strong and strongly contrasting American traditions came together in him. On his mother's side was the colonial family with its "respect for tradition" and on his father's, the pioneer family with "the most rugged kind of idealism." For the young Pound, the family avatars of the "pioneer spirit" and the "colonial spirit," respectively, were his father's father, Thaddeus Coleman Pound, and his mother's mother, Mary Parker Wadsworth Weston. In this family history he spoke most personally of "Ma Weston," who, through her mother, traced her ancestry back to Christopher Wadsworth. He came to America in the 1630s, as did his brother William, who was an ancestor of Captain Joseph Wadsworth, who saved the Connecticut Charter by hiding it in Charter Oak. Christopher's side of the family produced both Ezra Pound and Henry Wadsworth Longfellow. Pound described Ma Weston as "proud of the Wadsworth blood, and . . . responsible for maintaining the cultural heritage of the family." The psychiatrist reported:

She read Scott and Dickens to the patient, as a child, and continued to "pump romantic Colonial History" into him until the time of her death, [when Pound] was twelve years of age . . . . The death of this grandparent . . . was the patient's "first sorrow." Often this grandmother would write verse and prose for the patient, as a means of communication and education, but never felt she was

For further information about Pound's childhood and family history see Noel Stock's brief *Ezra Pound's Pennsylvania* (Toledo, Ohio: Friends of the University of Toledo Libraries, 1976), and J. J. Wilhelm's detailed *The American Roots of Ezra Pound* (New York and London: Garland, 1985).

producing literary monuments. As if, finding it difficult to convey the deep impressions left upon him by this indulgent grandmother, the patient initiated an elaborate discussion of American Colonial History, points out the significance of viewing his personality against such a backdrop, in order to get at the brass tacks of his upbringing.[1]

Such comments might encourage the suspicion that Pound's emphasis at this time on the quintessential Americanness of his roots and on his pride and interest in them were something of a put-up job in the hope of confounding those who wanted to label him a traitor. Yet it is easy to show that this is not so when we remember in what detail he had examined his family history in *Indiscretions,* written and first published in 1920.

Interestingly enough, Pound himself seems in the 1940s partly to have forgotten in just how much detail he had written about his relations, including Thaddeus, in *Indiscretions.* In a radio braodcast of May 9, 1942, for example, he said: "I . . . knew very little of [Thaddeus], till my dad come on along over [to Italy] and by chance brought a few scrap books" (*EPS,* 121), and he must have made the same point to the psychiatrist who was recording Pound's family history, since in it we read: "As a child, our patient saw very little of his grandfather, but learned a considerable amount about him many years later, in 1928, when the patient's father brought a scrapbook to Rapallo, Italy . . . . The patient noted that his grandfather's productions were concerned with political and economic problems and used a style of writing curiously similar to his own."

It is certainly not true that Pound "knew very little" of Thaddeus before 1928, as *Indiscretions* clearly shows, and what Pound describes in the 1940s as his discovery of his grandfather is in fact a rediscovery. After having read the news clippings in Homer's scrapbook—and in the light of his own situation in the 1940s—Pound sees the significance of Thaddeus from a new perspective, but neither his views at that time nor his comments in 1920 get at the full extent of the influence that his grandfather's example had on him. In *Indiscretions* Pound claimed to be interested in the details of his family history only for "their value as literary capital," saying, "My interest had suffered etiolation . . . . that is, to the extent that one had no intention of allowing these things to obtrude upon one's own future action."[2]

Although, as he writes *Indiscretions,* Pound claims to be seeing his family history as no more than "literary capital," the very fact that he has chosen to write about his material shows that it is of more than incidental interest to him. His decision, made later that year, to live in France rather than England shows that in deciding to write *Indiscretions,* he was in fact returning to his roots to reorient himself and to cast off the mask of the very persona behind which he had chosen to write the work.

The whole of *Indiscretions* is written in an arch manner appropriate to the persona of the aesthete he had chosen for his public appearances during his London years. He had, of course, been as activist in literary matters as his grandfather had been in politics and strenuously earnest on both economic and poetic matters (as he was always to be), but he needed some protective camouflage that would allow him to move around unscathed under the rather supercilious eye of Wyndham Lewis. A condescending but good-natured facetiousness had proved quite serviceable. But a strong moral earnestness was in the blood and, even as he was writing *Indiscretions,* the social activist was feeling increasingly constricted by the persona of the aesthete and the hedonist—as *Hugh Selwyn Mauberley* clearly shows.

When he writes: "It is one thing to feel that one could write the whole social history of the United States from one's family annals, and vastly another to embark upon any such Balzacian and voluminous endeavour" (*I*, 6), it is clear that, even though he chooses not to undertake the endeavor, he believes that it would be possible to do so. If the family history seemed less than absorbing in 1920, this was a reaction to an earlier period of considerable interest and influence, as he himself obliquely concludes:

Perhaps it may be held that the actions of one's ancestors, especially if recited to one in childhood, tend to influence one's character and materially to exhaust one's interest in a given subject or subjects. Given, then, that there may have been a certain intellectual interest in stealing charters pro bono (very romantically) publico; . . . or in timber, horse-fodder, mines, railways, ranching, agriculture, I might reasonably say that I had received personal and confidential reports on these matters at a very early age and that my interest had suffered etiolation.

He even modifies "etiolated" with "that is, to the extent that one had no intention of allowing these things to obtrude upon one's own future action" (*I*, 7). All the "matters" mentioned above—except for stealing charters— refer to the many and varied enterprises of Thaddeus and point to what must have been the main impression that the accounts of his grandfather's undertaking must have made upon Pound as a child.

Everything that Thaddeus did suggested action, energy, enterprise, and openness to and enthusiasm for new interests and ideas. In contrast, Pound's mother's side of the family seemed more sedentary and retrospec-tive, more concerned with preserving the legacy of the Wadsworth dignity than with ambitions for the future. Ma Weston, for example, "wanted [Isabel] to pair with someone who was prepared to live up to" the

Wadsworth "formalities." As Pound notes, "Such also is the snobbery . . . of the race, that all of us naturally cling to the greatest luxury we have known. . . . [Isabel] had seen the [Weston] star at its zenith, with the Nyack place and her uncle's intention to be a country gentleman and a patron of the fine arts; she can't have liked the collapse" (*I, 27*). Although Isabel was prepared to make an exception in Homer's case, Ma Weston "had 'other ideas about' Isabel," and a young man from Wisconsin whose overcoat "was neither of a cut nor of a timbre and colour combination that was then being, or had, so far as research can discover, ever been worn in New York" (*I, 21*), was not among them.

Isabel did, of course, marry Homer anyway but kept her fair share of grand airs. She was very concerned with appearances and cultivated formality of dress and manner. H. D. remembered her as "a beautiful woman, well-bred, somewhat affected in manner," adding, "One was inclined to be embarrassed and baffled by her little witticisms, her epigrams, as one so often was by Ezra's."[3] In her autobiographical novel *Hermione,* H. D. describes the mother of George Lowndes, her Ezra Pound character, as being "rather like a figure in a shop window, the sort of distinction you get from a wax figure wearing just the right clothes."[4] Pound called his mother "the Presbyterian Peacock."

In fact, the Weston reservations about the Pounds—particularly about Thaddeus—come through quite strongly in *Indiscretions* and markedly color Pound's presentation of his grandfather. Thaddeus's achievements are minimized by the vagueness of Pound's description of them and, although the offhand commentary is partly determined by the persona Pound has assumed for the purpose of writing this memoir, it is also clear that, at this stage, he is not aware of any particular similarity between his own sense of mission and the spirit in which his grandfather undertook his ambitious projects. Pound is both vague and misleading about Thaddeus's Union Lumber Company when he writes that his grandfather's lumbering amounted to having "a store from which he ministered to the material needs of Scandinavians employed by him to thin out the virgin forests of Wisconsin." He is similarly vague about Thaddeus's railroad building when he limits himself to the observation that his grandfather "undoubtedly fostered the advance of civilisation, had his name in large brass letters on the front of a locomotive; was probably president of the Wisconsin railway or some such corporation" (*I, 13*).

The fact that some of Thaddeus's visionary schemes proved themselves in later years to have been well-conceived is strongly tempered by the awareness that these same schemes proved ultimately to be of little

financial benefit either to him or to Homer, a point that we can imagine
Isabel emphasizing whenever Thaddeus was discussed in her house.

Entering Congress a "rich man," he "left it a poor one." . . . He left some
permanent work in plans for irrigation of the Western desert, made effective a
score of years after his agitation. He had opposed "nepotism" with the one
palpable result of not having pushed [Homer] into a soft Washington job. He
owned in latter 'eighties a few silver mines in "The Rockies" which were
"jumped," and fell into a litigation which was finally decided in his favour too
late for the decision to be of any use whatsoever. He owned still a farm, but the
fad for clipping the horns of milk-cows exercized maleficent influence upon both
the farm and the milk-route. He retained . . . a spring of the purest water
known to man [and] . . . the ability to regard possiblities rather than facts
which had served him in seeing a wilderness irrigated, still assisting him, he
continued to see "millions in it." [I, 14–15]

Pound tells how Thaddeus's successes at farming were compromised by his
failure to make sufficient allowance for the effect of the extreme cold
temperatures on his crop or for the fact that milk cows might not be better
for having their horns clipped, and we suspect the influence of Isabel's views
of the matter in:

It was perhaps natural . . . that [Homer] should be left to deal with sixty
sore-horned cows and a firm disinclination on the part of farm hands to milk or
to "monkey with" [cows] in that condition. And it was . . . natural that
[Thaddeus] should have landed [Homer] in said circumstances with no very
definite understanding as to what [Homer] should get out of it, beyond the use
of mansarded refuge . . . and some portion of the produce of the Chill Soil, and
of course the vast "possiblities," [I, 44]

In fact, Pound certainly knew in detail about the ambitiousness of
Thaddeus's enterprises and his success in getting things done. *Chippewa
County, Wisconsin: Past and Present,* in which Pound's "Legend of the
Chippewa Spring and Minnehaha, the Indian Maiden" appeared in 1914,
also contained a fifteen-page reminiscence by his grandfather which detailed,
among many other things, his considerble effectiveness in getting railroads
built.

Determined to bring rail service to Chippewa Falls, which at that time
was seventy-five miles from the nearest station, Thaddeus and Richard
Wilson spent the winter of 1862–63 in Madison lobbying for the charter
necessary to obtain a land grant for a railroad from Camp Douglas, via Eau
Claire, to Hudson. In 1870, with H. C. Putnam, Thaddeus began a
seven-year effort to link Chippewa Falls to the Camp Douglas–Hudson line
by laying a track to Eau Claire. Their first request to the country of
Chippewa for a subscription of $75,000 was bitterly opposed by livery men

and stage owners and was voted down, so Thaddeus organized many of the town's leading businessmen into the Chippewa Falls and Western Railway Company, with himself as president of the board. The city then passed a bond issue, but only $6,000 of the estimated total cost of $150,000 could be raised by cash subscriptions. Thaddeus borrowed the necessary money by issuing four-month promissory notes for a total of $25,000, payable to himself, depositing them with the First National Bank of Milwaukee. Having trouble both selling the bonds and finding rails for a reasonable price, Thaddeus eventually made contact with someone in Elmira, New York, with 1,000 tons of rails to sell, although he was obliged to borrow $15,000 from the seller to cover interim costs.

The day before the notes matured, the track was ready, and Thaddeus was given the city bonds, deposited them with the First National Bank, and settled all his debts. He interjects in his account: "Thus the first railroad was built to Chippewa Falls, with a cash subscription of only $6,000, supplemented by will and wit—inspired by an indomitable purpose to do a worthy and needful act, not for personal profit to the promoters, but for the public good. Can the reader name another enterprise more skillfully managed."[5] The eighty-year-old ex-politician is not averse to a little self-advertisement, yet his main point is highly relevant to our consideration of Pound's changing perception of his grandfather. All his railroad ventures were "not for personal profit . . . but for the public good," and while the lack of "personal profit" to the Pound family might well have been the emphasis of some of the family discussions of Thaddeus that Pound heard during his childhood and might have colored his feelings about his grandfather in 1920, after this date Pound was to be increasingly impressed by people who seemed to him to serve the public good in an unselfish way.

Thaddeus's final railroad project, completed in the summer of 1884, was on a large scale. Seeing the need for a direct east-west line for Wisconsin, he tried without success to persuade the president of the Wisconsin Central to build a line from Abbotsford west, through Chippewa Falls to Minneapolis–St. Paul. Discovering a blueprint in the president's office for a projected line through Eau Claire, which would bypass Chippewa Falls to the south, Thaddeus, determined to "circumvent any plans adverse to the interests of [his] city,"[6] took matters into his own hands, and conceived a plan for a railroad, not just between Abbotsford and St. Paul, but 275 miles across the whole state from Marinette on Green Bay to St. Paul. He contacted influential people in key towns along the route who met with him in Chippewa Falls to form the St. Paul, Eastern Grand Trunk Railway Company. Eventually the building of the line was divided up between Thaddeus's company, Wisconsin Central, and the Milwaukee, Lake Shore and Northern, and when the St. Paul Eastern ran out of money, Thaddeus sold it for enough to repay all the subscribers in full with a 10 percent profit.

While he was involved in railroad building, Thaddeus was working concurrently on several other major enterprises. With his brother Albert and Thomas L. Halbert he built a store—only the second to be built in Chippewa Falls—and then Pound and Halbert bought H. S. Allen's Lumber Company a year after it failed. They renamed it the Union Lumber Company and by 1870 it was taking down the Mississippi rafts of timber worth $40,000 apiece.[7] The operation was eventually ruined by an ice and log jam and was absorbed by the Chippewa Lumber and Boom Company.

"During the palmy days of the Union Lumber Co.," Pound and Halbert organized the First National Bank of Chippewa Falls, chartered on May 1, 1873, with Halbert as president and Thaddeus and Albert as directors. Originally their only competitor was Seymour's Bank, which was to fold in the panic of 1893. But on June 27, 1887, a group of shareholders met at the office of the Chippewa Lumber and Boom Company and by August the Lumberman's National Bank was chartered and open for business with Frederick Weyerhaeuser on its board of directors. Pound felt particularly bitter toward Weyerhaeuser, both because he credited him with ruining Thaddeus's lumber company and because of his dishonesty, as we see in Canto 22, where he writes of how his grandfather, "sweat blood / to put through that railway" while Weyerhaeuser, having permission to keep the timber he cut in the process of laying track for his railroad, "cut a road through the forest, / two miles wide, an' perfectly legal" (22/101).

Another of Thaddeus's enterprises was the Chippewa Spring Company, which provided bottled spring water for the cities of Chicago, Superior, and Minneapolis. The water was shipped in tank cars, some of which the company owned and some of which Thaddeus persuaded the Omaha Railroad Company and the Wisconsin Central to buy for him. Eventually the cartage charges proved to be too high for the business to be profitable.

Yet Thaddeus was never at a loss for new projects. At the age of eighty, just one year before his death, he was still advocating schemes for the prosperity and growth of Chippewa Falls, even though by then his home was in Chicago. The compilers of *Chippewa County Wisconsin: Past and Present* interviewed this "pioneer community builder," as they called him, when he visited the town in 1913, and he began his lengthy reminiscence by emphasizing how beneficial it would be for the "growth, population and wealth of the city" for a health resort to be built there. He also urged the importance of regulating the flow of the Chippewa River, both for flood control and to generate hydroelectric power. Although he anticipated skepticism about the suggestion, he stressed the importance of making the Chippewa navigable: "The completion of the Panama canal will emphasize the demand for the improvement of the Mississippi river and tributaries." The navigable rivers of America must be preserved as "highways of commerce, free for all the people of our nation" (413). In 1882, Thaddeus's last year in Congress, he had managed to have $100,000 of federal funds set aside for his plan to construct a reservoir system for the headwaters of the Chippewa for improved flood control and navigation, but his plans for the Chippewa were "defeated by the log and lumber interests"—presumably Weyerhaeuser again.

Having served as assemblyman for Wisconsin in 1864, 1866, 1867, and 1869—and as speaker in this last year—Thaddeus was appointed lieutenant governor in 1870 and 1871, becoming acting governor and being frequently referred to subsequently as Governor Pound. From 1876 to 1882 he was congressman for the Ninth District and showed himself particularly con-cerned with the responsible development of the country's natural resources. He was a strong contender for the post of secretary of the interior under Garfield in 1880 but was blackballed by Blaine, who, Pound claims, "declined 'to sit in the same cabinet with a man who was not living with his wife' " (I, 14). (To be more accurate he might have said "who was living with a woman other than his wife.") Thaddeus was to have his revenge in 1884, when he helped to defeat Blaine by playing the mugwump in transferring his support to the Democratic candidate Cleveland.

As chairman of the Committee on Public Lands in the Forty-seventh Congress, Thaddeus was able to introduce legislation for the improvement of harbors and waterways and in the Forty-fifth Congress was member of the Committee on Indian Affairs and author of the Indian Training School Act. Pound recalls his grandfather's view on this issue when, in Canto 22, he writes:

And he said one thing: As it costs,
As in any indian war it costs the government
20,000 dollars per head
To kill off the red warriors, it might be more humane
And even cheaper, to educate.   [22/101]

Thaddeus insisted that "the Indian, no less than any other person, should be amenable to and enjoy the protection of law, local and general, affecting the liberty, moral restraint and pursuit of happiness, vouchsafed to the citizen or other inhabitant."[8]

In his "Reminiscence," Thaddeus recalls how, when he first came to Chippewa Falls, the Chippewa Indians frequently came to the town to trade their furs, rice, and "fancy handiwork," and he shows his respect for the Indian when he adds, "It must also be confessed that some of the fascinating dark maidens were won to wedlock by the lonely white man, the evidence of which relation may yet be noted in our present generation, but not to the discredit of the dark race." Referring to the appointment of Ira Isham as constable, he comments that Isham "is yet alive, having reared a large family, not less respectable for being of mixed blood" and goes on to relate an instance of Isham's bravery in dealing with a drunken murderer.[9]

Thaddeus's humane attitude toward Indians is due, in part, to his direct knowledge of them but is perhaps reinforced by the strong Quaker tradition of his family. The Pounds had been Quakers for three generations before him. In *Annals of Our Colonial Ancestors And Their Descendants . . . ,* Ambrose Shotwell notes that Thaddeus's uncle Daniel Pound was an "esteemed minister of the Society of Friends" and describes Thaddeus's grandfather Elijah as "a conspicuous minister" among the Quakers. Elijah's father (also Elijah) of Piscataway, New Jersey, seems to have been the first of the Pounds to become a Quaker when, on June 16, 1757, he was accepted as a member of the Monthly Meeting of Friends for Woodbridge, Rahway and Plainfield, New Jersey. We also learn that he "was a member of the committee appointed by the Friends at Rahway in 1778 for the relief of sufferers under the laws against non-combattants, but being compelled to affirm his allegiance to the Continental Congress to avoid being thrown into prison, was therefore allowed to resign from the committee"[10] (6–8).

In the days of blatant political graft and corruption, of politicians like Blaine himself, who, while he was speaker, made $100,000 by acting as broker for the bonds of the Little Rock and Fort Smith Railroad, Thaddeus showed himself to be an honest and conscientious public servant, a fact to which Pound attaches increasing importance by the 1940s. The more strongly he is able to convince himself that his grandfather was working for the same economic goals as he himself, the more he is angered by a sense of waste at the thought of Thaddeus's sabotaged political career. Blaine was able to prevent Thaddeus from becoming secretary of the interior solely on an issue of private morality whereas, for Pound, Blaine himself represented the worst kind of abuse of public trust and indifference to the welfare of the nation, an immorality of infinitely more serious consequences than a decision to live with someone other than one's wife.

Pound had always criticized Protestantism for its "failure to distinguish between public and private affairs"—for willfully choosing to limit its discussions of morality to sexual morality. By 1937, in *Guide to Kulchur,* he was suggesting that matters of private morality were used as red herrings to turn attention away from gross immorality in the public sphere—that "pseudo fusses about the private lives of others" were not just "distinct from" but actually "an avoidance of trying to ameliorate public affairs, such as monetary abuses"[11] (*GK,* 194).

In 1943, prompted by a recent Democrat-sponsored commemoration of the fiftieth anniversary of Blaine's death, he devoted a whole radio broadcast to his grandfather's archenemy, taking as his text an open letter from Thaddeus to General E. Bryant which was run in many newspapers, including the *New York Evening Post* and the *Philadelphia Times*. In this letter, Thaddeus described Blaine as the embodiment of "most in American politics that is menacing to public morals and INTEGRITY in government" (*EPS,* 277), and as "a speculator, enjoying a fortune too great to have been acquired by honest industry . . . [who] sympathizes with and profits [from] speculative stock jobbing and gambling methods of acquiring wealth, methods which have wrought ruin, disgrace and business disasters beyond computation . . . unsettled values, placed the fruits of honest toil in the power of Goulds and Armours, to bear down and bull up in the markets, as whim or interest may dictate" (*EPS,* 278). Yet what finally seems to trouble Pound most is the lack of outrage, not only on the part of Blaine's Republican colleagues but on the part of the majority of the public, at such blatantly evident corruption: "The worst of it was that the public knew all about his slippery doings. He declared during the campaign that his life was an open book . . . . For the first time in our history a major political party nominated as its candidate a man who was known to be dishonest" (*EPS,* 279). And we sense here Pound's mounting frustration at what seems to him a comparable refusal, on the part of his contemporaries, to react with anger to even more blatant and more dangerous subversion of the public welfare.

Whereas the extent and nature of his grandfather's influence on him were, to a large extent, chosen by Pound himself, the influence of his parents was necessarily far more immediate and beyond his conscious control. In his comments to the doctor who was writing up Pound's family history, he emphasized how much closer he always felt to his father than to his mother: "My harmony with my father was unusual. I was my father's son in opposition to my mother. Most sons fight their fathers all their lives. My own case is farthest removed from the Oedipus complex" (file 1381c). At his first mention of his father in *Indiscretions,* Pound chooses for him the epithet "the naivest man who ever possessed sound sense" (8); yet it is unlikely that he was ever aware of the marked degree to which he shared this characteristic which seems to him so pronounced in his father and which will show itself in Pound most strongly in his ill-fated reliance on the good faith of Mussolini.

Although Pound clearly thought of himself as the opposite of naive, his naiveté differed from his father's only quantitatively and not qualitatively. Homer, with a good deal less education and sophistication than his son, was naive on a wider range of subjects; yet Pound, for all his sophistication in literary and artistic matters, had all the naiveté of a true, native-born and -bred American Jeremiah when the issue was reform and the perfectibility of society. Homer's naiveté seems, in addition, to have been thrown into relief by his comfortable un-self-consciousness—a quality that his son particularly drew attention to in *Indiscretions:* "Thad[d]eus thus bequeathed to his son, my father, the naive Euripides Weight [Homer Pound], a certain sophistication, a certain ability to stand unabashed in the face of the largest national luminaries, to pass the 'ropes,' etc., designed for restricting democratic ingress and demoralising the popular enthusiasm at processions" (15). We can imagine that Homer's oblivious insouciance was something of an embarrassment on such occasions to his adolescent son, and this is implied in Pound's allusions, later in *Indiscretions,* to Homer's visit to the Royal Mint in London with his "lanky whey-faced [son] of 16." Pound recalls the "lofty demeanour" of the official assigned to escort them on their rather irregular tour and how his manner seemed rather pointedly to indicate that "he was there through no fault of his own, or at least seemed to beg you (from an altitude) to consider that however suspicious his own presence there might be, it was nothing, oh! abysmally nothing, in comparison with the susceptibility [suspectibility?] of your own" (45–46).

It seems very likely that where Homer was strikingly un-self-conscious, Pound, as one would expect in a poet, was particularly sensitive to the impression that his father was creating. Perhaps to be the adolescent son of Mr. Homer Pound was to feel, albeit in a less extreme form, something of the embarrassment of being the son of Mr. John Dickens or Mr. John Joyce. And yet it was hard for Pound to set a distance between his father and himself because, unlike the pompous, improvident, and self-regarding fathers of Joyce and Dickens, Homer Pound was a paragon of kindliness. Pound seems to have decided early to disguise his self-consciousness with a mask of flamboyant arrogance, and it is likely that he took the cue for the formality of his manner from his mother's very studied and rather affected behavior. However, it was clearly his intention to set her values at defiance so that, where it was her intention to impress by overawing people with her rigorousness in observing the proprieties, it was his intention to impress by shocking people with the cavalier way in which he flouted the same proprieties. She had a local reputation for excessive "properness" and, naturally enough, as a child, finding her strictness rather oppressive, he probably found a variety of ways of registering his objection to her strict standards. One of these we see from a delightful reminiscence of a former schoolmate of his. When Carl Gatter, inverviewing Anna Corte, asked her what she remembered about Ezra Pound from the time when they were both nine together in Florence Ridpath's class at the Temporary Wyncote Public School, she said: "Well, I know it sounds funny, but he was always belching. This was because of his mother. He was a good boy. Of course we called him Ray."[11]

He certainly seems to have had a closer and warmer relationship with his father than with his mother and where in the St. Elizabeths family history he stresses this closeness, he speaks rather disparagingly of his mother: "She doesn't know a good book from a bad one and likes my early work better than my later. Perhaps this is a maternal attitude, for she has always wanted to keep me four years old. She doesn't particularly enjoy my presence, but came to Rapallo, Italy, in 1928, where she now lives with my wife."

Both his mother and his father were very actively involved in church work in a way that strongly reinforced the more general social influence of the American jeremiac legacy. Through his close involvement with this work, the influence of the jeremiac, reformist set of assumptions was so thoroughly internalized that it became an integral part of his view of the world. Its influence was so pervasive and fundamental that it was established at an unconscious level below that of his conscious schemes, resolves, and manifestos. Because this was so, we cannot take his rejection of certain outward forms of Protestant Christianity at face value. Unless we recognize how ineradicable the fundamentals of the jeremiac mind-set were for Pound, we might assume that it is Protestantism, or even Christianity, that he is rejecting when, in fact, he is only dissociating himself from certain attitudes common to members of the Protestant establishment of the small-town America of his youth—attitudes such as sanctimoniousness, parochialism, prudery, and particularly the kind of complacency that averts its attention from the task of social reform. It is also possible that some of his earlier attacks on Protestantism are an oblique criticism of his mother's rather rigid worship of the proprieties, and perhaps it is no coincidence that he chooses to make the bankers of Canto 12 (the "usurers in Excelsis" whom John

Quinn treats to the "dirty story" of the Honest Sailor) "ranked Pres-byterians"—members of his mother's church.

Moral earnestness was a strong component of his regular life from an early age. We find him at the age of five writing to Santa Claus to ask for a copy of Charles Kingsley's *The Water Babies* and in another letter to Santa for *Uncle Tom's Cabin,* although much later, when he was nineteen—presumably in response to some comment his mother must have made about Kingsley's book—he hastened to point out that he "did not like Water Babies."[12] Yet as proper and conservatively suburban as his parents were, there was an expansiveness and energy to their religious activities which set them somewhat apart from their neighbors and which has some bearing on the issue of Pound's antisemitism.

Nineteenth-century, un-self-consciously racist attitudes were unques-tionably part of Pound's childhood, as we have seen; yet this kind of pro forma antisemitism did not necessarily imply an actively discriminatory attitude and this was especially the case with Homer and Isabel Pound, whose religious convictions were not just concepts to pay lip service to but injunctions to be acted on. When the Pounds moved to 166 Fernbrook Avenue in Wyncote, they became members of the Calvary Presbyterian Church, where Homer taught Sunday school, was president of the Young People's Society of Christian Endeavor, and, having been elected an elder of the church in 1894, was very active in parish affairs. Isabel was vice president of the Women's Union. Their minister, the Reverend Carlos Tracy Chester, wrote short stories and articles and between 1889 and 1906 helped to edit the *Booklover's Magazine, Book Monthly,* and the *Sunday School Times,* and in 1909 Pound dedicated *Exultations* to him.[13] But in 1903 Homer and Isabel began their very active involvement with missionary work among the Italian immigrants of the Philadelphia slums. In the summers they lived at 502 South Front Street and worked at the Italian Mission, later to become the First Italian Presbyterian Church. The minutes for the January 7, 1903, Sectional Meeting of the Calvary Presbyterian Church note that "Homer L. Pound, feeling impelled by a divine call to enter upon institutional work in the city of Philadelphia . . . has tendered his resignation,"[14] and by 1905 he was superintendent of the First Italian Presbyterian Church (at Tenth Street and Washington Avenue), which by now had two pastors and a very full program: "Four Preaching Services every week, Sunday-School and Pastor's Bible Class, Kindergarten and Primary School, Sewing Class, Music Class, Boy's Club, Mothers' Meeting, Children's Meeting, Girls' Knitting Class, Dispensary, House-to-House Visiting."[15]

Pound appreciated the value of his parents' "practical Christianity" and helped in the work on occasion, as we see in the second of a series of four articles published under the title "Through Alien Eyes" in the *New Age* of January and February 1913. In the course of describing the South Tenth Street mission, Pound writes:

Children came there to learn wood-carving and modelling, and to give plays on a stage in the basement. . . . These Italians are for the most part sturdy peasants who make a living by working on railroads and as masons . . . . They come to the "church" for relaxation, for amusement, it is a decorative feature in their lives . . . . On the opposite corner there is an institution maintained by the Jews. Here you would find children huddled together, learning every sort of trade—shoe-making, the various specialities of tailoring, etc . . . . This wise and provident people, receiving its emigrants from Russia, from the afflicted districts, takes measures to prepare them as swiftly as possible to make their way among new surroundings, to acquire—and they do acquire—and buy up land and become rich in due season . . . . I point out the Jewish system of training as the wise means devised by one section of the poor, one nation of our country, to gain advantage over the rest . . . . If any work is done "interdenominationally" the Jew overruns it and gradually pushes out the others . . . . Acquisitive, he wants "culture," or anything else that he can get, free; and he has the foresight which is more or less lacking among the simpler, more sensuous emigrants. It is obvious . . . that an intelligent "lower class" would by instinct wish to learn trades and industries rather than "book learning." And it is obvious that this is a wise instinct, and that a sincere Government would try to give them facilities for acquiring such knowledge . . . . My impression of the few missions I've seen [in London] is that they are the old sort that teach the children to sing psalms and to honour their landlord. [276]

The antisemitism in this passage clearly involves a passive voicing of prejudice without any particular personal animus and with a lack of self-consciousness which would be impossible today. He concedes the wisdom of the Jewish approach to the training of the young; yet it is evident that his sympathies lie with the less "calculating" Italian peasants, whose easy-going ways, he feels, put them at something of a disadvantage in the immigrants' struggle for economic security. Behind these comments may well lie a sense that the Italians are mainly at a disadvantage in having a much less well-organized support system at their disposal than the Jews have. The Association of Jewish Immigrants at 931 South Fourth Street was able, by 1885, one year after its founding, to provide shelter for 848 and, in that same year, processed 900 job applications. This is, of course, something of a reflection on the services offered by the Presbyterian mission, which, although well-intentioned, was by comparison rather ineffectual.

Pound told his psychiatrist in St. Elizabeths that he "read the Bible regularly up to the age of sixteen years [and] characteriz[ed] the period between twelve and sixteen as that of the 'earnest Christian' " (1381g). We find plenty of evidence of this earnestness in his early letters to his parents. When, for example, in 1904 he changes his mind about transferring to the University of Pennsylvania from Hamilton, he writes home: "I really think it best and I don't want to chuck up something worthwhile for a little pleasure and comfort. [T]he doing what you don't like is more beneficial than the plush lined epicureanism of an effete society. I think I'll be more a man at the end of it" (*EPA*, 7/28/1904).

On several occasions he writes to his mother to give his opinion of the Sunday sermons at Hamilton: "Prex preached finely this A.M. on doing things *now* (*EPA*, 2/12/1905). "Square Root gave a bully Spiel. Mentioned the fact that the people who hitch to stars need to see that the traces are in good condition. Also several other things of more exalted sentiment. He i[s] a fine Seer of the inside of things" (*EPA*, 2/28/1905). Also, " 'Davy Dav' preached this A.M. and talked some idealized horse sense which is rare" (*EPA*, 3/3/1905).

In a letter to his father he speaks out strongly against the bigotry and injustice of Protestant anti-Catholicism. He has been reading about Japanese missions—a foreshadowing of his later interest in Joseph de Mailla and Séraphine Couvreur—until he could no longer stand the author's misrepresentation of the missionary work of the Jesuits:

This fuss about catholic form and ritual makes me tired. Do you go to a child in the infant class and preach infinite God? No. You tell it bible stories and show it pictures. The catholic church came when all men were as children, & gave them drama & made them worship wonderfully, by music, by cathedral building, by copying books, hour by hour, & year by year, when others were fighting. And the men who now try to tear down its structure are little better than the rabble who broke the stained glass of the cathedrals a few centuries ago. [*EPA*, 2/12/1905]

One of his most interesting—and longest—letters of this period is written in response to his mother's satisfaction at hearing that he had been making a rhetorical analysis of Emerson's "Self-Reliance." It is such a good index to his attitude toward the relative merits of modern and medieval literature, of Emerson's wisdom and biblical wisdom, and of the transcendant importance of Dante that it is worth quoting at some length:

Also madam you needn't begin to crow just because I happen to hear a little emmerson. He and all that bunch of moralists, what have they done? Why, all that is in their writings that's good is from the bible & the rest is rot. They have diluted holy writ. They have twisted it awry. They have it is true weakened it sufficiently for the slack minded & given vogue to the dilutation. The chief benefit of reading them is this. You can't trust a word they say & the exhileration produced by this watchfulness for sophistries is the only benefit. The joy I get from the mediaevalians is this. You current eventers think you're *so* modern & so gol darn smarter than anybody else that it is a comfort to go back to some quiet old cuss of the dark, so called silent centuries, & find written down the sum & substance of whats worth while in your present day frothiness.

I'm not yelling anti-progress, but it's good to know what is realy new. Only if you want to boast your progress stick to chemestry & biology etc. things that change per decade. But for love of right mercy & justice don't try to show off modern literature & brain quality.

Oh yes. "E"merson to make one think. (merely to detect his limitations). But find me a phenomenon of any importance in the lives of men & nations that you cannot measure with the rod of Dante's "Alegory."

Symbolize the development (the evolution if you will) of individuals & nations; the striving upwards of humanity, symbolize it so that your symbol shall be true for the ages.

Do it in emerson, do it with chemistry, do it with new discoveries in agriculture . . . untill you can show me men of today who shall excell certain men sometime dead, I shall continue to study Dante and the Hebrew prophets.

Also . . . I beg you not to think I praise Messire Dante Alleghieri [*sic*] merely because he wrote a book most people are too lazy to read & nearly all the rest to understand. Ecce homo. He fought in battles where he probably encountered much more personal Danger than Mr. Roosenveldt in Cuba. He also held chief office in his city & that for clean politics & good government.

Also he was a preacher who will rank with Campbell Morgan in extent of his influence & some centuries before Luther he dared put a pope in hell & a pagan without its gates & prophecy [*sic*] the fall of the temporal and evil powers of Rome.

He was incidentally a poet a lover & a scholar . . . although it is not recorded that he was President of a U.S. steel trust or the inventor of pin wheels.

Excuse me for not putting it more mildly.

Of course, if you don't want Dante, you can use a Bible it's even better. [*EPA*, February 1905]

At seven, Pound had attended the Chelten Hills School, run by the Heacock family and founded by Annie Heacock, an ardent suffragette whose influence made for a very enlightened attitude toward the abilities and goals of the girls who were students at Chelten Hills. During the time that Pound was there, for example, one of the entertainments offered the pupils was a dramatization of Tennyson's "The Princess," and the class prophecy for 1894 describes alumnae who have become a doctor, a professor, a writer, and a world traveler.[16] He stayed at the school for only a year or year and a half, but he did remain friends with Ned Heacock and with Esther and Priscilla Heacock, whom he saw for the last time on his visit to Pennsylvania in June 1969. It is hard to say how much influence the feminism of the Heacocks may have had on him, but it is certainly true that he was very much less sexist than the majority of his literary contemporaries.

In part 4 of "Through Alien Eyes," which he wrote for the *New Age* of February 6, 1913, his sympathy for independent and competent women does come through despite the deliberately flippant and blasé tone that he affects. He says how barbaric the treatment of suffragettes in England seems to an American and how perverse the public's reaction:

Half England shudders when a bill is brought forward for the flogging of pimps and half sits quiet in the face of forcible feeding and newspaper misrepresentations./ They say that the flogging would "brutalize" some one or other. As a matter of fact, the results of the bill will be two in number: it will send a certain number of men back to Brussels with great celerity, and the pimp will be replaced by the nation in this primitive form of insurance./ Yet the country still shudders and still injects soup through the female nose." [324]

He also argues that America offers women more scope to apply their abilities with the discipline of a professional—in social work, for example, which, he says,

has produced what is to my mind a very interesting type of woman . . . a woman of broad experience, of comprehension, usually of generous humour, a woman whose acquaintance with life has been first hand and various . . . the quality of whose comprehension is distinctive because her experience has not come to her solely or predominantly by the channels of sex . . . . Our women in civil life may be said to have some sort of human experience unconditioned by sex or caste . . . . A probation officer is eminently practical. She is perfectly aware than no two human beings are much alike. She is a person very different from the female member of a "Society for the Discussion of Social Problems." [324]

Pound was sincere in advocating independence and self-reliance for women and was personally attracted to women of what he called the "Artemis type," which he saw as to some extent peculiar to America. In *Patria Mia* he wrote: "There has been a deal of Artemis pose, and no one has taken much count of her in studying psychology. Yet among us, perhaps because we are a young and inexperienced people, there remains a belief in this type—a type by no means simple" (*SP,* 120). One thinks (and perhaps Pound was also thinking) of James's fascination with the independent innocence of Daisy Miller, although Pound had in mind a considerably less vulnerable kind of woman. H. D. in particular—Pound's "Dryad"—comes to mind; yet she is only one of several strong and self-reliant women to whom he was very close. For example, in 1907 he became strongly attracted to Mary Moore—more strongly so, it seems, than she to him. Recalling for Carl Gatter on June 1, 1970, the events of September 1907, she wrote: "A kiss on the forehead was as far and as passionate as our love-life went— though from letters written in Crawfordsville, to my consternation, I gathered that he was making plans for our marrying." She was, in fact, far too much of a free spirit for Pound to hold on to for himself. Mr. Gatter, making a note of comments made about her in 1970 by a nephew, wrote that "Mary had one affair after another. She is still very charming . . . . She tried to ditch [her husband] but he wouldn't let her. [She] has 3 children. She is about 82 & still drives a convertible (usually with top down). She carries a sleeping bag in the car and pulls off the road in the evening and sleeps in open fields and woods."

Since 1904 Pound had been very friendly with Katherine Ruth Heyman, a concert pianist fifteen years older than himself, and for a short while in Venice, in 1908, he undertook to be her business manager for European engagements. He seems to have thought of Marcella Spann, a close companion during his later years at St. Elizabeths, quite specifically as an Artemis figure, and it seems to be in tribute to her that he repeats three times in *Drafts and Fragments,* "And in thy mind beauty, O Artemis." But most important of all was Olga Rudge, another American musician, the mother of his daughter and his companion for forty-nine years, an extremely strong and independent woman. The self-reliance and stoicism of his wife during his confinement in St. Elizabeths greatly impressed all those who knew the bleak regimen she had imposed on herself by choosing to wait out these long years with him.

Unlike the other women in his life, H. D. has left a fairly detailed account of what it was like to be romantically involved with Pound, and her descriptions in *Hermione* and *End to Torment* of her perceptions of Pound's attitudes offer some interesting insights into his emotional nature in the early years.

Although *End to Torment* is straightforward biography where *Hermione* is fictionalized biography, we cannot simply assume that the former's account of the relationship between Pound and H. D. is the more reliable. Although, in the latter, the main characters are called Hermione Gart, George Lowndes, and Fayne Rabb, their circumstances, personalities, and interrelationships are virtually identical to those of H. D., Pound, and Frances Gregg. Even if one wanted to argue that H. D.'s purpose was not to offer a literal account of her relationships with Pound and Frances Gregg, her decision to portray these relationships in the way that she did is, in itself, significant. In addition, *Hermione,* completed in 1927, stands much closer to the events it treats than *End to Torment,* which was not written until 1958. When the accounts given in these two works conflict, as they do in some fundamental ways, *Hermione* can offer a more reliable guide. For example, the 1958 version of the reasons for the breaking of H. D.'s engagement to

Pound seems misleading. Pound had known H. D. since 1901, but before he offered to marry her, early in 1908, he had fallen in love with Mary Moore and considered himself engaged to her. Her unequivocal assurance, in late 1907, that she neither considered herself engaged to him nor wanted to be his wife came as quite a shock to Pound, who had overconfidently assumed, "You are going abroad with me next summer" He added, "We need spend no futile time in disputing the matter."[17] On February 14 he left Wabash after his landladies had informed the president of the college that Pound had allowed a stranded actress to spend the night in his rooms and almost immediately he began his courting of H. D. In February, she considered herself engaged to Pound, but her father refused to give his permission, and by March 7 she was written to Williams that the engagement is broken off. The timing here shows that H. D.'s attempt in *End to Torment* to make the breaking of their engagement Pound's fault really misrepresents the truth of the situation: "Did he want to break away from me? Of course he did . . . . He broke it by subconscious or even conscious intention, the little 'scandal,' the loss of a job was intentional?" (47).

In *End to Torment* she claimed, "I was separated from my friends, my family, even from America, by Ezra" (35) and describes him as "the whirlwind or the forked lightning that destroyed [her] human, domestic serenity and security" (48); yet this does not gibe at all with the account she gives in *Hermione* of Her's relationship with her family and her state of mind at the time when George was courting her. Here she describes in detail her feeling of claustrophobia in the company of her family, her sense of almost complete detachment from them, and her general disorientation as her surroundings come to seem increasingly unreal. As H. D.'s daughter comments in her introduction to *Hermione,* the narrative voice in the book is "frequently overwrought" (xi), and there is certainly no evidence in the book of the "human, domestic serenity and security" that George Lowndes is supposed to have destroyed. Instead we find Hermione acknowledging that "George, with his ribbons and his tatters of learning, was the one thing to save her from this dehumanizing process and she wasn't strong enough to [let herself be saved by marrying him]" (101). At this point she senses that to choose a life as an independent writer will be to make do without the humanizing influence that marriage to George would provide. She imagines how, now that she has chosen her independent and rather solitary course, "her feet would run, had run, would all her life run like a forest cat . . . like a cat gone thin and thinner and more gaunt and more dehumanized" (101), and this realization seems to have been prophetic when we turn to *End to*

Torment. Here a much later reengagement with the world around her after a period of hermetic withdrawal and depressive self-absorption is again associated with Pound and his life-affirming energy: "I am anonymous here or try to be. But talking or thinking of Ezra creates a human, humanizing bond. But this has only happened lately; I mean this simple natural approach has come to me since reaching and re-reading [David Rattray's 'A Weekend with Ezra Pound!']" (6–7). Her psychiatrist and close friend Erich Heydt had recently encouraged her to think about her early relationship with Pound and brought her some of Pound's books; and shortly after this a friend had sent her Rattray's article about a visit to Pound in St. Elizabeths. She writes: "Ezra was not consciously a love-image. But perhaps he had lurked there, hid there, under the years. In making me feel young and happy, Erich prodded him out" (17).

Particularly misleading is H. D.'s comment in *End to Torment* that "Frances Gregg had filled the gap in my Philadelphia life after Ezra was gone, after our 'engagement' was broken. Maybe the loss of Ezra left a vacuum; anyway, Frances filled it like a blue flame" (8). *Hermione* makes it abundantly clear that rather than stepping in to fill a vacuum, Frances Gregg—the Fayne Rabb of the story—was most instrumental in creating the vacuum. At the time that H. D.'s feelings for Pound were increasingly moving from ambivalence toward detachment, her feelings for Frances Gregg were mesmerizingly intense. She is far more strongly attracted to the Fayne Rabb of the story than to the George Lowndes. She speaks to her more openly and is both more excited and more intimidated by her than by George. Physical contact with Fayne produces a strong response but George Lowndes's kisses leave Hermione completely unmoved. In fact, in the climactic scene of the book—the point at which she has a revelation of her destiny as a writer—although the revelation is sparked by the lines of Swinburne that George quotes before he kisses her, when he says the word "Itylus" she thinks of Fayne.

Oblivious to George's kisses, she recalls how Fayne had looked at their first meeting and how this girl had "made walls heave and walls fall and straight lines run to infinity" in the polished floor. As she looks up into George's "grey-green forest eyes" she "recalled the dynamic splendour of [Fayne's] . . . star sapphires" (74–75). The recollection of Fayne's presence seems at least as necessary to her revelation about her destiny as George's words do. "I have tasted words, I have seen them . . . never had her forehead bent forward and, as against a stone altar, felt safety, I am now saved . . . . *The hounds of spring are on winter's traces* let her fall forward, there was hope in block of substantiated marble, words could carve and set up solid altars. . . . Her head rested heavy, dehumanized on George's shoulder" (75–77).

Fayne, who claims to have psychic insight, seems able to mesmer-ize Hermione in her present disoriented state of mind. Speaking of George Lowndes, Fayne tells Hermione, "*You* are not of him being pure, apart. . . . *He* is beneath you, below you. He has part and parcel of some other fortune. He is not for you." Hermione passively replies, "Yes, yes Fayne" (161), and she later tells Fayne, "I promise you I won't ever marry George, my swallow" (179). In *End to Torment*, H. D. tells how Frances's "chief object" in marrying an English University Extension lecturer was to ensure that she could go to Europe and join H. D. so that the three of them could live together in Belgium, where Frances's husband would be lecturing. When H. D. left her lodgings to join the newly married couple at Victoria Station, Pound was waiting for her and rode with her, insisting that she not go with them, saying, "There is a vague chance that [Frances] may be happy. You will spoil everything," and waited "glowering and savage" until the train left (8–9).

Significantly, after breaking her engagement to Pound, H. D. gives "Hilda's Book"—the collection of poems that Pound has written for her, copied out, and handbound—to Frances to keep for her and then seems to have forgotten about it until she heard in 1958 that it was up for sale (28).

Hermione also gives some interesting insights into Pound's habit of assuming a deliberately extravagant way of talking and acting and how his fundamental kindness and considerateness persisted beneath the mask. The complete reversal of her family's original disapproval of George shows how superficial the effect of his annoying mannerisms was. H. D. writes: "People hated George. George was *agaçant*. But people should hate with rea-son. . . . There was, as far as Hermione could follow, no reason for [her mother] to hate George so." The only reason her mother can give is the Wabash incident: "It's an outrage, not because George had a person to his room but because the university ladies *saw* him have a person . . . to his room" (44–45). Yet, in a short while, Hermione's family are won over. Her mother is pressing her to marry George and says, "I don't understand how people so misread George Lowndes" (121).

The mannerism which is especially annoying to Hermione is George's tendency from time to time to fall into "being Uncle Sam" (167). For example, when he first writes to her from Europe, his only comment is: "Hermione, I'm coming back to Gawd's own god-damn country" (28), and when he telephones her he speaks emphatically and constantly interjects foreign phrases. She thinks of him, on the other end of the telephone, as a "little far away miniature Punchinello shouting outside a tent . . . a harlequin sort of person with patchwork clothes with patchwork languages, bursting into Spanish or Italian or the sort of French that no one ever tried to think of speaking" (42–43). He falls into his Uncle Sam voice once again when they are walking in the woods and Hermione thinks how unnerving he is when he is being funny: "George, so beautiful, healing her by his presence was a hideous harlequin being funny on a woodpath. 'Noaaw this is fawrest *pri*-meval'" (66). He does this again later, when they are alone together: " 'Na-aow' (he was being Uncle Sam, he hadn't been for a long time, she thought he had forgotten) 'Little Miss Her Gart. I aoin't goin' to take any of this here fulsome flattery. I said your pomes were rotten'" (167). Yet it is important to notice that what prompts this response is Hermione's sudden comment, "Your mouth is very beautiful." Given her intense and abstracted manner at this time—she is on the point of a nervous breakdown —it is hardly surprising that in response to a comment like this he should fall into the habit he had adopted for masking his self-consciousness.

It is necessary to be aware, when we try to arrive at any conclusions about the significance of his Uncle Sam way of speaking in the radio speeches, just how early it was that he began to adopt this mannerism. In fact, it seems to begin with his adolescence since we find an instance of it in a letter that he wrote to his father when he was twelve (*EPA,* 7/5/1898).

His main reason, of course, for needing a protective camouflage of this kind is his highly sensitive and emotional, even passionate nature. Flamboy-ant and outrageous mannerisms allowed him an alternative to bottling up his strong feelings. He could be extravagant and demonstrative; yet, by displaying a personality other than his true one, he would run no risk of having his most intimate and intense feelings rebuffed or held up to ridicule. A sensitive and sympathetic person who cared very much about how people would react to what seemed most valuable and important to him, he assumed, through his adolescence and his early years in London, the manner of a person who not only did not care about the reactions of others, but would, if anything, prefer to shock and embarrass people than do otherwise.

When H. D. in *Hermione* writes of George Lowndes that "his curious beauty . . . made people hate him" (65), she draws attention to the fact that Pound's good looks did influence the way in which people reacted to him. Her comment here implies, perhaps, that people were simply jealous of him, but the effect of his "beauty" also goes beyond this. Such striking looks are themselves a kind of automatic flamboyance and make it unlikely that it will be easy for him to choose an introspective or reclusive way of shielding his emotional sensitivity.

A letter that Pound wrote to Viola Baxter in 1907 adds a little more to our understanding of his self-consciousness. It seems that she had written to accuse him of keeping himself unnecessarily aloof, either from her or perhaps from people in general and he replied:

As for "porcupine" & keeping away confidence: that is hardly fair. The beginnings of any art work are so full of faults that [it] is hardly fair to shove off on one's friends what editors can't stand. Also it is a very immodest form of mental undressing (& I am in all things modest; of course?) No, but until one is very sure that someone else has sufficient interest to pardon and—Oh well, one in one's art displays one by one the portions of one's anatomy stark naked & all one's weaknesses & varieties of idiocy come to the surface and one does not want—etc.[18]

For him, to write poetry is to reveal to public view both feelings which seem to him so intimate that to disclose them at all is almost comparable to stripping his body naked in his reader's presence, and thoughts which he fears might appear to his reader to be "weakness" and "idiocy." Although the beginning of the passage suggests that it is the possible artistic flaws of his poetry that make him reticent to share it with others, the rest of the passage makes it clear that it is really the confiding of his intense and intimate feelings that he shies away from.

Altogether the picture that H. D. draws of Pound as George Lowndes is a very sympathetic one. Although our initial impulse is to share her irritation with George's lapses into "harlequinism," once we realize how very disoriented and overwrought she has become, his occasional need to set some emotional distance between them seems understandable enough and we notice instead how genuine his strong feelings for her seem to be and how patient and considerate he is—not just with her but with her mother and with Fayne and Mrs. Rabb also. In *End to Torment,* H. D. acknowledges this sensitivity in him: "He himself, in a certain sense, made no mistakes. He gave, he took. He gave extravagantly. Most of the tributes to his genius, his daemon or demon, have come, so far, from men. But at least three women, whether involved in the emotional content or not, stand apart; he wanted to make them, he did not want to break them; in a sense, he identified himself with them and their art" (49).

By 1928, when his father arrived in Rapallo with the Thaddeus scrapbook, Pound had been deeply involved in the Social Credit campaign for fiscal reform for many years. Busy with his own writings on economics, he would have reacted with a shock of recognition to some of the turns of phrase that he found in his grandfather's writings:

The constitution provides that Congress shall "have the power to coin money and fix the value thereof. . . . Now the monstrous proposition is presented to turn the mints of this republic over to the owners of bullion . . . for their free use to convert silver into legal tender dollars, and pocket the difference between the commercial and coin value of the metal so coined . . . . Under its authority "to coin money and regulate the value thereof," the government must not alone determine the character of the money coined, but the quantity as well; and not consent either to the whim, caprice or interest of any man or class of men. [Homer Pound Scrapbook, p. 31]

Even though Thaddeus lived until Pound was twenty-nine, Pound's personal contact with his grandfather had been minimal. In *Indiscretions* he had written: "I have no recollection of Thad[d]eus, or of anything his save his beard" (33), but as he reads the scrapbook he feels a growing sense of kinship with this man who, as he is reminded, was "auburn-haired [with] grey eyes" like himself and who was noted for his oratory. Here Pound finds instances of his grandfather's "blood and thunder popularity that pushed him to the front" at political conventions:

Orators for months have thundered the land with arguments, logic, statistics and history, while the press has deluged every fireside with oceans of political literature . . . . Oratory is double-sided, but ever entertaining, while history treats of the decayed and buried past, out of which the present is born to new conditions and higher purpose. Our fathers did well in their day and generation, but reverently as we regard them we could not reap our grain with sickles, light our houses with tallow dips, nor convey our distant messages by footmen. Rather would they employ the multifarious agencies of which the present is so generously endowed, speaking through the universe by lightning—conquering distance by steam . . . conquering our manifold needs by the magic of modern invention. [31]

This is from an article jeremiacally headed "Sounds a Warning Note," and (the flooded firesides notwithstanding) Thaddeus's future-oriented enthusiasm comes through with considerable panache if not with any great originality. Pound's response to this passage would almost certainly be colored by the fact that Thaddeus is describing a phenomenon which takes a fairly prominent position in Social Credit theorizing: the idea of the unearned "increment of association" which a productive society has at its disposal as an inevitable part of its common cultural heritage, an idea which we will look at further in chapter 4.

From a hazily remembered bearded figure, Thaddeus becomes an increasingly substantial, even focal presence in Pound's thinking—one of the illustrious company of defenders of the American heritage whose example Pound is committed to emulate himself:

[T]his [is] MY war, and . . . my grandad [has] been in it before me. And we were and ARE BOTH on the same side.Last time I saw the old man, I must have been about 12 years of age. I can still see him settin' in our so called library in Wyncote in a big spring rockin' chair, facin' a funny patent iron coal grate that was under my greatgrandma's picture. Other side of the family that rather thought their side was superior . . . . I could write a whole American history by implication stickin' to unknown folks, in four or five families. But the WAR has been the same war. John Adams, Jefferson, Van Buren, and Jackson, and finally Abe Lincoln, V. P. Johnson, my Grand Dad. [*EPS,* 121]

After 1928, Thaddeus had ceased to be the relation whose schemes came to nothing and was instead, for his grandson, the type of the selfless public servant. In *Jefferson and/or Mussolini,* Pound shows by his placing of a comment on Thaddeus just how elevated a significance his grandfather had assumed in his eyes. Pound's main purpose in this book is to urge his view that Mussolini can only be correctly understood as a leader who shares with the great defenders of the American heritage the primary ideal of disinter-ested public service and constructive action:

Any thorough judgement of MUSSOLINI will be in a measure an act of faith, it will depend on what you *believe* the man means, what you believe that he wants to accomplish.
   I have never believed that my grandfather put a bit of railway across Wisconsin simply or chiefly to make money or even with the illusion that he would make money, or make more money in that way than in some other.
   I don't believe any estimate of Mussolini will be valid unless it *starts* from his passion for construction. Treat him as *artifex* and all the details fall into place. Take him as anything save the artist and you will get muddled with contradictions. [33–34]

In 1934 we find Pound at his self-appointed and ongoing task of the economic education of Mussolini, offering an instance of Thaddeus's fiscal self-reliance as an instructive example to the Duce. In a letter written to Mussolini on May 25, 1934, Pound enclosed a note of money scrip, issued by Thaddeus's Union Lumber Company, calling it a "souvenir of a neglected chapter of American economic history . . . a 'certificate of work done,' when my grandfather was laying a foundation for a city in the wilderness, before the arrival of the bank monopolies." He went on to claim that, since "the man who issued the money owned the merchandise, [n]aturally, the bankers were jealous and opposed to this primitive form, just as today they are opposed to the creative force of the State."[19] He elaborates on this further when he writes in 1942: "No one, perhaps, has ever built a larger tract of railway, with nothing but his own credit and 5,000 dollars cash, than that laid down by my grandfather. The credit came from the lumbermen (and in face of the opposition of the big U.S. and foreign steel monopolists) by printing with his brother the paper money of the Union Lumbering Co. of Chippewa Falls, bearing the promise to 'pay the bearer on demand . . . in merchandize or lumber' " (*SP*, 325).

Here we find hints of what Pound will shortly assert openly, that Thaddeus himself was working in opposition to the power of the bankers— an idea that immediately comes to seem problematic when we consider the fact that Thaddeus himself had been a banker. In a way that was to become increasingly characteristic of his thinking at this period, Pound was content to seize upon any evidence that seemed to fit with his preconceived ideas and to dismiss from his attention any that might conflict with them. From his observation that Thaddeus took issue with some of the same fiscal abuses that he himself was campaigning against, Pound was ready to move on to the unsupported assumption that his grandfather instinctively supported what would become key principles of Social Credit. By 1942, we find him writing in "A Visiting Card": "It was only when my father brought some old newspaper clippings to Rapallo in [1928] that I discovered that T[haddeus] C[oleman] P[ound] had already in 1878 been writing about, or urging among his fellow Congressmen, the same essentials of monetary and statal economics that I am writing about today" (*SP*, 325).

Presumably he has in mind Thaddeus's comment about the responsibility of the government to "determine the character of the money coined [and] the quantity as well" and to avoid catering to "the whim, caprice or interest of any man or class of men." Yet, one would need to overlook completely the context in which Thaddeus made this comment to be able to portray him as any kind of monetary reformer—let alone a Social Creditor. He was, in almost all respects, a thoroughly orthodox Republican, with all the conservatism that this implies. He was a staunch protectionist who claimed that "the policy of free trade betrays utter indifference to our own [trade] and may be characterized as international socialism"[20] and blamed the industrial depression of 1894 on the Wilson tariff of that year, which, in fact, although it purported to fulfill the Democrats' election pledge of tariff reduction, made such insignificant changes that President Cleveland denounced it and it became law without his signature. The only departure from Thaddeus's Republican conservatism seems to have been his support for "a fairly graduated income tax," which, he believed, "would create an annual revenue of sufficient magnitude to justify a revision and reduction of tariffs on importations." When the Supreme Court declared unconstitutional the 2 percent income tax authorized by the Wilson–Gorman Tariff Act, Thaddeus supported the idea of a constitutional amendment.

The idea of an income tax was the only plank of the Greenback or the Populist party policies that Thaddeus did agree with and, although Pound clearly wants to see his grandfather as a reformer in the Bryan mold, Thaddeus is unequivocal in his dismissal of the "boy orator of the Platte": "Another evil born of hard times, [is] the promulgation of false doctrines masquerading under the name of democracy, with Bryan as the Messiah of national Salvation . . . . This wiseacre assumes to have discovered a panacea for all our national and social ills, in the reformation of our monetary system." He dismisses the Populist call for the free coinage of silver as a "monstrous proposition . . . to turn the mints of this republic over to the owners of bullion . . . for their free use to convert silver into legal tender dollars, and pocket the . . . difference between the commercial and coin value of the metal so coined." It is in this context that he urges the authority of the government "to coin money and regulate the value thereof."

Although Thaddeus claims to be a bimetallist, by backing McKinley and denouncing Bryan in 1896, he is, without entirely seeming to realize it, backing the gold standard and an end to bimetallism. In general he is not very clear about the implications of fiscal legislation. He dismisses "the crime of '73" as a "tempest in a teapot" and mocks Bryan when he claims that "instead of accomplishing the disastrous work of demonetization of silver [it] seems rather to have demanatized many effeminate men." But the 1873 Coinage Act, which omitted—so quietly that many congressmen, President Grant himself, and even the press failed to notice—the provision that silver dollars continue to be minted, was indeed a de facto demonetization of silver and the end of bimetallism, considerably before the Gold Standard Act of 1900.

To be fair to Pound, we should note that the brief suggestions that Thaddeus was interested in fiscal reform are made only in passing and not with any intention of urging the point or convincing anyone of it. In his comments on Bryan, however, Pound is more eager to present him as a forerunner, not just in "the battle against gold" but also in the ongoing campaign for national control of credit. In a radio speech of July 26, 1942, he finds in Bryan's rhetoric exactly the emphasis that he wishes to capture himself: "The money power preys upon the nation in times of peace and conspires against it in times of adversity. It is more despotic than monarchy, more insolent than autocracy, more selfish than bureaucracy. It denounces as public enemies all who question its methods, or throw light upon its crimes" (*EPS*, 218).

Pound had already honored Jefferson and Lincoln for speaking out against the tyranny of gold. He frequently quoted Lincoln's "and gave to the people of this Republic THE GREATEST BLESSING THEY EVER HAD—THEIR OWN PAPER TO PAY THEIR OWN DEBTS," and Jefferson's observation to Crawford in a letter of 1816 that "if the national bills issued be bottomed (as is indispensable) on pledges of specific taxes for their redemption within certain and moderate epochs, and be of *proper denomination* for *circulation*, no interest on them would be necessary or just, because they would answer to every one of the purposes of the metallic money withdrawn and replaced by them" (*SP*, 159). Now he adds Bryan to his company of champions of economic democracy despite the fact that free silver was hardly an acceptable expedient to proponents of Social Credit, who believed that "all monetary metallism was a silly and arbitrary superstition" and that "to tether a nation's money supply to two metals was only slightly less foolish than to tether it to one."[21] Anxious to give recognition to Bryan's heroic stand against the power of the bankers, Pound claimed that Bryan was not as fiscally naive as his platform might indicate. In a radio speech of April 6, 1943, he says, "When Kitson met Bryan, Bryan already knew that the silver propaganda was an implement or a camouflage over a major issue, that namely of the control of the national credit, or the national power to buy . . . . It had been almost impossible to get any large scale propaganda against the fetish value of gold save by ballyhoo about silver. By [1878] silver ballyhoo was already necessary to get in a motion to keep at least some of the NON-Interest bearing national debt in circulation as currency . . . . Bryan denounced the cross of gold, but needed support from the silver interests, and it was insufficient" (*EPS*, 271–72). This point is recorded cryptically in *The Cantos* in the line, " 'Window-dressing' as Bryan admitted to Kitson" (97/673).

It is tempting to dismiss Pound's contention that Bryan was aware that the free silver propaganda was a camouflage for a more thoroughgoing reform of the control of the national credit and that he had acknowledged as much to Mr. Kitson. Yet when we investigate this further it turns out to be quite possible. Arthur Kitson, an English engineer and inventor of the Kitson Light, was working in America, where he became a friend of Thomas Edison. In 1894 he published *A Scientific Solution of the Money Question,* in which he insisted that "money is a *social* instrument and morally belongs to the people . . . . It is redeemed every time it is accepted by the public for goods and services, and needs no gold redemption." He also argued that, although bimetallism was somewhat better than monometallism, both should be done away with. After reading this book, Bryan became friendly with Kitson and persuaded him, despite the latter's reservations about bimetallism, to campaign for him in 1896 and, on one occasion in Philadelphia, even to debate the postmaster-general for six hours.[22]

Even if the Populist position on silver was essentially heretical to a Social Creditor, the spectacle of Bryan's campaign against the combined money and power of Wall Street and the Republican party could not fail to be a heartening one to an advocate of monetary reform. With the support of the common people alone he had come close to defeating the power of the vested interests and succeeded in giving Wall Street what the Social Creditor Gorham Munson called "the biggest scare in its history" (129). It was Munson's hope that "Wall Street has probably not forgotten the scare and does not rule out so easily, as do some historians, the possibility of another national election which like 1832 and 1896 will turn upon the Money Question" (131).

By 1944 Pound was still doggedly reiterating the need for monetary reform, even though it was evident to him that the particular battle he had been fighting was clearly lost. He thinks of his grandfather now as, like himself, another would-be reformer who, having faced insuperable obstacles, had finally to accept the fact that his work had come to nothing. He begins "America and the Second World War" with this observation:

The historical process has been understood at various times, but this understanding on the part of a diligent minority fighting for the public good is again and again thrust down beneath the surface. In 1878 my grandfather said the same things that I'm saying now, but the memory of his efforts has been obliterated. The same applies to the revelations of men like Calhoun, Jackson and Van Buren. Forty years ago Brooks Adams assembled some very significant facts, but his books were not widely read. He had no vocation for martyrdom, he confessed with irony.[23]

Visionary Economics

2

To
A. R. Orage
(1873–1934)
who had no axe but truth to grind
and with it struck at the root
while thousands hacked only at the
branches of economic evil.
[Gorham Munson's dedication to
Aladdin's Lamp]

On the evening of November 5, 1934, A. R. Orage gave a talk on Social Credit on the BBC. In Rapallo, Pound picked up the broadcast and shortly afterward he recalled how his friend's "voice came over the radio, curiously gentle and patient, without the fire I had known or the sharp snap and crack of the sentences, but very clear, as the transmission was mostly good, though the last sentence went with a crackle (thunder probably in the Alps)" (*SP*, 4, 38). At the time of hearing the broadcast, Pound, like the other friends of Orage who were listening, was not aware of the reason for the absence of Orage's customary fire and energy that they noticed. Orage's biographer, Philip Mairet, explains how Orage had been suffering from severe chest pains for several months and how "whilst he was speaking at the micro-phone, the pain attacked him with agonizing intensity and he feared he could not go on. He lengthened a natural interval between two sentences, however, the pain diminished, and he finished his performance correctly; so that those of us who were listening felt only a vague intuition that something was slightly wrong with Orage's voice or manner."[1] That same night Orage died in his sleep.

To the reader who is working through the file of the Pound/Orage correspondence in the Pound Archive at the Beinecke Rare Book and Manuscript Library, it is a shock to come without any warning upon a telegram, dated November 7, 1934, reading, "Orage died Tuesday please write obituary appreciation urgent newengweek. London." Yet the immedi-ate shock of Orage's death was by no means its most serious impact on Pound. Orage's common sense, clarity of insight, and ready criticism were crucial stabilizing influences for Pound, and once they were removed, Pound's decline into confusion and self-deception was swift. In his letters to

Pound in the 1930s, Orage was unfailingly frank in his criticisms of those ideas of Pound's with which he did not agree and he made no bones about the fact that he was "very dubious . . . of the economic value of [the] great M!"[2]

Consciously, Pound did not doubt that his own understanding of Mussolini's motives was more realistic than Orage's, because he believed that, since he was seeing the Fascist economic program at first hand, his view of it was likely to be more accurate than Orage's impressions from a distance. Yet unconsciously the misgivings of a person whose incisive perceptions he had admired for so many years was clearly an influence that he could not discount. We see the weight that Orage's misgivings carried with Pound from his attempt in his obituary for Orage and in his memorial article "In the Wounds" to try to satisfy himself that the differences that Orage saw between his own economic ideals and those of Mussolini were more apparent than real. In his obituary Pound writes: "As to the corporate state, I believe [our] differences were more a matter of time and location than of any root disagreement. [Orage] died exactly one month after the speech to the Milan workers. It was natural that he should not see this in the same light that I do, or rather that he should have estimated it differently, as a victory, certainly, but perhaps not yet fully as the great and final collapse of Scarcity Economics" (*SP,* 438). In "In the Wounds" it is clear that Pound wants to insist on Mussolini's right to be seen as an enlightened economic thinker comparable to Orage and Major Douglas, and this is the point of his assertion that "three great men studying reality from three different angles, but without personal vanity, whatever their initial oppositions, are bound to converge in measure as they attain complete understanding" (*SP,* 445). The juxtaposition of Orage and Mussolini is particularly significant in the following passage from the same article:

Orage's last words over the radio, emerging for Rapallo from the crackle of Alpine thunder were: "In the gap between Price-values and Income is enough gunpowder to blow up every democratic parliament."

Adnuit. That was a fine sentence to die on.

Mussolini is erecting an assembly *more representative* than the old model parliament; he is working against the "gap" by a human Italian system, which he has himself stated was not "an article for export," all of which needn't prevent the intelligent foreigner from learning the truth about Italy, or perhaps acquiring a little of Italy's cultural heritage. [*SP,* 442]

The death of Orage meant the silencing of the cautionary voice that Pound respected most, and it left him in a position made doubly vulnerable by the fact that he was now bound to turn even more unequivocally to Mussolini as the one person who seemed to him, even if by default, most able to take over the position of economic leadership that Orage had left vacant.

For us, Orage has become an elusive figure. The story of his dynamic and visionary intellect and its catalytic impact on the young London intellectuals of the nineteen-teens has, for most people, been dropped from the record almost without trace. There is even very little clue to the charismatic qualities of Orage in Pound's two obituary pieces, partly because Pound did not willingly or readily write on personal matters of this kind but even more because, at the time of their writing, he had already turned so far toward what he saw as Mussolini's practical measures to carry the spirit of Orage's vision of reform into action. Yet, although Pound gives us few clues to the nature of Orage's influence, unless we are able to arrive at some insight into this matter, we are almost bound to misunderstand the spirit in which Pound first approached and then became committed to the cause of economic reform.

Even when he was alive Orage, who had such a decisive formative influence on those who knew him personally, was an elusive presence to most of those outside this inner circle, but now it is true to say that Orage is unknown largely because Social Credit is unknown. He was much more than a Social Creditor, but ultimately he considered Social Credit to be so important that, if he could not make the public see its importance, he was content not to be seen at all. His great achievement was as a magnetic center of intellectual inquiry who galvanized the minds around him into action, gave them a new self-confidence and independence of speculation, and then, through rigorous criticism, challenged them to set increasingly ambitious intellectual goals for themselves. This he was able to do because the breadth and depth of his learning were greater than theirs. His journalism, because of its occasional nature, provides us with only a very incomplete sense of his intellectual stature. Shaw judged him to be the most brilliant editor of the past century and Eliot "the finest critical intelligence of our day" (Mairet, p. 121); that he was very much more is clear from the obituary tributes in the *New English Weekly* for November 15, 1934. It is worth quoting Edwin Muir's tribute at some length, particularly as it expresses so eloquently points that are made by so many of the other contributors:

[H]is character . . . was all of a piece; and the quality which steadily shone through it, in private and in public, was the great and rare quality of disinterestedness. . . . He gave out constantly an active and enlightened good-will such as I have never met in any one else and his chief aim was not so much to influence one's opinions as to make one understand one's own thoughts and realize ideas and aims of which one was only half-aware. He carried friendship on to the plane of high intelligence, without losing its human warmth; and his work as a public man was only the final expression of this disinterested and enlightened friendship, for he was passionately concerned for the good of his country and of mankind. In his writings and his comments on the contemporary state of the world that passion was displayed . . . in an intense and steadfast employment of the reason. . . . As a commentator on the most important and urgent problems of contemporary civilization he maintained for many years a standard of pervasive reason approached by nobody else. . . . He did not weary of continuing in the face of perpetual discouragement and of frequent misunderstanding; he resolutely went on doing good to his fellow man in spite of them. . . . His "Notes of the Week" represented a standard of what comment on public affairs should be, and there is nothing left to take their place. That is a loss not only to civilization but to the steady and informed goodwill on which the hope for the future of society rests, and of which Orage was the purest and most disinterested representative in his age.[3]

A. J. Penty, the founder of guild socialism and one who had worked very closely with Orage between 1900 and 1919, said of his friend that his "great achievement was to create a centre of free intellectual discussion which in our time has led to nothing less than a revolution in thought on social questions" (113). This revolution was the incremental effect of a large number of personal interactions with individual writers and thinkers, all of whom had benefited, and some to a very great degree, from Orage's interest, enthusiasm, and advice. A partial list of contributors to the *New Age* acts as a kind of mirror for Orage. All the following are better known than Orage himself and yet the fact that all of them in some way or another found his support an occasion for gratitude and his judgment and insight worthy of their serious consideration is a telling reflection on his authority and influence. Among the already famous were Shaw, Chesterton, Belloc, H. G. Wells, Havelock Ellis, and Arnold Bennett. Those at an earlier stage—or at the beginning—of their careers were Katherine Mansfield, H. D., Richard Aldington, John Middleton Murray, Michael Arlen, T. E. Hulme, Herbert Read, Edwin Muir, G. D. H. Cole, Wyndham Lewis, and, of course, Ezra Pound.

Orage could act as an "unwobbling pivot" at the center of so much diversified intellectual activity because of the breadth of his knowledge and vision and his ability to establish a judicious balance among divergent intellectual positions. His own deepest interests—religious mysticism and social reform—carried his thoughts in very different directions, and yet with his own enthusiasms, as with the enthusiasms of others, he was able to maintain an equilibrium through his pragmatism, his common sense, and what Edwin Muir called his "incorruptible adherence to reason." T. S. Eliot saw Orage's "restless desire for the absolute" as the quality which gave him his forcefulness as a spokesman for reform and understood that, because Orage saw both that "any real change for the better meant a spiritual revolution; and . . . that no spiritual revolution was of any use unless you had a practical economic scheme," he was able to bring together very different kinds of reformers who would otherwise have "no common ground of action."[4]

The two strains of social activism and religious inquiry ran side by side in him from the beginning. As a boy he read Ruskin, Carlyle, Arnold, and Morris, and as a young schoolteacher in Leeds he was simultaneously interested in Platonism, labor and socialist political theory, theosophy, and the ideas of Nietzsche, but in every case his interest was analytical and, when he saw occasion for it, adversarial. As his biographer, Philip Mairet, explains, Orage "believed in a higher state of being and awareness . . . and to him that was the meaning of life," and yet he "wanted to analyze every 'phenomenon' into its rational or psychological components" (18–19). His essay, "Consciousness, Animal, Human and Superhuman," a digest of lectures he had given for the Theosophical Society, was, Mairet says, "much too rational in spirit to be congenial to theosophists," who, "attracted by the prospect of mysteries and magical revelations," want to immerse themselves in "the warm sea of optimistic speculation where nothing remains real but everything possible."

Orage's relentless insistence on subjecting all his provisional beliefs to "trial by reason" made him as unorthodox a socialist as he was a theosophist. Although the *New Age* was a socialist paper—its subtitle was "An Independent Socialist Review of Politics, Literature and Art"—Orage had serious reservations about the "accepted Socialist dogma of the benevolent State" (42) and was very careful not to give his editorial support to one brand of socialism in preference to any other. "Socialism" was, in fact, a very imprecise label for a wide variety of only loosely related movements and causes, as Orage pointed out, with his characteristic wit and incisiveness, in the following pronouncement:

It was . . . a cult, with affiliations in directions now quite disowned—with theosophy, arts and crafts, vegetarianism, the "simple life," and almost, one might say, with the musical glasses. Morris had shed a medieval glamour over it with his stained-glass *News from Nowhere*. Edward Carpenter had put it into sandals. Cunninghame Graham had mounted it upon an Arab steed to which he was always saying a romantic farewell. Keir Hardie had clothed it in a cloth cap and a red tie. And Bernard Shaw, on behalf of the Fabian Society, had hung it with innumerable jingling epigrammatic bells—and cap. My brand of socialism was therefore, a blend of, let us say, an anthology of all these, to which from my personal predilections and experience I added a good practical knowledge of the working classes, a professional interest in economics which led me to master Marx's *Das Kapital* and an idealism fed at the source—namely Plato.[5]

The *New Age* provided proponents of all the varieties of socialism with a forum and also with a good chance of being attacked in print by other contributors with opposing views.

It was not until he met C. H. Douglas in 1918 that Orage found a set of economic truths to which he could give his wholehearted support, and from then on he focused his efforts toward social reform upon the theory of Social Credit. Similarly, in the teachings of Gurdjieff he found for the first time a spiritual dicipline which satisfied his very high standards of integrity. Even if the premises of Social Credit were correct, as he earnestly believed them to be, he knew that this was no guarantee that they would ever be imple' mented, and when in 1933 he discovered Gurdjieff's teachings, he decided to postpone his campaign for economic refort to free himself to spend a year at Gurdjieff's institute outside Paris, near Fontainbleau. After this period of rigorous mental and physical discipline, he went to America, staying mainly in New York, where he gave lectures on the aims of the institute to audiences whose enthusiasm he found stimulating (Mairet, p. 95).

After six years in America he decided to return to England and, within a year, had taken up the Social Credit cause where he had left off, this time as editor of the *New English Weekly*. From then until the year of his death he chose to hold in abeyance matters of philosophical and religious speculation because, as he explained to Mairet, "if I were to take up philosophy again it would not be possible to carry on the work I have to do" (Mairet, p. 116). Yet at the beginning of 1934, his friend noticed that he "relaxed this rule, discussing various philosophical and psychological questions, not didactically, but with a kind of detached, agnostic apprecia' tion." Orage continued, until the time of his death, to reject the possibility of any certain knowledge of ultimate religious truths: his mind "was peacefully active in discussing these problems; he seemed to have reached something positive in his final conclusion as to their insolubility" (117).

Orage's great endowment of "negative capability" persisted until the end of his life. He maintained his thoughtful equilibrium in this calmer mood as he had before in the more intense and passionate pursuit of his twin goals of spiritual enlightenment and social reform. He remained the "unwobbling pivot" until the end as Pound, who himself was to suffer so greatly for lack of just such a capacity for "holding fast in the middle," was able eventually to recognize:

> But the lot of 'em, Yeats, Possum and Wyndham
> had no ground beneath 'em.

> Orage had. 不 [98/685]

In his last years, Pound was able to see even more clearly the value of Orage's wisdom and to appreciate that its value was determined by the root from which it sprang:

> Orage held the basic was pity
> *compassione* [111/783]

This intensely humane, idealistic, intelligent, imaginative, and pragmatic thinker was not merely responsible for converting Pound to Social Credit. His influence was much more thoroughgoing than we have realized or even than Pound himself would have realized. Both in introducing Pound to new intellectual interests and in opening his eyes to new dimensions of interests that they found they already held in common, Orage more than anyone else provided Pound with his real "post-graduate education." The "lecture rooms" were the basement of the A.B.C. restaurant in Chancery Lane, where every Monday afternoon Pound and other contributors to the *New Age* joined Orage in reading the proof sheets of Tuesday's number; the Café Royal, which he often adjourned to later; and the Kardomah Café in Fleet Street, where this same group met once a week for further discussions.

During the period in which he was in close contact with Orage, Pound underwent a profound change in the perception of his own poetic and intellectual priorities—a change which he appraises retrospecitvely in *Hugh Selwyn Mauberley*.[6] When he knew Orage before the war, he was very much the self-consciously bohemian aesthete, with his velvet jacket and calculatingly histrionic gestures. His primary concerns were his own brand of poetry, Wyndham Lewis's brand of painting, Henri Gaudier-Brzeska's brand of sculpture, and any aesthetic theories, such as those of T. E. Hulme, which could offer interesting hypotheses about those qualities of these brands of poetry, painting, and sculpture that gave them their authenticity and dynamism. Almost certainly Pound would have moved beyond his bohemian aesthete phase in his own good time, but, as it happened, he was not to have the luxury of taking his time about it. World War I sabotaged the vorticist enterprise, killed both Gaudier and Hulme, and left Pound deeply grieved at the loss of Gaudier, altogether bewildered and angry and needing to find an explanation that would make some sense of this cataclysmic, international tragedy. When in 1918 Pound, through his association with Orage, discovered Douglas's theory of Social Credit it seemed to him to be the explanation that he had been hoping to find. Yet it would be wrong to assume that Pound's conversion to Social Credit was necessarily doomed to have catastrophic consequences—that it was a hasty, arbitrary, and ill-considered decision which he made only because, at a particularly vulnerable time, he came under the influence of Orage and Douglas.

The Social Credit vision fulfilled exactly the requirements of the jeremiac imperative which Pound had carried with him as an ineradicable part of his heritage and, although his state of mind after the war probably made him more aware of this than he was before, he and Orage were very similar in their intellectual enthusiasms, temperament, and moral earnestness. To the extent to which Pound resembled Orage in temperament and social conscience, he differed from Wyndham Lewis. Although Pound had been very much under the influence of Lewis before the war, it was not Lewis's views but the dynamism of his creative energies and the forcefulness of his intellect that mainly attracted Pound. The two men were temperamentally very different and Lewis's misanthropy, cynicism, authoritarianism, and absolutism were the antithesis of the humanitarian, millennial, and democratic instincts which Pound shared with Orage.[7] Hulme called for "a complete reaction from the subjectivism and relativism of humanist ethics" and the establishment of "the objective character of ethical values" and "an order or *hierarchy* among such values, which it also regards as absolute and objective";[8] Orage strongly mistrusted such absolutism and the authoritarianism that it implied. He countered Lewis's and Hulme's attack on relativism with the following assertion: "Everything depends on time, place and circumstance, and there is no rule that can be absolutely applied. What we need, therefore, is a balanced judgement to know, in any given case, what things or what men are of the greater value. To assume beforehand that either is always to be preferred is to abdicate the office of moral judgement and to put ourselves in a kind of mortmain to an authoritarian theory" (*NA*, 4/13/16).

Pound shared Orage's fundamental optimism about human nature and belief in the basic decency and common sense of ordinary people, and this unspoken optimism was the ground of the instinctive bond between himself and Orage. It seems likely that Pound, who in his lack of reflectiveness was almost the antithesis of Orage, gave little if any conscious thought to the temperamental reasons for his affinity with the man whom he thought of primarily as a superb editor. Before the war Pound's sense of closeness to Orage was limited, not just by his even greater closeness to Gaudier and Lewis but also because one of his main interests was his poetry; and Orage's tendency to recur to the great English poets of the eighteenth century as the exemplars of poetic excellence made his views on poetry of limited interest to Pound. When the tragedy of the war made an exclusive preoccupation with poetry seem an irresponsible, effete, Mauberleyan hedonism, Orage was there as the best possible kind of model. Here was a highly literate, intelligent, judicious thinker who was convinced of the extreme importance of the arts but also aware of the pressing need for the kind of reform that, in relieving the twin miseries of poverty and war, would revitalize the arts also.

Before we consider further their shared preoccupation with social reform, it is worth noticing that they are even alike in their underlying fascination with the mystical. Even though Orage's pursuit of the mystical was far more sustained, disciplined, and programmatic, Pound's mysticism—as impressionistic and ad hoc as it might have seemed—persisted as an undercurrent which, when it came to the surface in the form of a public profession, showed itself to have remained there essentially unquestioned. He was to tell the psychiatrist who prepared his family history for the St. Elizabeths records that "from the ages of sixteen to twenty-four, he came under the influence of mysticism" and that after this he became what he called an "aesthetic pagan" and then a "Confucianist."[9]

Both Orage and Pound were strongly drawn at an early age to Platonism. Orage had formed a Plato Group in Leeds and said in the *New Age* for December 11, 1913, that he had spent seven years on the study of Plato (Mairet, p. 177). Pound was particularly interested in the Neoplatonists, as is abundantly clear from his writings, and even the "Confucianism" of his later life was heavily "neoPlatonized."[10] Although Orage's roots were English and Pound's American, there is a strong trans-Atlantic impulse in both of them. Pound, remaining always essentially American, nevertheless pursued his jeremiac vision of social reform most directly in England and Italy, whereas Orage, although he did not become Americanized, nevertheless found that America provided a particularly stimulating and receptive environment. When Pound came to England, the center for millennial change seemed to have shifted from America to London. As Wallace Martin writes in *The New Age Under Orage,* the 1910 and 1911 issues of the magazine were full of articles suggesting that a "new age" was, in fact, at hand.[11] He quotes Allen Upward's observation: "It is a sign of the times that so many of us should be busy studying the signs of the times. In no other age since the birth of Christianity has there been manifested the same devouring curiosity about the future, and the same disposition to expect a new earth, if not a new heaven" (*NA*, 1/26/11). Orage's view was, predictably, cautionary:

If I were asked upon what I rely for the renaissance of England, I should say a miracle, but it does not follow that because we cannot define the causes of miracles, miracles are not therefore to be understood. They can be understood easily enough if they are regarded as works of art instead of works of logic . . . . The miracle that may therefore be confidently anticipated in England is not necessarily one that we cannot sense in advance or cannot even deliberately create. We can both divine what it will be and prepare for its coming. [*NA*, 10/10/12]

Pound's views of the didactic function of literature were shared by Orage, who believed that "literature affects life for better or worse" (*NA*, 12/25/13) and who could have been speaking for Pound when he wrote, "Decadence, for me as a critic, is absence of a mission, of a purpose, of a co-ordination of powers; and its sign manual in style is the diffuse sentence, the partial treatment, the inchoate vocabulary, the mixed principles." Orage's conviction of the moral responsibility of artists toward their society confirmed and intensified Pound's own sense of his jeremiac obligations. Already inclined to be eclectic in his interests, Pound was also encouraged by the example of Orage to make his broad range of interests even broader, particularly in the direction of exploring concrete proposals for social change.

To the extent that Orage was influential in shaping its principles and its program, Social Credit reflected the ideals of guild socialism, with its call for industrial self-government by workers and its aversion to bureaucracy and political control of industrial affairs. Orage had been interested since 1906 in the possibility that the organization of the medieval craft guilds might suggest ways of redefining workers' rights and responsibilities that would allow them self-government in their work. To him, autocratically organized industry was an anomaly within a political democracy. Between 1912 and 1915, he worked with G. D. H. Cole and S. G. Hobson to incorporate part of the old guild concept into a set of practical proposals for workers' rights in industry.

A series of articles by Hobson, heavily edited and revised by Orage, were the basis of their coauthored *National Guilds* (1914), which was first serialized in 1912 in the *New Age*. The guild socialists believed that "men could not be really free as citizens unless they were also free and self-governing in their daily lives as producers."[12] They believed that, freed from pressing financial anxiety, people could be trusted to make sensible choices for themselves about the quality of their lives, and they objected to what they saw as the overly utilitarian, paternalistic, and state-worshiping approach of the Fabians—an objection which Pound frequently repeats in his writings.

Orage's respect for the dignity of the working classes and his concern for the suffering of the poor was not a sentimental indulgence but sprang from a strong sense of identification with their predicament. He had grown up in poverty himself, and in his attitude toward the suffering caused by poverty, he was unfailingly realistic and practical. Eric Gill, who valued and shared his friend's pragmatic humanity, wrote:

We both saw that "a starving man needs food, not instruction"—that the state of the modern world is not so much due to crime as to folly, though, truly, a folly almost criminal—that the immediate enemy is not so much ill will, deliberate wickedness, as extraordinary stupidity, a gross and ridiculous ineptitude in our system of finance—that religion and poetry cannot possibly have effect and bear fruit, material or spiritual, while a poverty as unnecessary as it is unholy condemns millions to misery, and a financial system as antiquated as it is ridiculous compels the rest of us to an insane and war-provoking commercialism. [*NA*, 11/15/15]

For the Social Creditors as for the guild socialists, their concern for the workers went beyond the solely materialistic issues of wages, hours, and benefits to the ethical matter of the quality and dignity of life of the workers as individuals. Yet, although their ultimate goal was the shaping of a more humane society, their means of accomplishing this were to be pragmatic rather than proselytizing. They would not aim for a change of heart on the part of those powerful people to whose self-interest the well-being of the common people was being sacrificed. Or, as Pound says in "ABC of Economics," "Economics, as science, has no messianic call to alter the instincts" (*SP*, 259). They would simply take practical, legislative steps to make it as difficult as possible for the powerful and corrupt to find opportunities to exercise their greed at other people's expense. The Social Creditors believed that Douglas's statistics showed that not only were there no safeguards against such exploitation but that the present fiscal systems of Europe and America had, from the first, been set up in such a way as to maximize the opportunities for powerful individuals to "faire passer ces affaires / avant ceux de la nation" (38/192) and to do so with the minimum risk of disclosure or interference.

Of Orage, Pound wrote in "In the Wounds": "He was a moralist, and thence an economist" (*SP*, 447), reminding us of how different the advocates of Social Credit were from our current notion of economists. We think of an economist today as a statistician rather than a moralist, as trying—often rather defensively—to explain what is happening in the present by juggling data, the implications of which are far from clear, and by hazarding hypotheses over which there is bound to be strong disagreement. The Social Creditors were visionary economists in the sense that their attention was mainly fixed on the future. Economic truth was not a set of theories and tables to be jealously guarded and defended against rival theories but a powerful instrument of social change—a vision of how a just and efficient economic system should be.

Social Credit took its beginning from the analysis of figures—from C. H. Douglas's observation on the account books of the Royal Aircraft Works at Farnborough—yet, from Pound's point of view, as we see in his review of Douglas's *Economic Democracy,* "it is in the underflow of protest against the wastage of human beings that we find the author's true motive power" (*SP*, 211). And for Pound, as for Douglas, it was Orage who supplied the visionary quality to the statistical basis of Social Credit. Orage was quick to see the human implications of Douglas's theorem: to see how, if current monetary policy were adjusted to eliminate the anomaly that Douglas had uncovered, the quality of life for large numbers of people could be significantly improved.

The implications of Social Credit theory were optimistic, humane, democratic, vital, liberating, and future oriented. That its vision of social reform could elicit the unequivocal assent of a mind as discriminating and inclined to skepticism as Orage's and could stir his ambitious imagination should make us wary of dismissing Pound's enthusiasm for Social Credit as pointlessly eccentric. Perhaps the strongest appeal of the theory to Pound was its highly optimistic insistence that abundance of production was a fact of life and that the gross economic injustices everywhere apparent were entirely the effect of managing a condition of abundance according to fiscal practices premised on scarcity. From the Social Credit point of view the facts of the case were established beyond discussion. As Pound wrote: "Probably the only economic problem needing emergency solution in our time is the problem of distribution. There are enough goods, there is superabundant capacity to produce goods in superabundance. Why should anyone starve? . . . And the answer is that nobody should. The 'science' or study of economics is intended to make sure no one does" (*SP*, 234–35).

The hallmark of Social Credit thinking—the characteristic that made it both visionary but also likely to be dismissed as too simple to be true—was its attention to first principles. Dispensing with preconceptions and unburd-ened by the traditional economist's need to take the current situation as a given and to work always with reference to that—either in rationalizing it or in suggesting variations on it—the Social Creditor could approach fiscal theory as an ethical matter. Social Credit thinking showed that economic theory could have, as Orage said, "deep roots in psychology and philoso-phy"[13] and could be as appropriate and worthwhile a study for writers and artists as for scientists and engineers. To the extent that it went back to first principles and set aside the whole body of received economic "wisdom," it made possible insights of a visionary nature; however, it also was very unlikely that these insights would be acted upon, since those with the power to affect economic policy were so irreversibly committed to the received wisdom that Social Credit had set aside. The problem with instituting a Social Credit economics was not that it would be complicated, but that it would remove a fiscal structure whose very complications were the source of profit to so many powerful people. The main problem with the Social Credit ideal was that it was an ideal—that it insisted on taking an idealistic approach to the one area of human activity which offered the greatest temptation to greed, deception, and self-interest.

The basic Social Credit tenets were both logical and straightforward. As Orage said, "The theory is at least no more difficult to understand than a thousand and one others which people claim to understand; and, in comparison with the theory of the Gold Standard, for instance, upon which there appear to be millions of experts, it is elementary. Anybody who in one and the same breath professes to understand the existing Money-system and to be unable to understand Douglas is either wrong about the first or has never given his mind to the second."[14] The very idealism and simplicity of Social Credit's premises, in fact, have the paradoxical effect of making them seem suspect, just because they are so different from the extreme complexity and uncertainty of orthodox economics. Put in the simplest way, these premises are that the productive capacity of the industrialized nations is more than adequate to manufacture everything necessary to ensure a high standard of living for all the people of these nations; that, since the "problem of production" is solved, the economist's paramount concern must be distribution; and that the primary function of money is to be a facilitator of distribution.

Social Credit proposals were not only reasonable but also very modest in the extent of change that they asked for. As Orage wrote in the third part of "An Editor's Progress,"

Major Douglas . . . was anything but one of the usual money-cranks . . . . He
had no such absurd notion as demonetizing gold or denouncing the financiers, or
nationalizing banks. His constructive proposals . . . concerned mainly the only
practically important question asked by every consumer—the question of price;
and beyond a change in our present price-fixing system, there is in his proposals
nothing remotely revolutionary. For the rest, everything would go as now.
There would be no expropriation of anybody, no new taxes, no change of
management in industry, no new political party; no change, in fact, in the status
or privileges of any of the existing factors of industry. Absolutely nothing else
would be changed but prices.[15]

The Social Creditors believed that there would be little profit and great
danger in Marxism's revolutionary approach to economic reform, and their
insightfulness is well corroborated by their warnings of the dangers that
they believed would follow from an ideology that encouraged class revenge.
Their aim was not to overthrow the present system but to overhaul it. The
pressing need was not for radical new concepts but for a more accurate
perception of the principles according to which the present situation
actually worked. The first step was to admit the extent of general ignorance
about money, to concede the truth of Orage's contention that, "as much as
men love and realize the value of money, not more than one person in a
million—and this is even a generous estimate—either knows or cares where
money actually comes from, how it is actually made, what it is actually
composed of, or what forces actually regulate its circulation and amount."[16]
When Pound found John Adams expressing the same view, Adam's
statement assumed for Pound a talismanic power and he quoted it as
corroboration from the highest possible authority:

All the perplexities, confusion, and distress in America arise, not from defects in
their constitution or confederation, not from want of honour and virtue, so
much as from downright ignorance of the nature of coin, credit, and circulation.
[GK, 354]

The idea that the root of the problem was ignorance was guaranteed to
appeal to Pound's fundamentally optimistic view that once ordinary people
could be shown the truth of a situation, they could be relied upon to act in
accordance with basic decency and common sense. From beginning to end,
Pound saw his role as a Social Creditor as removing economic ignorance
through education. It seemed as though it should be an easy matter to dispel
economic ignorance by disseminating the basic principles of Social Credit,
since these principles were so self-evident and straightforward. It was
particularly frustrating to Pound to discover how impervious to education
most people were in the matter of economics—not because any of Douglas's

basic principles were hard to grasp but because of an almost universal lack of interest in "the nature of coin, credit and circulation." People were perfectly content to think of money as a commodity rather than a "ticket" and to assume that the power of the privately owned banking system to issue credit at interest and to expand or contract the money supply was a fact of life—something that only a crank would think to question.

Douglas's A + B theorem, from which the whole of Social Credit thinking sprang, was less valuable in itself than for the incentive which it provided to rethink the logic of the bases of traditional fiscal practices. Today, in a time of runaway debt, when "orthodox" economic theories are increasingly showing themselves unable to explain or predict the behavior of the economy and when there is violent disagreement among economists upon virtually every national economic policy issue, such an incentive continues to have value.

Douglas's key theorem was simple and self-evident. As assistant director of the Royal Aircraft Works at Farnborough during World War I, he noticed a basic fact, one which had been there all along for anyone to see, and realized that it had very significant implications. As he worked with the account books he noticed that every week the amount paid out in wages and salaries was less than the price value of the goods produced in that week. In other words, the factory never generated enough purchasing power to buy what it produced. This observation he formulated as his A + B theorem. Including in group A payment made to individuals in the form of wages, salaries, and dividends, and in group B payments made to other organiza-tions to cover the price of raw materials, bank charges, and other costs, he spelled out the fact that the prices of goods produced must always be at least A + B and so prices must always be more than A alone; that is, than the purchasing power available to cover them. The gap between A (purchasing power) and prices must be bridged by some other source of "money," either loan-credit or export credit. With this situation necessarily duplicated in every factory, the gap can never be closed and, in fact, becomes progressively wider as wages are paid out, week by week, and spent, while it may be several weeks before the product which the wage earners have been manufacturing is completed and reaches the market.[17]

Faced with this inevitable insufficiency of purchasing power, industry has no recourse but to try to borrow its way out of the problem and, as we see only too clearly today, an untenable situation becomes only more untenable as an increasingly higher percentage of earnings must go to pay interest on debts. When the deficiency of purchasing power becomes severe enough, there is a full-scale depression and the economic situation in the

1920s and 1930s certainly seemed to support Douglas's contention that the inadequacy of purchasing power would make the economic systems of the West unworkable. The collapse he predicted was averted by the war (which he also predicted) and the large-scale spending it required, but the fact that this spending entailed massive indebtedness only postponed rather than solving the problem.

Because industry and business cannot generate sufficient purchasing power to keep the economy healthy, we have come to accept the idea that government spending will help to fill the gap; yet this has led to indebtedness of astronomical proportions. We are now facing budget deficits far too great to be significantly lessened either by taxation or by cutbacks in government spending for social programs. If there is no change in the present policy of relying on deficit spending and of the government paying interest to privately owned banks for the privilege of borrowing enough money to maintain distribution of goods at even modest levels, there can be no hope of halting, let alone reversing, the escalation of debt. Today the threat of unmanageable debt is a serious international problem, as we see from the mounting anxiety about the difficulties of heavily indebted Third World countries in times of recession. Having been encouraged to borrow heavily during the 1970s, these countries now find it progressively difficult to pay interest and refinance principle. If they reach the point of being unable to continue servicing these debts, the international economy will suffer severely.

The fundamental differences between Social Credit thinking and orthodox economic practice concerns the appropriateness of debt financing. The Social Credit position is logically unassailable. With plenty of raw materials and power, with the benefit of the "cultural heritage" of the cumulative scientific and technological achievements of the past and because of the "increment of association"—the great advance in efficiency that results from workers collaborating in the manufacture of products—the country has almost unlimited productive capacity. This was abundantly clear, for example, from the level of production achieved during both World War I and World War II, when so many of the usual work force were no longer even involved in the productive process because they had been drafted for military service. From the Social Credit point of view there should be such an inevitable connection between what a country produces and its money that, if there is no shortage of industrial capacity, it is nonsense to talk about a real shortage of money. If there is too little money to get the goods distributed, then this is an artificial shortage which should be remedied by having more money printed—not by banks, who have no title to the country's productive capacity, but by the National Treasury, acting as steward of the wealth of the whole people.

The conditioned response of the orthodox economist is to cry "inflation," but the Social Creditors had an answer to that, as Pound pointed out in the "Finale" section of his "ABC of Economics," where he wrote:

Within twenty-four hours of writing the above I find that R. H. C. [Orage] (in *New English Weekly* for 16 June 1932) has at last found an expression simple enough to be understood by almost anyone, save possibly Maynard Keynes . . . . "Would you call it inflation to issue tickets for every seat in a hall, despite the fact that the hall had never before been filled, or more than a fourth of the seats sold, because of there not being enough tickets available? Inflation would consist in issuing more tickets than there are seats." [SP, 262]

The Social Creditors realized that an economic system which could preserve for money the status of a medium of exchange and prevent it from being used as a commodity—that is, maintain a direct link between the nation's money and its productive capacity—was bound to be a stable and equitable system. Such stability would improve the quality of life for the majority. Of course, for the minority, who under the present system have the scope to amass personal fortunes through speculation, it would be most unwelcome since speculation requires instability.

The present economic situation shows how vast accumulations of debt have followed from the progressive distancing of "money" from any tangible source of real value. Banks, for example, routinely "create money out of nothing" in that they can legally lend out, and collect interest upon, nine times the amount of deposits they take in. Through "deficit spending" and through access to "credit," the government and individual citizens are constantly spending "hypothetical money" which they do not actually have. The indeterminate status of this "owed money" seems to have encouraged a cavalier assumption that the indebtedness which it creates is itself almost hypothetical. Pound would have found entirely predictable, in this context, the ubiquitous use of the word "credit" rather than "debt" on the part of lenders and of economists insisting on the health of the economy.

Keynesian economics provides what is now thought of as an "orthodox" legitimation for government indebtedness, but, at the time when it was initially relied upon to provide a rationale for increasing the deficit spending that President Franklin Roosevelt had already been forced to have recourse to by the catastrophic conditions of the Great Depression, it was seen as a "heresy." It was adopted, not because there was a logic to its practice, but only by default—because the "orthodox" economic recourses had shown themselves incapable of keeping the economy functioning.

To adopt deficit spending as a temporary, emergency measure seems reasonable, yet to continue to rely on it to an ever increasing degree seems to require some more rigorous theoretical basis than the observation that "it seems to work." At the time of this writing, it no longer even seems to be working. In America the concept of "wealth" has probably never been further distanced from the actuality of "creation of a marketable product" than it is today. Both official pronouncements about the health of the national economy and many people's perceptions of the health of their personal finances have been conditioned by the tacit assumption—all the more dangerous for remaining unexamined—that "prosperity" can be defined as "access to 'credit.'"

The ubiquitous use of "credit," with its primary connotation of "ability to pay" in those cases where "debt" with its connotation of "obligation to repay" would be the appropriate term, is both symptomatic of and instru-mental in creating the vast and still growing accumulation of indebtedness in the country. Under cover of the spurious idea that availability of credit is a sign of national economic health, debts have been allowed to escalate to a dangerous level. In 1981, it had taken 189 years for the national debt to reach 1 trillion dollars; within four years it had doubled. In September 1985, for the first time since 1914, the United States became a debtor nation, spending more abroad in dividend and interest payments than it got back through ownership of foreign stocks, bonds, and property.

The illusory nature of "wealth" or "prosperity" which is not directly tied to the creation of a marketable product is being dramatically demon-strated by recent economic events, for example, the behavior of the stock market. Between the third quarter of 1982 and the second quarter of 1987, the Dow Jones Industrial Average rose 169.8 percent while the GNP rose only 39.0 percent. By far the greater part of these stock gains were the result, not of productive investment, but of mergers, takeovers, and leveraged buy-outs financed by "junk bonds." In these transactions, the losers suffer from being bought out or swallowed up, but the "winners" also are often left in a potentially highly vulnerable position because of the enormous debts they must entail to finance these takeovers. This takeover mania had, in the words of Boris Yavitz, former dean of the business school of Columbia University, made "the markets a casino rather than a capital formation mechanism."[18] The fragility of stock values created under such conditions was only too dramatically demonstrated by the market crash of October 19, 1987.

The rapid growth of the U.S. foreign trade deficit and government measures to attempt to control it show graphically what should have been obvious all along: successful productivity is the only sound way to improve a country's balance of trade. When competitor nations are operating with wealth that *is* based upon high-quality productivity, successful marketing, and accumulation of capital, then quick fixes for a trade deficit will obviously involve risk. To attempt to cure the problem of the U.S. trade deficit by devaluing the dollar is to try to minimize the symptoms of the problem without addressing the problem itself. Devaluation can shrink the value of the debt and can even make American products more affordable overseas, but to shrink the debt in this way is to shrink the value of American assets across the board so that foreign business can use its real profits to buy up American assets at bargain basement prices.

The simplicity and logical obviousness of the economic proposals of the Social Creditors may seem easy to dismiss as naive in comparison to the sophistication of current economic theories. Yet this very sophistication has now become highly suspect in view of the recent manifest inability of economic experts to provide reliable predictions of the consequences of economic policies. One could argue that the economic naiveté most damaging to a nation is for a government to imagine that financiers will ever voluntarily put long-term considerations of the overall health of the national economy above the short-term considerations of maximizing personal and company profits by all possible means—and on those grounds reduce regulation of the transactions of the financial community.

The Social Creditors were far from naive in their thinking on safe and constructive borrowing. Although they were strongly opposed to heavy reliance on debt financing, to levels of interest which they considered usurious, and particularly to the idea of the government's having to pay interest to the banks, they did believe that there was a legitimate role for the borrowing of money at interest. As Pound wrote in "The Enemy is Ignorance," "That industrial concerns and plants should pay interest on their borrowed capital is just, because they serve to increase production."[19] but the need to go into debt should arise only when very large sums of money are necessary for investment, and these debts should be able to be paid off once the project for which the money was borrowed is completed and in operation.

The main Social Credit innovations concerned money for use as purchasing power, and the Social Creditors felt that it was logical to suggest that, since this kind of money served a different function from money as capital, it could take a different form. In "A Visiting Card," Pound defined capital as " 'productive undertaking,' or the securities of such an undertaking, i.e., securities that presuppose a material basis which yields a produce that can be divided periodically, paying interest (share interest in monetary form) without creating inflation, which is a superfluity of paper money in relation to available goods" (*SP*, 330). The idea of a "material basis which yields a produce" is crucial to Pound's thinking about the distinction between legitimate interest and usury. With the Social Creditor's knack for getting down to the usually disregarded bases of economic transactions, Pound pointed out the simple, but very important fact that "the practices of rent and interest arise out of the natural disposition of grain and animals to multiply. The sense of right and justice which has sustained the main practice of rent and interest through the ages, *despite* countless instances of particular injustice in the application, is inherent in the nature of animal and vegetable" (*SP*, 256). And yet money itself does not have this reproductive capacity, so there is no basis for charging a substantial rate of interest for the borrowing of money. Pound was pleased to find Shakespeare making this same point when in *The Merchant of Venice* he has Antonio ask Shylock: "Or is your gold . . . ewes and rams?"

Banks clearly have a very useful function and are a benefit to the whole community, provided, Pound felt, they are content to let their transactions reflect in a realistic way the actual productive activity of the community they serve. He makes this point at some length by devoting Cantos 42 and 43, the opening Cantos of *The Fifth Decad,* to the founding of the Monte dei Paschi Bank in Siena. The bank was founded to remedy the specific problems resulting from a shortage of currency:

OB PECUNIAE SCARCITATEM
                    borrowing, rigging exchanges,
licit consumption impeded
                    and it is getting steadily WORSE
others with specie abundant do not use it in business. . . .
                    . . . and everyone remains here without work
few come to buy in the market
                    fewer still work the fields.   [42/213]

to correct this situation, the Grand Duke Ferdinand II of Tuscany and the Grand Duchesses Maria Maddelena and Christina provided 200,000 scudi for the founding of the bank. Security for a 5 percent interest on this capital would be provided by income brought in by the grazing lands south of the city and by "the persons and goods of the laity." The General Council of Siena, in drawing up their plan for the bank, specified that:

. . . any citizen shall have right to deposit
and to fruits therefrom resultant at five percent annual interest
and that borrowers pay a bit over that

for services . . .
and . . . that the Magistrate
give his chief care that the specie
be lent to whomso can best use it USE IT
to the good of their houses, to benefit of their business
as of weaving, the wool trade, the silk trade

and that the bank

could accept specie from . . .
. . . .
. . . companies and persons both public and private
                                      WHOMSOEVER
not requiring that they have special privilege
because of their state or conditions but to folk of
ANY CONDITION   [42/209–11]

Cantos LII–LXXI, the next sequence of the poem, also opens with the
Monte dei Paschi Bank as he reminds his readers:

And I have told you how things were under Duke
                                      Leopold in Siena
    And of the true base of credit, that is
                                      the abundance of nature
with the whole folk behind it.   [52/257]

It seemed clear to Pound that the closer the connection between
product and money as representation of the product's value—or between
work performed and the money token of that—the less scope there was for
falsification and corruption. He felt that the paper money that the State of
Pennsylvania issued before 1750 was bound to provide a more just and
efficient basis for the economic life of the colony than British currency
would and that, by banning it in 1751, the British government was serving
the interests of British creditors and merchants at the colony's expense.
Pound could look to his own family history for an instance of a particularly
direct connection between "money-tickets" and the source of their value.
He had in his possession several of the "certificates of work done,"
exchangeable for merchandise or lumber," that Thaddeus had printed to
keep his own Union Lumbering Company functioning smoothly. Drawing
attention to their worn condition, he frequently offered them as evidence of
how effective a very simple system of money tickets could be, sometimes
enclosing them in letters—for example, when he wrote to Mussolini—
when he wanted to argue the practicality of using an alternate currency to
speed up distribution.

It seemed only logical to the Social Creditors to pay some attention to the process by which the principle of a close and necessary connection between money-tickets and the items whose value they represented came to be abandoned. Gorham Munson in chapters 5 and 6 of his *Aladdin's Lamp* is our most lucid and informative guide to the Social Credit position on this issue as he explains the process "whereby the function of creating money has been alienated from the makers and owners of real wealth, and vested in the custodians of wealth" (69).

Munson prepares his readers to be much more objective and critical than usual in their thinking about the present banking system by pointing out the duplicity and outright corruption that were involved in its establishment from the first. He emphasizes the readiness of Hamilton, the prime mover in this enterprise, to sacrifice the principles of democracy and justice to the interests of wealthy and politically powerful individuals. Before submitting to Congress a proposal that the government redeem the severely depreciated soldiers' pay certificates at face value, he tipped off his powerful friends in time for them to send agents to buy up these certificates in the South and the country districts before wind of this new proposal got there. When Madison tried to remedy this injustice by a provision to share between the original owners of the certificates and the speculators who had bought them up, the difference between the depreciated value and the redeemed face value, his proposal was voted down by congressmen, many of whom, it was later established, themselves held these securities. This pattern repeated itself over the matter of the federal assumption of the state debts and generated strong hostility to the North on the part of the southern states, either because, as in the case of Georgia and the Carolinas, many of their state securities had been bought up by northern speculators or, as in the case of Virginia, they had virtually liquidated their debts and resented the plan to tax the whole country to pay off the large debts of the northern states.

Yet it was the chartering of the Bank of the United States which showed both the full extent of Hamilton's ability to turn his own predilections into national policy and the arbitrariness of the process by which the United States came to have a privately owned banking system. He was shrewd enough to see that two predictable weaknesses would give him the leverage he needed over a sufficient number of his political associates: the greed which makes it easy to put private interests before the interests of the country and the confusion that surrounds the whole subject of banking and finance in most people's minds. By playing on these weaknesses, Hamilton was able to overcome the objection that it would be unconstitutional to give a privately owned bank a monopoly in issuing money and controlling the nation's economy. Madison had serious doubts about the constitutionality of Hamilton's plan, as had Washington, whose own misgivings were backed up by the written opinions of Jefferson and Randolph. Once the Bank was chartered, the names of its directors were announced and there was a great outcry at the discovery that several of these men were leaders of the Congress which was responsible for the Bank's creation.

From the first, Hamilton's dealings with the Bank in his capacity as secretary of the treasury were fraught with deception and pretense. Even to supply the $2 million which constituted the 20 percent of Bank stock that the government would own, Hamilton chose to "invent" $2 million worth of spurious drafts on Dutch banks which, by juggling this sum back and forth between the Bank and the treasury, he was able to turn into unsecured government notes to be paid off to the Bank at $200,000 annually. Just before the first payment came due, he introduced a bill to authorize the president to negotiate a $2 million loan from the Bank, but Congress, thoroughly suspicious of such an unnecessarily large loan, refused and passed resolutions requiring Hamilton to submit reports on his management of the country's finances. Although resolutions of censure were introduced against him, they were voted down by the House of Representatives.[20] Considering Hamilton's responsibility for transferring the right to issue money from the government to "private dealers-in-debt" as itself a kind of treason, Munson sees Aaron Burr as less of a traitor than Hamilton and notes that William Carlos Williams is disposed to be more generous in his estimate of Burr also.

Jefferson (and the Jeffersonians) were highly critical of Hamilton's treasury policy and Munson felt that the Jeffersonian and Hamiltonian traditions were in direct opposition to each other. Whereas the American political order is democratic and derived from faith in the decency and common sense of the people, the economic order is an elitist one tending to authoritarianism, based upon special privilege and substituting for a desire for equality the principle of the exploitation of the majority by the financially powerful minority. Munson called the irreconcilability of the Jeffersonian and Hamiltonian traditions "the Great American Contra-diction." The Social Creditors saw themselves removing this contradiction by insisting on "economic democracy" which would complement the political democracy.

The dangers to democracy of a national debt funded by a private banking system were very clear to Jefferson, as we see from a letter that he wrote to John W. Eppes on November 6, 1813—a letter to which Pound several times refers:

At the time we were funding our national debt, we heard much about "a public debt being a public blessing"; . . . This paradox was well adapted to the minds of believers in dreams, and the gulls of that size entered *bonâ fide* into it. But the art and mystery of banks is a wonderful improvement on that. It is established on the principle that "*private* debts are a public blessing." . . . Here are a set of people, for instance, who have bestowed on us the great blessing of running in our debt about two hundred millions of dollars, without our knowing who they are . . . or what property they have to pay this debt when called on; nay, who . . . to fill up the measure of blessing . . . receive an interest on what they owe from those to whom they owe; for all the notes or evidences of what they owe, which we see in circulation, have been lent to somebody on an interest which is levied again on us through the medium of commerce.[21]

Jefferson not only criticized the Hamiltonian notion of a large, banker-funded national debt but was also able to see a constructive alternative to it in the idea of interest-free government money. On June 20, 1816, he wrote to William Crawford, secretary of the treasury, to suggest that "if the national bills issued, be bottomed (as is indispensable) on pledges of specific taxes for their redemption within certain and moderate epochs, and be of proper denominations for circulation, no interest on them would be necessary or just, because they would answer to every one of the purposes of the metallic money withdrawn and replaced by them."[22] Munson, with his usual clarity, spells out Jefferson's reasoning like this: "Since any debt of a government must, according to bankers' own precepts, be eventually paid out of taxes, and since it is the assurance of tax revenues that backs up the interest-bearing government debt which the banks hold, then if the government issues its own money and puts the assurance of tax revenues behind it and pledges its redemption by taxes, this money is just as good as bankers' money because the same thing covers it, and in fact it is better, for it need not bear interest" (106).

The next major battle in the campaign against Hamiltonian finance was Jackson's contest with the Second Bank of the United States and its director, Nicholas Biddle, a contest that Pound makes the focus of Cantos 88 and 89. Jackson vetoed the Bank's premature recharter and, despite Biddle's power plays of restricting credit to the point of producing a depression and then expanding credit before the presidential election, Jackson won the election and the Bank was routed. By January 8, 1835,

Jackson liquidated the national debt and, in his farewell address of March 4, 1837, he recalled what had been at stake in his campaign against Biddle's Bank. This Bank, he reminded his listeners,

possessed the power to make money plenty or scarce at its pleasure, at any time and in any quarter of the Union, by controlling the issues of other banks and permitting an expansion or compelling a general contraction of the circulating medium, according to its own will . . . the power to regulate the value of property and the fruits of labor in every quarter of the Union and to bestow prosperity or bring ruin upon any city or section of the country as might best comport with its own interest or policy . . . . Yet if you had not conquered, the government would have passed from the hands of the many to the hands of the few, and this organized money power from its secret conclave would have dictated the choice of your highest officers and compelled you to make peace or war, as best suited their own wishes. The forms of your government might for a time have remained but its living spirit would have departed from it.[23]

Lincoln's attempt to compete with the power of the banks was not so successful. He believed that it should be possible for the government to resolve the problem of financial stringency that was the consequence of the Civil War by instituting the kind of interest-free government money that had seemed entirely logical to Jefferson. In a letter to Colonel E. D. Taylor written in December 1864, he credits Taylor with the origin of the greenback and shows his own enthusiasm for this kind of money:

When troublous times fell upon us . . . and myself surrounded by such circumstances and such people that I knew not whom to trust, then I said in my extremity, "I will send for Colonel Taylor; he will know what to do! . . . You came, and I said to you, "What shall we do?" Said you, "Why, issue treasury notes bearing no interest, printed on the best banking paper. Issue enough to pay off the army expenses, and declare it a legal tender." Chase thought it a hazardous thing, but he finally accomplished it, and gave to the people of this Republic the greatest blessing they ever had—their own paper to pay off their own debts.[24]

Although the greenbacks are customarily dismissed as an instance of unsound finance, Munson contends that the fact that they rapidly depreciated was not a reflection on the soundness of the concept but the result of their vulnerability to manipulation by the banking interests. Their Achilles' heel was what he calls the "trick-exception clause"—the limitation that they would be legal tender for all debts *except* duties on imports and interest on the public debt"—which enabled the bankers to depreciate them in terms of gold. Munson also points out that at the time when they were depreciating in value, all the other money in the country was also, and that after 1864 they rose steadily in value up to the end of the war (52–56).

The government's wartime need for money led to the National Banking Acts of 1863 and 1864. Chase, the secretary of the treasury, who had thought the greenback scheme hazardous, felt that the safest course was to ask the banks to help in selling large amounts of government bonds and urged these acts on Lincoln and Congress. By providing national chartering and regulation of private banks and specifying minimum specie reserves, these acts made possible a uniform currency, but the banks took care to ensure that when they bought government bonds, this was on terms very favorable to themselves. They were allowed to collect not only interest from the government but a second interest on 90 percent of the amount of these bonds through the provision that this amount could be lent at interest in the form of notes.

Chase came to regret his role in pressing for this legislation: "My agency in procuring the passage of the National Banking Act was the greatest financial mistake of my life. It has built up a monopoly that affects every interest in the country. It should be repealed. But before this can be accomplished the people will be arrayed on one side and the banks on the other in a contest such as we have never seen before in this country."[25]

Lincoln, writing to William P. Elkin on November 21, 1864, expressed the same forbodings about the vulnerability of the American people before the power of the bankers:

It has indeed been a trying hour for the Republic; but I see, in the near future, a crisis approaching that unnerves me and causes me to tremble for the safety of the country. As a result of the war, corporations have been enthroned, and an era of corruption in high places will follow, and the money power of the country will endeavor to prolong its reign by working upon the prejudices of the people until all wealth is aggregated in a few hands, and the Republic is destroyed. I feel more anxiety for my country that ever before, even in the midst of war.[26]

Yet, as Munson points out, it was not clear to those politicians like Jackson and Lincoln, who opposed the banks, what alternative system might be less liable to abuse. Jackson did consider the possiblity of government ownership of a new bank, but could not find an answer to the objection that political considerations might interfere with the bank's commercial functions. In fact, as many subsequent instances have shown, nationalization of banks fails to remedy the inadequacies of the old system since the problems are built into the system, regardless of who is running it. The Social Creditors believed that a new conception of the banks' function was necessary and that their system, built upon this new conception, would function in a mechanical and self-correcting way that would virtually eliminate opportunities for the greed and self-interest of the few to operate at the expense of the majority.

The Social Credit system had three main requirements: that the government assume the issuing of all kinds of money, that the just price be established, and that provisions be made for issuing a national dividend. The existing banking system would remain, but as the agency through which the government would issue and withdraw money. The government would also establish a National Monetary Authority, one of whose responsiblities would be to collect the data from which the just price and the national dividend could be calculated. The first step would be to compute the amount of the country's "Real Capital Assets" (the money value of agricultural lands, forests, minerals, buildings, harbors, communications, irrigation, developed water power, public works and so forth) and also the "Capitalized Value of the Population" (including earning power, value of production, value as consumers—as these are calculated by life insurance companies.) This inventory of the country's "abundance" would establish the amount of "real wealth" that could legitimately be monetized and provide a figure to act as an upper limit for the amount of money that the government could issue.

The monetary authority would also keep records of total production and of total consumption from which the just price would be calculated. The just price would equal cost price multiplied by consumption over production so that if the level of consumption stood at $\frac{3}{4}$ of the level of production, prices would be reduced by $\frac{1}{4}$. The logic behind this is that "if we have on one side values of a certain amount, they must be exactly balanced by money in consumers' hands if the goods to which the price values are affixed are to be cleared."[27] The Social Creditors claimed that a major flaw in traditional economic theory was the erroneous assumption that incomes always automatically generated sufficient purchasing power to cover cost of products. The just price would correct an inevitable insufficiency of purchasing power which traditional economics refused even to concede existed.

The most revolutionary Social Credit proposal was the idea of a national dividend. This would be a percentage (Douglas suggested an initial 1 percent) of the real capital assets account, to be paid equally to all citizens—adults and children—of the country except those whose net income was more than four times the amount of the dividend.[28] The amount of the national dividend would automatically act to adjust the level of the just price, since to increase the amount of the dividend would be to raise the amount of consumption relative to the amount of production and so reduce the amount of the retail discount.

In addition to ensuring sufficient purchasing power to maintain a healthy level of production, the national dividend would be particularly effective in helping to relieve the increasingly serious problem of insufficient employment. On this subject the Social Creditors were particularly far-sighted, and our present situation bears out their contention that the same progressive sophistication of technology that is constantly increasing our productive capacity is simultaneously responsible for reducing opportunities for employment. We see ample evidence now that seems to suggest that full employment is no longer a reasonable expectation, even though, by talking as though high real levels of unemployment are a temporary aberration, we have chosen to evade the responsibility of addressing a genuine problem and attempting a serious solution.

If full employment is no longer a possibility, it is essential that some form of income other than wages alone be available to people. Otherwise we are ensuring that there will always be an underclass of people who, although there never was an opportunity for them to work, are kept in poverty and stigmatized as unworthy of any better fate, as though they were unemployed by choice. A problem that mechanization had already made considerable when Douglas, Orage, and Munson were writing will inevitably be made much more serious by the revolution in data processing and the increasing sophistication of robotization that high tech microelectronics has made possible. We are so loath to abandon the assumption that full employment will always be the norm that we assume that any major advance such as high tech is bound to return us to this norm; yet this assumption seems not to be justified. As Robert Lekachman pointed out in 1983, "According to a Data Resources study commissioned by *Business Week,* high tech in the next decade will give birth to fewer than half of the two million jobs that vanished in manufacturing during the last three years."[29]

It is especially perverse that those very inventions that provide the community with easier and more efficient means of production than manual labor does should cause hardships for some members of the community. It was even more perverse, in the opinion of the Social Creditors, to persist with the traditional wage system when the system of national dividends would remove these hardships. Orage explains the logic of the new system very succinctly:

Social Creditors believe that as the Wage-system becomes obsolescent, thanks to the progressive depopulation of Industry, Dividends should gradually take the place of wages; so that as the Machine displaces Men, the Wage-income previously paid to the displaced men, continues to be paid to them by the Machine that has displaced them. If the Machine does the work of one hundred men, its production is obviously enough to pay one hundred men's wages. The Dividend is the logical successor of the Wage.[30]

The Social Creditors also realized that with decreasing opportunities for employment, is was necessary for people to overcome their instinctive mistrust of leisure. If people could be convinced that a national dividend was a more logical and humane alternative than hard-core unemployment, they would also have to become accustomed to shorter working hours and increased leisure.

Orage himself saw increased leisure as not only a necessity but also as an entirely positive development for the society as a whole. He points out: "Leisure, restricted though it has been, has nevertheless given us all the values of Civilisation, as well as some of the values of Culture. Civilisation may be said to be the creation of Leisure, just as Culture may be said to be the right use of Leisure."[31] Yet, with his customary realism, he was well aware of the strong psychological resistance that most people have to the prospect of more leisure for everyone and to the optimistic projections of the Douglas plan. In "The Fear of Leisure" he lists eight reasons for this resistance: "The Fear of Scarcity. The Moral Associations of Work. Hatred of the Principle of Something for Nothing. Class-hatred, on the one side, and Class-revenge on the other. The deep-rooted convictions that Man is not meant to be happy, that any prospect of happiness is too good to be true, and that even if the conditions were created for happiness, human nature would soon spoil them. The Will to Power . . . the control over the lives of others . . . The Fear of Leisure [and] Fear of any change whatever."[32]

Pound's one significant departure from Douglasite theory was his advocacy of stamp scrip as an alternative to a national dividend. The purpose of stamp scrip, as set down by Silvio Gesell in his work *The Natural Economic Order,* was to ensure that money was kept in circulation by arranging for it to lose its value if it was hoarded. People were to be required at regular intervals—he suggested the first of each month—to attach a stamp costing 1 percent of its value to each note of currency in their possession, so that the longer the money was held, the less its value became until the cost of the stamps canceled out the face value of the note. The stamps would substitute for a sales tax and provide the government with a source of income, and Pound liked the fairness of the idea that "this form of taxation . . . can only fall on persons who have, at the moment the tax falls due, money in their pockets worth 100 times the tax itself" (*SP*, 347–48).

Pound did not become interested in Gesellite *Schwundgeld,* or "shrinking money," until after 1933. The "ABC of Economics," in other respects his most complete statement of his economic views, makes no mention of it, although it is true, as he says in "The Individual in His Milieu: A Study of Relations and Gesell," that the ABC "left a place for Schwundgeld" (*SP,* 277). This "place" is his observation that "one hundred gallons a minute through an inch pipe at one speed can equal one hundred gallons through a different pipe at another speed—the bigger the slower, the faster the smaller, etc. A small amount of 'money' changing hands rapidly will do the work of a lot moving slowly, etc." (*SP*, 254).

Pound liked stamp script because it was an "unhoardable" form of money, a medium of exchange which was stripped of its "privileged status" vis-à-vis perishable commodities in being made "perishable" just as they were. It also satisfied his didactic bent: "I am particularly keen on Gesell, because once people have used stamp scrip they HAVE a clear idea about money. They understand tickets better than men who haven't used stamp scrip . . . . I don't say you HAVE to use Gesell's method. But once you understand WHY he wanted it you will not be fleeced by bank sharks and 'monetary authorities' WITHOUT KNOWING HOW you are being fleeced. That is WHY Gesell is so useful as a school teacher" (*SP, 296*).

In fact, it seems safe to say that Pound was drawn to the idea of Gesell's scrip more for philosophical than for practical reasons. He liked it because it was "usury-proof," whether it was practical or not. It did become clear to him that it could work only as an auxiliary means of exchange, and as long as this was so it would be hard to stop people from using other forms of money. Its most promising use would be an interest-free way of financing public works projects and other services useful to the state. On one hand he was aware of certain practical limitations to its use, but on the other was the temptation to treat its failure to be implemented as the result of a banker's conspiracy. His thinking about stamp scrip cannot fail to be colored by the fact that, so soon after he learned about it, he had seen at first hand how it had been sabotaged.

In late summer of 1935, he made an expedition with James Laughlin to the small town of Wörgl in the Austrian Tirol to find out for himself how stamp script had actually worked. When Michael Unterguggenberger became mayor in December 1931, the town was on the verge of bankruptcy. Local unemployment meant that many municipal taxes had gone unpaid for several years and even federal taxes were in arrears. In July 1932, a committee of four, led by the mayor, decided to issue 12,000 schillings' worth of Gesellite scrip (or *Notgeld*) in vouchers of 1, 5, and 10S. The speed with which this scrip circulated can be seen from the fact that between August 1932 and November 1933, the town had spent 100,000S on public works, although only 12,000S of Notgeld were in circulation. In this short time, back taxes were paid up, bank deposits were in excess of withdrawals by 60,000S, all the badly deteriorated town streets were repaired, a new concrete bridge was made over the river, the town hall was renovated, a ski jump was built, and the business of local shopkeepers increased significantly. But in January 1933, the Austrian National Bank charged the mayor and corporation with violating the federal law that gave the bank sole right to issue banknotes. The mayor ignored the court ruling against him but was charged a second time and, when he took the case to the Appeal Court in November 1933, it was judged a criminal offense and the scrip was liquidated. Soon after this, Engelbert Dollfuss came to power and Unter-guggenberger was imprisoned for two weeks because of his "political opinions."[33]

In 74/441, Pound recalls his visit:

> the state need not borrow
> as was shown by the mayor of Wörgl
> who had a milk route
> and whose wife sold shirts and short breeches

and on whose book-shelf was the Life of Henry Ford
and also a copy of the Divina Commedia
and of the Gedichte of Heine
a nice little town in the Tyrol in a wide flat-lying valley
near Innsbruck and when a note of the
small town of Wörgl went over
a counter in Innsbruck
and the banker saw it go over
all the slobs in Europe were terrified
"no one" said the Frau Burgomeister
"in this village who cd/ write a newspaper article
knew it was money but pretended it was not
in order to be on the safe side of the law."

The danger point here lies between the two lines "and the banker saw it go over / all the slobs in Europe were terrified." Pound could not resist the temptation to give the sabotaging of this colorful, local, small-scale, and very concrete manifestation of sound finance a significance that was far too sweeping—and sinister. In one mood he saw stamp scrip as education, in another he saw it as "counter-usury," a weapon in the guerrilla war of the monetary reformers against the "enormous, secret, unacknowledged" privi-lege of "the merchants of money" (*SP*, 274). As early as October 1935, he was writing of the Wörgl experiment in the same spirit in which he was to think of it at Pisa in Canto 74: "At Woërgl . . . a working (therefore workable) system was only interrupted by brute force, the Austrian government playing catspaw to the international thieves' and murderers' association, by no right, by no justice, by brute stupidity and malevolence, with force on the spot and the power of preventing very wide publicity of their infamy from spreading outside their own tyrannised borders" (*SP*, 277–78).

Some of Pound's friends tried to warn him against being lured from the safe road of Social Credit by the ignis fatuus of Gesellism but, characteris-tically, he paid little attention. John Hargrave, the leading Social Credit activist in Britain, in a long and very informative letter of January 6, 1935, rejected Gesell's approach as too indirect and insisted that "a good strong dose of Douglas *neat* is what is wanted" (*EPA*). Orage, in a postscript to a postcard written to Pound on June 12, 1933, was even more emphatic: "PS./To hell with Woergl!" (*EPA*).

Orage was very eloquent in projecting his vision of a time when grinding poverty or interminable financial anxiety for many would be replaced by economic security and productive leisure for all, but as we have seen, he was well aware of the obstacles that threatened to keep this ideal time permanently in the realm of the visionary. His realism saved him from the disillusionment that was eventually to warp the thinking of many of the adherents of the Social Credit cause, but it was frustrating to someone like John Hargrave, who was particularly strongly committed to political activism. In a letter that he wrote to Pound on January 26, 1935, Hargrave recreated an exchange with Orage in Brenton's *New Age* office. To Hargrave's accusation "I think you want to have a revolution without having one," Orage conceded, "Yes, I think I do." Then "Orage began to put forward [the] idea of a sort of Big Brother Movement [which would allow him to be] . . . a personality who gathered people around itself and just suggested gently what they should do—never by chance giving an order." Hargrave continued, "It was clear to me . . . that Orage would not face the pain of giving an order to someone else, and the physical strain that political action demands. His chemistry was Big Brother . . . he tended to think *about* action [which] is always fatal at the moment of action."

As it turned out, Douglas himself was to prove completely incapable of providing the leadership to translate his theory into effective political action. He was able to present his theory at several forums but this was not enough.

In 1921, the draft scheme for the mining industry that he presented to the British Labour party received an adverse report. In 1920 he went to America as a consultant to founders of labor banks; in 1923 in Ottawa he testified at hearings for renewal of a bank charter act, and in 1923 he gave evidence to the Macmillan Committee on Finance and Industry. In 1933 in Birmingham there was a public debate between Douglas and R. G. Hawtray of the British treasury. In 1933 and 1934 he made a world tour during which he addressed large crowds in Australia and New Zealand, gave evidence before the Agriculture Committee of the Alberta Legislature in Canada, spoke at the New School for Social Research in New York, and attended a supper for senators and congressmen which was given in his honor by Senator Bronson Cutting. On his return to England, Douglas realized that presentation of his theory was no longer enough, so in June 1934 in a meeting at Buxton, he announced a program of political action which led to the founding of the Social Credit Secretariat, of which he became chairman. But the secretariat decided to limit its activities to collecting signatures and pledges as a way of influencing members of parliament rather than mounting a propaganda campaign to stir up public support.

One Social Creditor, Robert J. Scrutton, organized a petition to be presented directly to King George V. Even more than his father, the future Edward VIII was known to be convinced of the need for social reform, and Pound's high hopes that some progress could be made in instituting Social Credit once Edward became king—"It may depend on one man / . . . as in the case of Edwardus" (87/563)—were not just a personal idiosyncracy but a strongly held belief among Social Creditors. As it happened, these hopes were to be abruptly dashed by the death of George V and the abdication of Edward.

In a letter to John Hargrave on the subject, Pound writes with his characteristic urgency and hyperbole:

If you don't move NOW you are OUT for all time. . . . You will never get another King with decent instincts and a will or at least a passive willingness to improve the condition of the people . . . . I have no proof that Ed/ has ability, but he is human . . . USURY is AGAINST LIFE. against fertility. Usurers' pimps are against LIFE in poor and life in palace.[34]

John Hargrave was an ideal contact for Pound. An even more indefatigable correspondent than Pound himself, Hargrave gave him a very detailed and reliable view of what was happening in Britain in Social Credit circles. In some ways the two men were rather similar, most notably in their optimism, their energy, and their strength of will—although Hargrave was much more practical and more in touch with the facts of the social and political realities around him than Pound was. Like Pound, he was a writer as well as a social reformer and came from a family with a strong Quaker background. His childhood, like that of Orage, gave him a firsthand acquaintance with poverty. He also wrote proudly to Pound of the "streak of fighting Genghis Khan blood" that he inherited from a grandfather on his mother's side who came to England as a student refugee after fighting in Hungary under Kossuth. In 1935 he published his sixth novel, *Summer Time Ends,* which Williams reviewed very favorably in the *New Democracy* of November 1.

Unlike Pound, Hargrave was very strongly committed to and adept at practical action. He had been one of Lord Baden-Powell's close associates in the Boy Scout movement and, on August 18, 1920, founded his own "camping, handicraft and World Peace Movement," which he called the Kindred of the Kibbo Kift (from two dialect words meaning stick—or cudgel—of great strength), which was to provide training in woodcraft, camping, and nature craft as a way of counteracting the effects of overcrowding in the cities. In 1924 Hargrave discovered the works of Douglas, and in 1929 the movement adopted Social Credit. This increasingly became its main focus and a Green Shirt wing organized itself, with the purpose of carrying the Social Credit message to the young and the poor. On October 30, 1932, the Kinsmen and their Green Shirt associates joined the hunger marchers' demonstration in Trafalgar Square carrying a green and white banner with the slogan Abolish the Means Test and Issue the National Dividend—Not Less for Some, but More for All! In January 1933 the Kibbo Kift was reorganized as the Green Shirt Movement for Social Credit, whose program had three demands: "Open the National Credit Office, Issue the National Dividend to All, Apply the Scientific Price." In 1935 the Green Shirt Movement changed its name to the Social Credit Party of Great Britain and Northern Ireland.

Hargrave, who prided himself on his expertise in organizing demonstrations, told Pound that he had made a systematic study of "Techniques of Revolt" (letter of January 6, 1935) and was able to get a good deal of publicity for the Social Credit cause. One demonstration that received considerable press and radio coverage was the Social Credit party's ritualistic burning of a wheat sheaf outside the London Board of Trade on January 10, 1939, where representatives from twenty-two countries were attending a meeting of the International Wheat Advisory Committee. The demonstrators carried signs reading They Burn the Wheat We Want to Eat and marched up in formation. His followers were well-organized and loyal and many were arrested for acts of "civil disobedience" such as painting Social Credit slogans on the Bank of England or shouting them in the House of

Commons. Hargrave himself used the same kind of disruptive technique when, on July 20, 1938, he publicly broke with Douglas and "amid riotous circumstances at Chiltern Court, London . . . invaded a dinner of Dougla-sites, climbed on a table, and repudiated 'any claim made by or on behalf of Douglas and/or Secretariat-group to political leadership of the Social Credit movement.' "[35]

Pound was enthusiastic about Hargrave's strategy for taking the cause to the common people: "thank god / SOMEone HAS studied revolt as such . . . a SEEN action out weighs all the talk. S/C/ has got to get OUT of Bloomsbury and into the East End" (EPA, 1/21/35). He was also ready to give whatever support he could to the whole business of mounting impressive parades, to which Hargrave attached so much importance. Hargrave insisted that the uniforms, the marching, the singing, and what he called the "pageantry equipment" of drums and flags all be smart and impressive and warned Pound that handmade equipment would make a poor impression. He asked Pound to agree to "present" one of the green, white, and black Green Shirt flags which would have Presented by Ezra Pound, 1935 embroidered on it. Pound did not have to pay for it but was to send a "Letter of presentation" to be read at its dedication.

Hargrave also asked Pound to write some Green Shirt marching songs and wanted some contributions to his weekly Message From Hargrave, preferably a foreword of support for the Green Shirts and a regular column to be called "Ezra Pound's Pound" or "Ezra Pound's Corner." The idea of the marching songs appealed to Pound and he rose to the occasion, offering as one of his credentials the observation: "I wuz riz among nigguhs / the uneven forms of the camp meetin . . . dos jes get right down into my blood / regular strophes BORE ME//" (EPA, 1/21/35). In something of the same vein, led by his enthusiasm beyond the limits of the practical, he offers Hargrave the unintentionally amusing suggestion that it might also be possible to attract public attention to the Social Credit message through the use of music hall routines (EPA, 1/26/35).

Hargrave manages, also unintentionally, to be every bit as amusing in what has to be one of the most rousing calls to write that a poet ever received. On February 12, 1935, he writes to Pound:

I want you to write a book (big or small) of Green Shirt Cantos. . . . Stuff it full of meat: product of intellect. Never mind if we don't know what your allusions may be exactly—don't be simple. We shall "get" you by . . . the word-music coming out of you. By telling US what you feel, you can shape the whole S.C. movement in Great Britain, and give it fire and passion. . . . The Prophet Ezra preaching to the Green Shirts! You can make us shout back at you in mass-chorus. . . . Take the Green-Shirts as a centre-point for an Epic World-Shout! It'll be like shouting a Great Poem over the mike (you speaking-singing-shouting to an invisible audience . . .). Ezra, if you can and will & do write *that* for us—we shall get power to fight and win. It's your *job* as a bard, a poet, a wordmusic-maker to do this. . . . I bet you've never been asked before to do a real job which *is* your real job by living men who need your help to go into action?

Pound, naturally enough, politely declined this invitation to turn his poetry into Whitmanian chant: "Cantos 31/41 are about as solid economically as anything can be / (I don't know if you saw 38 when Orage printed it.) But I don't see it going big in Lambeth" (*EPA*, 2/20/35). Yet his certainty that his Cantos cannot be used as a vehicle for this particular kind of jeremiac exhortation does not necessarily mean that he rules out the possibility of making an "Epic World-Shout" altogether. In fact, we could say that he follows this directive of Hargrave's very closely if we apply it, not to his poetry, but to his radio broadcasts. As it happens, part 2 of Hargrave's suggested outline for a set of "Green Shirt Cantos" begins "THIS IS EZRA POUND speaking . . . (*EPA*, 2/12/35). When we think of the Rome Radio broadcasts and consider Pound in 1944 in Rapallo, printing up posters and "banners" with maxims from Confucius and economic reform slogans, we might do well to resist the automatic assumption that he is imitating the techniques of Fascist propaganda and recall the placards of the Green Shirt movement and Hargrave's call to Pound to make the Epic World-Shout of economic reform.

Hargrave was adamantly anticommunist and even more adamantly anti-Fascist. He insisted that Social Credit could provide the complete solution to the problems that had made people turn to communism or fascism in despair of finding a better solution. He coined the term "Third Resolvent Factor" to emphasize the ability of Social Credit to make pointless the "Left-Right Conflict." Hargrave's Social Creditors assumed a highly patriotic position at the time of World War II: taking a strong stand against Mosley's thugs, urging the government to be militarily more aggressive and to use more effective propaganda, and criticizing the Bank of England for slowing down arms production by not making debt-free money available for more rapid armament.

The clearness and directness of Hargrave's message appealed to a wide range of people, not just to the poor, the young, and the workers but also to servicemen and artists. He was said to have three thousand supporters in the air force, and we can see from the following tribute paid to him by Augustus

John the "visionary" quality of his message, which appealed to writers and artists like Eliot, Williams, and Pound:

Turning neither to the "Right" nor to the "Left," [Hargrave] offers a clean-cut program of national recovery which joins to the aspirations of the Spirit a new and rational technique of economics, and, by the methods of Science, the resuscitation of the soil we live on. The leader of the Social Credit Party announces the Gospel of Peace, Freedom, Leisure and Abundance; a Light for the disinherited of all lands, and sounds the trumpet-blast of a New Order, home-grown but of universal application. In this sign we shall conquer.[36]

The Social Credit movement in America may not have provided as colorful a character as Hargrave, but in Gorham Munson it found an eloquent leader of exceptionally fine intellect. Orage himself was personally responsible for introducing America and Munson to Douglas's theories, as Pound reminds Hargrave in defending Orage against the charge that he was too little concerned with putting Social Credit ideas into action: "Last time I kussed at Orage fer theosophy-WhichWhat, I was reminded that it was in America he got the wherewithal fer new start [to start the *New English Weekly*] / he also planted the Soc/Cr seed over thaaar. He had fought 20 years in Eng / needed vacation" (*EPA*, 1/21/35).

It was not until the end of his stay in American that Orage spoke publicly on Social Credit. Early in the spring of 1931 he gave four lectures on credit to about fifty people at the New York School of the Theatre, several of whom—including Munson himself—were to become the leaders of the Social Credit movement in America. In 1932 Orage's *New English Weekly* began publication, and the New Economics Group of New York was established with Munson as one of the founding members. The group published some pamphlets, drew up a general Social Credit Plan for New Jersey, and published the Social Credit journal *New Democracy*, which Munson edited.[37] Pound had given James Laughlin an introduction to Munson, who put him in charge of the Social Credit and the Arts, department which Laughlin chose to call New Directions. In 1938 Munson founded the American Social Credit Movement with the object of encouraging political action. Already, on August 23, 1935, Congressman T. Alan Goldsborough had introduced into Congress a Social Credit bill drafted by the New Economics Group. The bill was given a two-day hearing in the spring of 1936 and, after being revised by the technical studies department of the American Social Credit Movement, the Goldsborough bill was reintroduced into Congress in 1937 and received protracted hearings before the House Banking Committee although it was not, finally, reported out of committee. (Munson includes a draft of this bill in the Author's Workshop section of *Aladdin's Lamp,* pp. 362–63.) Also in America, Hugo A. Fack kept Gesell's message before the public, both by publishing an English translation of Gesell's *The Natural Economic Order* and a monthly magazine, *The Way Out,* out of San Antonio.

Social Credit as a political force rather than just an economic theory is most likely to be associated with Alberta since it was here that a Social Credit party actually came to power. In 1935, William Aberhart's party won fifty-seven of the sixty-three seats in the Legislative Assembly, and the Social Credit party remained in power for thirty-six years. They were replaced by the Conservatives in 1971, and, on March 31, 1982, the Social Credit party formally decided not to run any candidates in the next election. Yet ironically, the party was never able to institute any permanent Social Credit measures, partly from the lack of clear direction in the early days of Aberhart's premiership but mainly because the Social Credit legislation that was finally proposed—such as the issuing of Gesellite "Prosperity Certificates"—was declared illegal and unconstitutional by the dominion courts.[38]

Douglas's failure to go promptly to Alberta, as expected, to advise Aberhart was widely criticized as a characteristic instance of his general failure to provide the Social Credit movement with effective political leadership. Douglas's own defense was that Aberhart had already decided to be guided by orthodox financiers before he would consult with Douglas and so there was no point in his going to Alberta at all.[39] In January 1937, John Hargrave tried to galvanize the Alberta Social Credit party into demanding some genuine Social Credit legislation from Aberhart, and two commissioners were sent from England as advisers, but then the dominion courts moved in to disallow the legislation.

William Carlos Williams kept a photograph of Orage in his attic study, and by early 1934 Williams was actively committed to the Social Credit cause and began to contribute to *New Democracy.*[40] On January 15 of that year, the magazine ran his article "Social Credit as Anti-Communism," and on October 15, 1935, he wrote a strongly positive review of *Jefferson and/or Mussolini.* In 1936 Munson invited him to be one of a team of Social Credit speakers to attend a conference sponsored by the Institute of Public Affairs in Charlottesville, Virginia. Williams, asked to present an artist's point of view, gave a talk entitled "The Attack on Credit Monopoly from a Cultural Viewpoint," in which he reiterated many of Pound's favorite points about Van Buren, Confucius, Hamilton, and Jefferson, spoke of his own difficulties in publishing his work under the present economic system, and warned that American communists were seriously underestimating the violence that would be involved in any proletarian revolution.[41]

Williams was much disturbed by the drift toward antisemitism that he saw in Pound in the late 1930s and tried to warn him against it, without success. Douglas also turned to antisemitism in this period. He had been writing on Social Credit for twenty years with no sign of an antisemitic bias, but in the late 1930s he started to emphasize what he claimed to be the racial causes of world economic problems. As soon as Munson saw that Douglas had taken this tack, he insisted on a complete separation between the American Social Credit movement and Douglas, and he warned strongly of the dangers of treating the matter of economic corruption as though it were a racial issue by including in *Aladdin's Lamp* a chapter entitled "Anti-Semitism: A Poverty Problem." Hargrave, determined to safeguard his party against the antisemitism of Douglas and some of his followers, issued a formal statement on the matter on March 5, 1943. "The SCP is against any kind of anti-Semitic propaganda, or the development of any racial antago-nism. Any Member or Associate Member who deviates from the Party Line . . . is liable to have his or her membership terminated by direction of the Founder and Leader of the Party."[42]

Yet Pound's correspondence shows that, before 1935, even though Douglas had begun to turn to antisemitism in this way, Pound had not. In June 1934 we find Orage responding to a letter in which Pound had passed on to him, from W. E. Woodward, a warning that "any trait of anti-Semitism in Douglas is *necessarily* fatal" (*EPA*, 6/11/34). Orage points out in his response that, while Pound is warning him about what, at this stage, is "a trifle of anti-Semitism" in Douglas, Pound is simultaneously urging Orage to try to work with other economic reformers who are, unbeknownst to Pound, extremely antisemitic. Orage makes his own position clear when he writes: "Douglas thinks that Jewry is *organically* incapable of seeing Social Credit; but . . . I'm not impressed. After all, there are lots of Jewish Social Creditors (not Munson except by marriage), & there's Waldo Frank to begin with" (*EPA*, 6/29/34).

To a large extent, where reformers turned to antisemitism, they did so out of their sense of frustration and disillusionment with their lack of progress toward their goals. This is evident in the case of Father Charles E. Coughlin, "the radio priest," with whom Pound was in correspondence. It was entirely consistent with Orage's thoughtfulness and perceptivity that he, in contrast, should have been so clear about the fallacy of any "conspiracy theory" explanations of the Social Creditors' lack of progress and so clearly aware of the real explanation:

A sufficient number of people can certainly be got to understand the Douglas Theory at least as a theory. A dozen good parliamentary draughtsmen, in consultation with Douglas himself, could certainly draw up the statutory orders necessary to start the Plan in practice. But neither a sufficient number of people will trouble to understand the Plan, nor will any responsible official draught a clause of an enabling Act, *until,* by one means or another—despair of the existing order or hope of a new order—the objectives, implied in the Plan, are earnestly and unequivocally desired. . . . I am so far from thinking that any grand conspiracy could succeed against the community without at least the passive consent of the community itself that I even believe that the Grand Conspirators, if they exist, are only the conscious agents of the unconscious hopes and fears of their victims. And, in my judgement, if the world becomes subjected—as it appears likely to be—to the Grand Dictatorship of Finance, it will be because an overwhelming majority of its population will approve of that form of control, as, at any rate, the lesser of the two evils of world-dictatorship, on the one hand, and a Douglas Social Credit Commonwealth on the other.[43]

Orage, unlike Pound, by not being given to overoptimism, was saved from the recourse of paranoia.

One of Pound's most fundamental mistakes would prove to be his failure to dig deep enough in his attempt to expose the roots of economic injustice. Perceptive about its nature, he failed to understand its root cause and "motive power." He failed to consider that the socially destructive forces which he deplored did not originate with corrupt institutions but proceeded from the inescapable defects of human nature—from greed, selfishness, and love of power. We see that he finally became aware of his mistake from his July 1972 foreword to his *Selected Prose, 1909–1965*: "re USURY: I was out of focus, taking a symptom for a cause. The cause is AVARICE."

Pound and Mussolini: "The Coming of War: Abyssinia"

3

"No longer necessary," taxes are no longer
necessary
in the old way if it (money) be based on work done
               inside a system and measured and gauged to
human
                                       requirements
inside the nation or system

and cancelled in proportion
                     to what is used and worn out
á la Wörgl. Sd/ one wd/ have to think about that
but was hang'd dead by the heels before his thought in
proposito
       came into action efficiently

[78/481–82; Chinese = *tao* "the process"]

Imprisoned at Pisa, Pound, against all the evidence, persisted in his belief that the system that had worked at Wörgl could have been made to work in Italy and that there was still a chance that, had he not been killed, Mussolini would have instituted the economic reforms that Pound wanted to see. Pound needed to believe this because of the role that he had chosen for himself and that he would continue to perform—despite its complete inappropriateness—even after Pisa through the twelve and a half long years at St. Elizabeths. If we can understand how he conceived of this role and how inevitable it was, in his eyes, that he should accept its responsibilities, we can go a long way toward understanding his actions and reactions during his years in Fascist Italy.

    The year of Mussolini's invasion of Abyssinia, 1935, was a fateful one for Pound. The invasion confronted him with irrefutable evidence that Mussolini was not the champion of world peace that he had claimed, and Pound had believed him, to be. To renounce Mussolini at this stage would require Pound drastically to revise the role that he had arrogated to himself, and this he was unable to do. Instead he evaded the responsibility of conscious moral choice. He committed himself by default to a strategy of unconsciously motivated evasion of the truth about Mussolini, and rationalizing away the evidence of the Duce's bad faith. In October 1935, the same month as the invasion, Pound published an article in the *Criterion* that provides valuable clues to his conception of this all-important role he felt he had no choice but to accept. "The Individual in His Milieu" begins:

Twenty years ago little magazines served to break a monopoly, to release communication, mainly about letters, from an oppressive control, and they now wither on the stalk because they refuse to go on from where the late Henry James was interrupted. H. J. perceived the *Anagke* of the modern world to be money. . . . The diseased periphery of letters is now howling that literature and poetry in especial, should keep within bounds . . . [or] "respect itself," which phrase is perverted to mean that literature should eschew the major field by omitting and leaving untackled . . . the subject [of money]. [*SP*, 272]

Pound's role as prophet of economic reform is clearly, in his view, merely a continuation of his role as reformer of poetry. We have already seen how far he considered his efforts to "purify the dialect of the tribe" to be the fulfillment of a moral imperative and an essential means of safeguarding the society by ensuring the integrity of its main means of communication. After World War I, it became clear that "cleansing [the] language" was not a stringent enough measure to protect the West from the recurrence of such a catastrophe. Once he heard Douglas's promise that his system of economic reform could cut to the very root of the causes of war, it was not just logical but even inevitable that Pound would give the Social Credit cause priority among his allegiances.

Yet he overlooked the very real differences between being the focal point of the Imagist movement and being a central authority on the reform of the economic systems of America and Europe, which was, in fact, how he now saw himself. "The Individual in His Milieu" makes clear how felicitously he had chosen to deny these differences: "The truth about economics had had no warmer welcome than had a few simple and known facts about the tradition in metric and poetry during a couple of preceding decades. The parallel would be comic were it not freighted with tragedy, death, malnutrition, degradation of the national health in a dozen countries" (*SP*, 280). Even the gesture toward recognition of the disparity between the magnitude of the poetic changes he effected and the economic revolution he projected is withdrawn. He chose to see no reason why he should not be able to have as much impact on the world of international finance as he had had in the London literary world before the war.

Particularly after the death of Orage, Pound took upon himself the grandiose role of one-man clearinghouse for all the "serious" economic reform movements of Europe and America. He credited himself with an international perspective of greater breadth and discernment than anyone else's and with an overarching and synthesizing vision which would enable him to reconcile the various reformist factions by pointing out how the strengths of each could be capitalized on and how their superficial differ- ences could be shown to be immaterial. His strongest qualifications were his incontrovertible sincerity and goodwill and his indefatigable energy, but he had, of course, set himself a task that no one could accomplish.

He suppressed any awareness that the talent and effort necessary to produce good poetry and the expertise and influence necessary to recon- struct the economic systems of the West were of a different order of magnitude and that to have succeeded in the first was no guarantee of success in the second. From his jeremiac perspective, he was both qualified and obligated to be an economic reformer, but his tendency to fall into ranting overstatement in the writings in which he does insist that this is so, clearly reflects the tension that comes from a discrepancy between apparent certitude and unconscious misgivings. In "History and Ignorance," for example, we sense the defensiveness behind the panicky assertions:

The "Manchester Guardian" howl that poetry should be a lavender sachet bag, and omit all the major content of the Divina Commedia [that is, its concern with economic and social justice], comes well from fake pacifist quarters.
Pacifists who refuse to investigate the economic causes of war make common cause with the gun sellers. . . . Naturally the bastards who do not want truth . . . want to eliminate the whole major domain of writing . . . from the scope of the poets. . . . This degradation . . . obviously plays into the hands of the people who wish to maintain slavery, and to whom any perception of truth re social or *any other* kind of relation, is a menace.
The maintainers of mass murder and mass malnutrition have in these people very useful, if unconscious, allies.[1]

Yet when he is writing on purely literary matters and sending criticism and advice to other writers, there is frequently no trace of this kind of ranting. For this reason, a selection of letters that are predominantly on literary subjects alone, such as Paige has made, gives a very misleading impression of Pound's state of mind in the late 1930s. The "History and Ignorance" article was written in 1935; yet none of the Paige letters, even though they run through 1941, shows any evidence of the ranting which, in the 1935 article, so strongly conveys Pound's paranoid state of mind.

Presumably, Paige deliberately chose to omit from his collection those letters which show Pound in an obviously disturbed state of mind and yet this has the unintentional effect—surely the reverse of the one he intended—of ultimately creating a more negative rather than a more positive impression of the poet. Many of the readers of Pound who know his letters are likely only to know those in Paige and from these they will take away the impression that even in the late 1930s Pound was substantially lucid, reasonable, and in control of his emotions. When they turn from these letters, in which what he says seems so clearly under his conscious control, to the radio speeches, it would seem to be a reasonable assumption that the broadcasts also are a straightforward expression of his conscious and considered opinion. If this were so, we ought to judge Pound far more harshly than we would if we realized that the broadcasts were, on the contrary, the product of a mind whose perception of its surrounding reality was seriously distorted and which was moved much more by unconscious compulsions than by considered, conscious purpose.

The degree to which his commentary on purely literary matters *is* free from ranting and the predictability with which any economic topic will draw him into involuntary tirades might well make it hard to believe that it is simultaneously possible to exercise self-control and discretion on one subject and to be incapable of self-control on another. Yet this is exactly the case with Pound. The fact that his state of mind progressively declined during the 1930s and 1940s is beyond question; yet the matter of tracing that decline is very much complicated by a constant side-to-side movement as he swings from energetic optimism to frustration and angry paranoia and then back again. Although his thinking, whenever he discussed economics, showed how seriously distorted his perception of reality had become, his lucidity and reasonableness on the subject of his own writing and his literary interests led people to minimize the extent of his disorientation in this other area. As we shall see, it even led the psychiatrists at St. Elizabeths to discount the possiblity that his paranoia could really be the psychotic state which it both seemed and almost certainly was. They were unable to help Pound because they were unaware of the reasons for his mental state. But, to have understood these reasons would have required them to make themselves familiar in some detail with his literary and economic ideals, with his expectations for reform, and with his perception of the situation in Italy from 1924 on.

The critic trying to decide what to conclude about Pound's essential nature from his post-1935 broadcasts and writings must take into account both the above considerations and also the kind of moral choice Pound made in 1935. Most crucially at issue is the difference between choosing deliberately and consciously to adopt an antisemitic position and coming to hold such a position as a consequence of having evaded the responsibility of making a conscious choice on an unrelated issue. It is easy to assign blame when consciously, unapologetically, and out of deliberate ill-will a person chooses to call for antisemitic measures, but in Pound's case the point at which he started to make his antisemitic statements was at a considerable remove from the original act of choice about whether to renounce Musso-lini. It is clear that, at the time when he had to choose, he could not even have foreseen what state of mind his evasion would reduce him to, let alone have chosen it in advance. While this makes his antisemitic statements no less immoral in absolute terms, it needs to be taken into account if we are attempting to arrive at conclusions about the essential nature of his personality and character on the basis of his having made these statements.

Whenever Pound's speeches are at issue, it is common to find considerable resistance to the idea that they show Pound to be a man driven at some level by hatred. This resistance is not merely apologist. When those who knew him personally, Jews as well as Gentiles, argue that they cannot reconcile the picture of Pound as rabid antisemite with the kind and generous-spirited man they knew, and when students of his writings insist that they cannot find even latent evidence of hatred and meanspiritedness in his pre-1930s' writings, they are responding to the observable facts of the case. Any decisive judgment of his actions must allow for the fact that we are not dealing with an instance of conscious and deliberate moral choice but with the avoidance of choice and the inevitably self-destructive consequences of this kind of evasion.

Rather than choosing to act in an inhumane way, Pound chose evasion over confrontation and, in so doing, unwittingly placed himself in a situation in which his ability to make responsible moral judgments would necessarily be impaired. An examination of Pound's state of mind at the time of the Rome Radio broadcasts shows how the attempt to protect oneself by evading information that threatens to be painful and by adopting an alternative, false explanation is likely to be a self-destructive act, entailing more pain and confusion than would be involved had the reality of the situation been faced squarely. In Pound's case, the considerable inventive and persuasive abilities of his unconscious were enlisted in the task of rationalizing away all the evidence of how the political situation in Italy really was after 1935 and of maintaining the impression that the expurgated version that remained was an accurate representation of the current reality. Repressing his awareness of the mounting evidence of Mussolini's duplicity and corruption, Pound found himself supplied with plenty of inventive rationalizations; yet the deep mental instinct toward health—manifested in the impulse to register honestly the facts of a situation as they were—constantly acted as a threat to the persuasiveness of the rationalizations that were being supplied. This meant that either the rationalizations had to be made more sophisticated and inventive or the observable facts of the situation had to be blocked out. We see both these processes at work in Pound as the 1930s move to their end until, by the time of the Rome Radio broadcasts, he was psychologically incapable of registering accurately the nature of the international situation and the roles played by Mussolini, Churchill, Roosevelt, Stalin, and Hitler.

When we study the anger of the Pound of the late 1930s, we are discovering not "how he had really been all along," but what his state of mind had become as a consequence of trying to evade the need to make a responsible moral choice on a specific issue at a specific time. The general principle of the self-destructive consequences of evasion is illustrated in a magnified form in the case of Pound, both because of the intensity of the pressures he was subjected to and because of the extremity of his tempera-ment. Qualities of personality which, exercised in pursuit of a worthwhile goal, would have a highly positive influence served only to aggravate an already deteriorating situation once his perception was unreliable and his goal ill-judged. This was especially true of his tenacity and of his capacity for quick and decisive action, both of which were bound to carry him further than a less tenacious and impulsive person would go. They not only carried him as far in a self-destructive direction as they would have in a constructive one, but their negative effect was even greater as a result of his tendency to intensify his activity to an even more frenetic pace as the pressures upon him increased.

Similarly, the intuitive abilities upon which he so prided himself were also to prove as much of a liability to him in his attempt to appraise the political situation as they had been an asset in his poetic judgments. When he was making decisions about his own poetry or judging the writings of others, his intuitive reactions were usually reliable and his method of singling out and juxtaposing "luminous details" was effective. Yet this way of registering the insights of the "direct and shooting mind" works only as long as the mind remains discriminating and preserves a sense of balance and proportion. If no sound understanding or careful appraisal of its general context lies behind his selection of a significant detail, the gist no longer embodies a general truth but becomes dangerously impressionistic.

The very ideogramic approach which had allowed him in his poetry to set up complex interrelations of echoes and resonances in a way that deepened and amplified the significance of the whole was now being used with the opposite effect. Seizing upon details with no proper attention to their context, he was allowing himself to settle for dangerous oversimplifications of complex situations. As the pressures upon him increased, his reactions to what seemed to him significant details became increasingly extreme. One negative instance was likely to lead to a blanket condemnation or impassioned denunciation, while a positive sign could be taken as grounds for unrealistic hope and fulsome praise. For example, an Associated Press dispatch from Calgary giving an accurate and sympathetic account of Aberhart and Social Credit seemed to him grounds for new faith in the American press as a whole: "The New York account of ALBERTA is proof of one high ideal . . . that has sprouted in American journalism, namely that the press is there to PRINT NEWS and not to think for its readers, or prevent their getting matter to think from" (*NEW*, 9/19/35). At this point, in 1935, he was very anxious to find grounds for optimism, particularly about what was happening in America and he was ready to believe the best of Roosevelt: "The passage of the utilities holding company bill . . . constituted a triumph for the Administration. . . . For this victory alone Roosevelt deserved re-election" (*NEW*, 10/10/35).

This tendency to give undue significance to isolated facts inevitably magnifies and aggravates his lack of balance. When an optimistic sign appears, his hopes rise unrealistically high so that when they are disappointed he feels that more has been lost than in fact has, and his mood swings further than it would otherwise have toward frustration and anger. For this reason the course of the decline of his mental state is not a gradual and steady deterioration. His constant vacillation between unjustified optimism and frustrated annoyance makes it hard to generalize about his mood at any one time. Even in the late 1930s we can find him writing in a perfectly reasonable and lucid fashion on literary matters, particularly when he is writing to good friends.

That he was unconsciously aware of how vulnerable his abuse of the ideogramic method left him is strongly suggested by his almost obsessive harping on the need for clear definition. His advocacy of specificity, clarity, and precision began, of course, with his propaganda for Imagism. Once he was campaigning for Social Credit, it became essential to redefine key economic terms as accurately as possible to expose the muddled thinking which underlay traditional economic practice, masking its inadequacies and illogicalities and obstructing reform. But increasingly in the 1930s and after, he spoke of clear definition as though it were a panacea for all of society's ills. His optimism about Roosevelt, for example, was based on the belief that if the president could be made to see the logic of the Social Credit position, he would only have to communicate his insight to the American people in a clear and simple way and the necessary reforms would be implemented more or less automatically in response to the will of the people. Writing to Father Coughlin on August 29, 1935, about the idea of making Social Credit a plank in the Democratic election platform for 1936, Pound concedes that it is only a "thousand to one chance" but expresses his belief that if Roosevelt could be won over, his ability to clarify the issue for the American people would constitute a reforming force of great power: "There is no need for the President's taking ACTION, IF he will show (and thereby SHOW to the people) that muddled thought is NOT the straight road. I mean get him to break his thought clots. . . . It doesn't require appointments, jobs, commis- sions to untangle these clots and clogs. He can commit this en[o]rmous ACT of enlightnment over the radio in three minutes, and let the obscurantists wriggle."[2]

That he had this exaggerated notion of the power of clarity is partly a testimony to the strength of his wish that there should be some decisive way of salvaging an increasingly hopeless-looking situation, but it is also an evasive maneuver. To extol the talismanic power of the clear definition and to be so quick to excoriate people on the grounds of failing to make precise discriminations seems suspiciously like projection in someone as guilty as Pound was at this time of seizing upon details that supported his preconcep- tions and leaving out of account other equally pertinent pieces of evidence that would have challenged his reading of a situation.

His optimism proved to be a weapon that he could turn against himself. This "castiron faith in life" that Williams had commented on to his mother back in 1906[3] and from which Pound's whole sense of jeremiac mission sprung was liable to become a dangerous overoptimism in someone as little disposed to reflection and calm appraisal of facts as Pound was. He paid far too little attention to obstacles and problems and discouraging data and assumed that what seemed to be contradictions would ultimately be reconcilable. Rejecting cold analysis in favor of intuition, he failed to see that what he accepted as his intuitive grasp of how things really were was no more than the illusory projection of his highly optimistic and strongly willed idea of how he wanted things to be. He continued to hope on the flimsiest grounds and discounted discouraging evidence so readily that his optimism was left with no foundation. He was even less disposed to modify or retreat from the idea that his highly positive goals would be achieved because the alternative was so painful to contemplate. To abandon his faith that economic justice could be achieved was very hard, but to concede that a second world war might not be averted or that the leader whom he believed to be most strongly committed to the cause of peace and economic justice could be acting in a way that could lead to war were almost unthinkable.

To be fair to Pound, it is important to recognize that there were several reasons why he should have continued to be optimistic about the state of affairs in Italy, even when optimism was no longer justified. The regime's effective use of censorship and propaganda and the readiness of the majority of Italians, until 1939, to accept the accuracy of what they were being told, obscured much of the most persuasive evidence for condemning Mussolini's actions. Also, Mussolini did change direction and his on-again-off-again belligerence was a definite departure from his original insistence that Italy's ambitions must be national revitalization, not international adventurism. As Mussolini had written in *The Doctrine of Fascism,* in a passage that Pound had marked in his own copy: "The Fascist State expresses the will to exercise power and to command. . . . [Yet] an imperial nation, that is to say a nation which directly or indirectly is a leader of others, can exist without the need of conquering a single square mile of territory."[4]

There were certainly significant grounds for optimism about Italy when Pound moved there in 1924. Both his temperament and his millennialist expectations would have made it very unsatisfactory for him to live as an embattled outsider in a cultural and political climate that he found stultifying or depressing. He was not suited to be an "enemy" in the manner of Lewis. He felt compelled to leave England when the postwar disillusionment and torpor set in and soon found Paris equally uncongenial in its own way. Decadence and dissolute living held no appeal for him and the aimless drifting and self-absorption of the Lost Generation of Americans who had gravitated to Paris after the war was as far as it could be from his jeremiac reformism. More than anything else, it would have been his underlying moral earnestness which made him feel ill at ease with the prevailing ambience of the literary and artistic community and prevented him from being un-self-consciously assimilated into it.

Pound was not a Left Bank type, but Olga Rudge, remembering Pound's Paris years, recalls her regret that, unlike herself, he was not a Right Bank type either. Although she was born in Youngstown, Ohio, her mother brought her and her two brothers to Europe when Olga was very young. Olga had been placed in a Catholic boarding school in Selbourne when she was only four and a half, and after she left at the age of twelve had lived in Paris, where she had no further formal schooling but concentrated on studying the violin. She remembers how much antisemitism was a matter of course in Paris after the Dreyfus case and how Jews were not received in many salons. She tells how when her mother, a singer, wanted to give a concert and reception, she felt it necessary to have two receptions, one for her antisemitic friends and one where her Jewish landlady, who was musical herself, would not be snubbed. Feeling very much at home in Paris herself, Olga Rudge regretted that Pound was not able to stay there, though she understood why he found Italy so congenial by contrast.

Pound needed to feel that his vision of social justice could be achieved in reality. He could not settle—as Orage could—for the satisfactions of enlightenment and increasing wisdom alone. He wanted his vision to be made manifest in the daily lives of people in general, and Italy seemed to be the only country that offered any prospect of this. Here he could live among the monuments of his favorite culture and surrounded by a pleasant, optimistic, generous-spirited people at the hopeful beginning of a new regime, full of promise, which had already improved the living conditions of the common people in very obvious and tangible ways. He would have been thinking of his own decision to move to Italy when in 1944 he wrote, "It is intellectual cowardice if one is afraid to formulate one's own concept of society. This is all the more so at a time full of possibilities, at a time when the formulation of a new system of government is announced" (*SP*, 350). Of course, it was much cheaper to live in Rapallo than in Paris and this was certainly a consideration for Pound, living as he always had to "on a shoestring." In fact, as a consequence of Mussolini's economic policy, the cost of living went down as rents were lowered and prices controlled. Yet, as advantageous as it was to Pound, the financial benefit of living in Italy was not a primary consideration. It is essential to realize that Pound's interest in the Fascist regime was exclusively confined to its economic policies. As we can see very clearly in "The Italian Score" (*NEW*, 5/23/35, p. 107), when he writes about "Fascism" he is dealing only with its social and fiscal programs. Here he gives Italy's "Score": "40 hour week," "rotation of work" rather than the dole to deal with shortage of jobs, government monitoring of banks, the "Great Guild Council," in which workers are represented by a member of their own trade, rent cuts, lower interest rates, premiums for large families, controlled prices, "premiums for growing grain and draining swamps," and the use of public credit for housing and recreational facilities. Even though, as he readily concedes, these measures do not constitute Social Credit, he believes that they do represent significant progress toward the view of money "as a MEANS not an end."

His virtually exclusive preoccupation with economic matters was the major reason that he paid very little attention to the militaristic side of the regime, but even when he did consider this, he insisted that it was no cause for concern for Americans and for the British, who could adapt what was most positive in the Italian experiment to the particular conditions of their own countries with no risk. It seemed obvious to him that differences of national temperament would automatically ensure that the more "histri-onic" characteristics of fascism would have no appeal: "There is no more danger of squadrismo, of a love of military drill (other than an occasional serio-comic parade) in the U.S.A. or in England (with an occasional Coronation or Lord Mayor's Show) than there is of legal requirement for Javanese temple-dancing in Essex or Philadelphia for the entire populations thereof" (*NEW*, 10/15/36, p. 12). He felt that the parades, uniforms, and rousing speeches that were the public face of fascism were just unimportant trappings, and it annoyed him that the British and American press insisted on treating them as fascism proper. He wanted Americans to see that "what they call fascism is mainly what the Duce set out to eliminate from Italian life, namely the de facto tyranny of irresponsible finance . . . with irresponsible power constantly and silently shifted from constituted au-thority into secret departments of government in the interests of private juntas and bank-boards." He assured them, "I am heartily opposed to everything I have seen labelled or called fascism OUTSIDE of Italy" (*NEW*, 7/25/35, p. 285).

It seems increasingly likely that Pound's enthusiasm for Mussolini's economic and social programs will prove to have been better founded than has generally been supposed. The invasion of Abyssinia, the alliance with Hitler, the ineptness of Mussolini's conduct of the war, and his decline into chronic self-contradiction, vacillation, and lying have made historians fall into the assumption that because he was incapable of responsible judgment later in his career, he must have been from the beginning. This assumption has remained unexamined by even such an eminent scholar as Dennis Mack-Smith and the problems that result can be seen in his biography of Mussolini. Eventually this study forces the reader to challenge the plausibil-ity of its portrayal of Mussolini. Had the Duce been as unrelievedly erratic and indecisive and as unreflectingly impulsive as Mack-Smith paints him, it would surely have been impossible for him to have achieved anything at all. It seems most likely that with Mussolini, as with Pound, a definite decline occurred as the direct result of choices made in the mid-1930s. Mussolini's fatal choice was his reversal of his original resolve to avoid military adventurism. Pound's fatal choice, of course, was his refusal to face the full extent and the implications of Mussolini's change of direction. Since Mussolini's involvement of Italy in a military alliance with Germany was an act of bravado and did not spring, as in Hitler's case, from a genuine desire for war, he was set on a course which, begun in defiance of reality, would lead him to greater and greater lengths of self-deception.

When, as in Hitler, we find a true "will to war," military preparedness is undertaken with determination, and "making war" is the principal focus of energy and enthusiasm, compared to which the fact of conquest is almost of secondary importance. Mussolini's attitude toward war making was very different. He wanted to be seen to be a conqueror but had no enthusiasm for the process of conquest. Fighting was to him the regrettable price that must be paid before one could be acclaimed as a conqueror, and when Hitler put pressure on him to commit Italy to making war in fact, Mussolini tried to back away. In May 1939, although he was speaking publicly of Italy's readiness for war, he sent a belated message to Hitler to say that he would prefer to postpone their war until 1943."[5] Although on July 24, 1939, he assured Hitler that if, in the führer's opinion, the time was right for war with Poland, Italy would be "one hundred per cent ready," within a few days he sent Count Galeazzo Ciano, his minister for foreign affairs, "to explain that such a war would be complete folly—that they had better wait at least four years—if not seven or eight."[6] By September he had tried unsuccessfully to arrange another peace conference and then simply decided not to fight, calling Italy not "neutral" but "non-belligerent."[7] This degree of ambivalence about making war helps to explain why Mussolini made no serious commitment to military preparedness and was content to give out grossly inflated figures of combat-ready troops and matériel.

It is not surprising that in their outrage at his alliance with Hitler and their scorn at his inept conduct of the war and his increasingly erratic and self-contradictory behavior, most people have been only too ready to dismiss Mussolini as a "histrionic clown." In fact, this is even an essentially just appraisal of how he was after 1939. Yet for a historian to assume—as most have been content to do—that his conduct of the war was typical of his implementing of his prewar domestic policies is seriously to misrepresent his achievements in social reform.

In *Italian Fascism and Developmental Dictatorship*, A. James Gregor provides an impressive and substantial corrective to the prevailing unexamined assumption that fascism under Mussolini was merely an ad hoc and makeshift patching together of policies. He is well aware that his research is being undertaken against the current of "received wisdom" about fascism, and that the view that fascism is "opportunistic, anti-ideological, anti-rational, and consequently devoid of programmatic and strategic content is most difficult to dispel," even though it is "significantly untrue."[8]

Gregor shows in persuasive detail that, rather than being essentially reactionary and conservative, Italian fascism was revolutionary and developmental:

Fascism was the heir of a long intellectual tradition that found its origins in the ambiguous legacy left to revolutionaries in the work of Karl Marx and Friedrich Engels. Fascism was, in a clear and significant sense, a Marxist heresy . . . creatively developed to respond to the particular and specific needs of an economically retarded national community condemned, as a proletarian nation, to compete with the more advanced plutocracies of its time for space, resources, and international stature. [121]

The fact that under Mussolini fascism had formulated a specific philosophy of social reform and "had identified its economic interests with impressive emphasis and specificity" (97) is of great relevance to our thinking about Pound's attitude toward Mussolini. Mussolini's economic policy was Pound's virtually exclusive interest, so when we find Gregor commenting on "the almost complete absence, in English, of any serious study of Fascist economic policy" (315), we realize how likely it is that Pound's enthusiasm about Fascist progress toward social justice through economic reform will have been misjudged.

When we are assessing Mussolini's achievement it is essential to consider how retarded the country was economically when the Fascists came to power. Italy, "still largely agrarian and artisan, innocent of a modern bourgeoisie, beset by regionalism and provincialism, malintegrated and maladministered" (91), provided for many of its people a way of life essentially feudal. Under the Fascists Italy was modernized and industrialized according to "a long-range economic program that was reasonably well articulated in the [Fascist] doctrinal literature of 1921 and 1922" (127). This, in turn, was rooted in the social philosophy of the revolutionary syndicalists, who had a definite and clearly formulated economic program and whose doctrines Mussolini as a young man had largely adopted for himself.

When the Fascists came to power, they were faced by problems of labor unrest, shortage of new investment capital, confused tax laws, recent collapses of some of the largest banks and industries, and low agricultural productivity.[9] The greatest threat to the country's economy lay in its deficit of 6 billion lire, which required an annual interest payment of 400 million lire. The Fascists addressed these problems with impressive efficiency. They balanced the country's budget by 1925, achieved "a rate of savings and capital accumulation unsurpassed until Italy's 'economic miracle' of the 1950's" and, doubling the country's industrial output by 1929, gave Italy a higher rate of industrial productivity than France, Germany, or England (Gregor, pp. 142–43).

By 1926 Mussolini was preparing for a second phase of economic reform, "the construction of an insulated economy, an economy capable of sustaining itself against the impostures of the plutocratic and capitalist powers" (147). Foreign ownership had always been a great burden on Italy, undermining national pride as well as subverting national wealth, and Mussolini was determined to modernize and industrialize Italy for the benefit of its own people. He encouraged the reduction of exports by a sharp devaluation of the lire which made them uncompetitive and used controls to limit foreign imports. By arranging tariff protection for the chemical, textile, metallurgical, and mechanical industries, he encouraged them to expand and modernize.

It is easy to see why Pound would be enthusiastic about these developments, since they seemed to be founded upon the same philosophy of economic nationalism that the Social Creditors subscribed to: the idea that a government's first responsibility was to make sure that the "natural abundance" of a country should be developed for the benefit of the citizens of that country. The setting up of an "insulated economy" would be, from a Social Credit viewpoint, an effective impediment to intervention by "international finance," and Pound found additional reason for optimism on this score in Fascist banking legislation. In 1926, Mussolini began the process of centralizing banking and established a government *Istituto di Emissione* to issue all national currency. The state gradually increased its control over banking and by 1937 the *Istituto per la ricostruzione industriale* "controlled over forty-four percent of all Italian capital stock, and almost eighteen percent of the total capital of the nation. For all intents and purposes, the credit system of the nation was under the control of State and parastate agencies. By the end of the 'thirties, approximately eighty percent of the credit available in the Italian economy was controlled directly or indirectly by the State."[10]

Although Pound realized that measures of this kind did not, strictly speaking, constitute Social Credit, some of the differences were attributable to the fact that, because Italy's industrialization was so much more belated than England's its economic policies must be geared toward production first before it could concentrate, as England or America now could, on distribution. Mussolini's social welfare programs also seemed to Pound to be undertaken in the spirit of Social Credit, even if they did not qualify as Social Credit proper: "The family allowance provisions approach steadily nearer and nearer to C.H. Douglas' Social Credit principles. They do not constitute, obviously, a national dividend per capita as Douglas proposes, but they are definitely consumer credit. On February 11, 1941, they were extended far beyond the working class and made to include college graduates, sons and daughters of professional men, who weren't yet earning their own livings."[11]

The success of Mussolini's social welfare legislation was, in Pound's opinion, a persuasive reason for his faith in the Duce's commitment to domestic reform. As soon as he came to power, Mussolini established the eight-hour work day and then went on to regulate child labor and work for women and to improve working conditions. The Labor Charter of 1927 set up a far-reaching program of state insurance benefits for accident, unemployment, maternity, and occupational disease and established vocational and technical training. In December 1925, a maternity and child-welfare agency was set up to provide obstetrical and pediatric services, nursery schools, dispensaries, and food rations, one of the consequences of which was a decline of more than 20 percent in the infant mortality rate between 1922 and 1936. Government funding of education was significantly increased; many new schools were built and public elementary school attendance increased by 25 percent between 1922 and 1935.

The government also made a significant investment in disease control. The incidence of malaria was reduced through the reclamation of swampland, and a concentrated effort was made both to improve the treatment of and to prevent tuberculosis. Pound seems to have been particularly interested in the campaign against TB. He developed an interest in the claims of a Dr. F. Tweddell to have discovered a simple cure for TB. There are two pamphlets by Tweddell in Pound's library—"The Need of Calcium Therapy in Tuberculosis," and "Immunity to Tuberculosis among workers in Sulphur Dioxide"—and in a *New English Weekly* article for October 24, 1935, Pound claimed that Tweddell's cure was being deliberately kept from the public. This article, "Again the Rev. Coughlin," includes an obituary paragraph that notes the "tragic loss" of the American Social Creditor Robert Tribby, who had died from tuberculosis on August 1 and continues:

One can also comment . . . bitterly on the usurer's triumph in quenching scientific curiosity as to Dr. Tweddell of Plandome, Long Island, whose CURE for tuberculosis remains unadvertized because it would put so many institutions and salaried physicians out of work. Men in a million dollar tubercular hospital are NOT interested in curing the disease by anything as simple as a flit-squirt and a preparation of simple chemical like borax, whereof two dollars worth would last the patient till cured. [26]

In 1938 Pound wrote to Williams asking if he could do anything to arrange some institutional support for further research into Tweddell's theories, and Williams, though clearly impatient with Pound's naive assumption that medical researchers would be ready, just for the asking, to make available their time and facilities to some unknown doctor with yet another "cure" for TB, relented, as he usually did with Pound, and said that he would do what he could.[12] Even as late as November 1944, with the kind of only minimal awareness of the actual political situation which had all along been customary with him, Pound was still reminding the regime of its social duties. He writes to Fernando Mezzasoma, the minister of popular culture: "I do not know who represents the Central Italian peasants . . . . The abuse heaped upon these people has done much to alienate their good will . . . . The government has done nothing to eliminate the tubercular germs from milk . . . but I don't believe that pasteurization would be popular here. Do not abandon the periphery!"[13] Even at this late hour, when fascism was in its death throes, it remained for Pound what it had been all along—the will to improve the lives of the common people.

Yet Pound had been impressed, from the beginning, that Mussolini was prepared to look beyond the need to improve the living conditions and physical welfare of the people to consider in addition the contribution that culture and the arts could make to the quality of their lives. In May 1925, the Dopolavora organization was founded and was highly successful in making a wide variety of cultural activities available to the working class. It sponsored and funded "music recitals, excursions, sporting events, films, radio, theatrical and folklore presentations, educational courses and national ceremonial displays."[14] In June 1925, the Istituto nazionale fascista di cultura was established, and Camillo Pellizzi, who was made president of this institute in 1939, was a particularly good friend of Pound's. His respect for and attraction to Pellizzi was yet another instance of Pound's instinctive affinity for people of intellectual excellence and original and creative thought. That Pellizzi respected Pound suggests that Pound, during his Italy years, was not merely despicable.

Giovanni Bechelloni, in his obituary for Pellizzi, describes him as "mild and cultured, reserved, solitary and proud."[15] Pellizzi, like Pound, was a highly original and independent thinker, and any attempt to categorize his political views is bound to falsify them. As Bechelloni points out, "Even though his role in fascist culture was at the highest level, he was never truly a fascist; just as, after the Second World War, even though his role in the development of Italian sociology was at the highest level, he was never truly a sociologist. He had, in fact, that rare ability to participate in [*stare dentro di*] something without committing himself to it completely, always capable of that critical detachment and subtle irony that characterizes the great intellectual." In an important sense, both Pound and Pellizzi saw Italian fascism from a distance. In the 1920s and 1930s Pellizzi was living in England, where he taught Italian literature at London University and published the *British-Italian Bulletin,* and he returned to Italy only for vacations. Pound, living mainly in Rapallo, was kept from an intimate acquaintance with the true nature of fascism partly because of his isolation "in the provinces" but even more by the fact that he saw the Italian situation through the eyes of an American and not with the insights of an Italian.

Both Pound and Pellizzi began with very optimistic expectations of fascism's potential for positive social change and were loath to abandon them. Pellizzi came from a family of socialists and his admiration for Mussolini dated back to the Duce's socialist days. From 1919 on, he contributed articles to the *Popolo d'Italia* and got to know Mussolini personally. While he was in London, Pellizzi regularly wrote for the *Corriere della Sera,* but from then on his contacts with the regime were largely confined to his friendship with Dino Grandi and Guiseppe Bottai. On the few occasions that he did see Mussolini, Bechelloni tells us, the Duce's attitude was one of "respect mixed with curiosity and suspicion." This comment reminds us of Pellizzi's own observation about the suspicion with which Pound was viewed by some of the high-ranking officers of the regime at the time of the Rome Radio broadcasts.

Upon his return to Italy in 1939, Pellizzi was given a Chair of History and Fascist Doctrine and was appointed president of the Institute of Fascist Culture. He was known to be a highly independent thinker, and the very fact of his appointment as president was testimony to the truth of Gregor's observation that "Fascism was rather casual in exacting ideological commitments from its functionaries," and that Fascists were rarely prepared "to sacrifice what they thought to be expertise for political enthusiasm" (Gregor, p. 323). Although Pellizzi was dismissed from the university after the war, he later resumed his university teaching when the first chair of sociology in the country was created for him in the Cesare Alfieri School of Political Science in Florence. In 1960 he founded *Rassegna italiana di sociologia,* a quarterly publication which remains a leading sociology periodical in Italy.

One of Pellizzi's acts as president of the Institute of Fascist Culture was a particularly eloquent statement of his independence of any Fascist "party line." In 1938, after the passage of the racial laws, an attempt was made to confiscate and burn books that were either written by Jews or that could be considered anti-Fascist. The confiscated books were sent to Pellizzi's institute to be examined and burned, but instead of burning them, Pellizzi had them stored and carefully catalogued. When the partisans seized and destroyed the institute's entire library, they unwittingly destroyed "the richest, the best catalogued and most cosmopolitan anti-fascist library in Rome."[16]

His association with Pellizzi must have confirmed Pound's faith in Mussolini's regime in many ways. That the regime would give a position of power to an intellectual of Pellizzi's caliber must have seemed to Pound a testimony to the seriousness of its commitment to cultural excellence, and that a person as discriminating and disinterested as Pellizzi accepted this position must have suggested that he still retained his initial optimism about the regime's potential—at least in the area of cultural improvement. In a letter to Pound of April 6, 1936, Pellizzi gives his view of the current situation in Italy and, although he admits important impediments, still believes that optimism is justified. The major impediment seems to him to be "the nullity of [the] middle class." The "real" Italy is the "one big fellow at the top and an *excellent* popular raw material," but whoever are worthwhile from the middle class are either excluded from the regime or, if they are included, are "sworn in, regimented, at the beck and call of any second-rate lieutenant in chief." Although he is eager to correct Pound's mistaken impression that worthwhile middle-class intellects have any "free play" as things now stand, he is also careful to insist that he does see reason for optimism:

All this will change, improve; but it will take time. Also I am convinced that a policy vastly different from this one would be impossible; it was no better before, it was much worse in every substantial way; and now we have so many new things which are good, so much that is coming and growing—No other nationals, not even Russians, have gone through a period of so intense civic and social experience as the Italians of my own generation (I was born in '96). And more is to come, if God preserve us—[17]

That neither Pellizzi nor Pound was a party-line Fascist but rather an independent thinker with a genuine concern for the welfare of the common people is strongly attested to by the fact that the group of leftist, dissident Fascists, whose views Pound was sympathetic toward when he attended their meetings in Felice Chilanti's apartment in 1941 and 1942, also saw in Pellizzi an intellectual who would be qualified to be their official spokesman. Pound had been introduced to the group through the economist Odon Por, a

Hungarian who had taken refuge in Italy from the fascism of his own country and whose economic views coincided closely with Pound's own. Por was a contributor to *Domani,* the group's biweekly newspaper, which had been suppressed in August 1941 by order of Mussolini. In it Chilanti had called for "the overthrow of the capitalist system and the creation of a new order free from plutocrats and usurers,"[18] and he described the *Domani* group as "Fascists 'in continual crisis,' innocent, disappointed, indignant, rebellious, idealistic—even mystical." He says, "We were Anarchist-Fascists . . . Catholic-Fascists or Communist-Fascists or Liberal-Fascists. We reinvented everything, rediscovered for ourselves concepts of Anarchy, Communism, Liberalism, Christianity. Even our Christianity was 'rein-vented.' " Chilanti felt that Pound was drawn to the group because he could see that, like him, they had invented an economic system of their own "subordinated to higher laws." They listened with great respect as he spoke to them about Confucius, Jefferson, Picasso, and Piero della Francesca and he listened equally attentively to their theories:

The war has been lost . . . . We have to get out of the war before the catastrophe is irremediable . . . . The industrialists are [responsible], who sell the state cardboard shoes and tinfoil tanks . . . . They are also [responsible] for the war because they wanted it to start, and guilty for the defeat, which came from the sordid souls of usurers and profiteers. . . . Ciano was the go-between for the Anglo-Americans and those who were truly responsible here . . . the mastermind of a treacherous plot which cost the Italian people dearly . . . the accomplice, the bondsman of those enemies of the Italians who had already committed the crime of using reactionary sabotage and corruption to keep Fascism from developing into a superior social order, the triumph of spiritual values. [241]

The problem, they contended, was not Mussolini himself—he was being frustrated in carrying out his policies by the corruption or inefficiency of his subordinates. Wanting to believe, as Chilanti's group did, that a "pure" form of fascism could bring into being the new society that he wanted, Pound embraced the same kind of rationalization:

and as to poor old Benito
          one had a safety-pin
one had a bit of string, one had a button
     all of them so far beneath him
half-baked and amateur
          or mere scoundrels
To sell their country for half a million
          hoping to cheat more out of the people . . .
the problem after any revolution is what to do with
your gunmen.   [80/495–96]

Chilanti's group was, in fact, planning to act on its theory of the "betrayal of Mussolini's ideals." Ciano wrote in his diary for March 22, 1942, of being visited by a young man from the Fascist University Group who "said that he had been approached by a journalist, Felice Chilanti, who suggested that he join a super-Fascist insurrectional movement, the purpose of which would be to eliminate all rightist or conservative elements in the party, and to impose upon the Duce a violent[ly] socialistic policy. Everything was thought out—attacks, seizure of the ministries, death of Ciano."[19] Although no one in the group told Pound outright that a conspiracy was planned, Chilanti thought Pound probably worked this out for himself. When, as Mary de Rachewiltz records in *Discretions,* he praised the dissidents for being "wide-awake" yet concluded that they were "too violent for his taste" (p. 166), it seems likely that he was registering his disapproval of violent action such as a plan to murder Ciano.

On April 1, 1942, most of the members of the group that Pound had met were arrested. Chilanti was sentenced to five years' imprisonment. In his account of his interrogation, in his autobiographical novel *La paura entusiasmante,* he is asked why he had included on his list of new ministers Camillo Pellizzi as minister of people's culture. He gives as a his reply: "Why him? Because he is a man who reads books, Mr. Commissioner, and without books there can be no culture."[20]

Pound continued to correspond with Pellizzi after the war, writing from St. Elizabeths in a way that showed how his highly idiosyncratic (and usually highly simplistic) diagnoses and remedies had persisted substantially unchanged since the war years. On September 14, 1944, Pound had written to Fernando Mezzasoma, minister of popular culture for the Republican government at Salo asking that the fourteenth-century arches in the main plaza at Rapallo not be torn down, as had been ordered from Genoa, and also asking that cement and calcimine be sent to the evacuees in the mountains surrounding the town so that they could make cisterns for storing water.[21] In St Elizabeths on October 9, 1952, he is still reiterating the same themes: "Yu damPHoolZ [should] start planting wot I tell yu/ à la 'alberi e cisterni' [trees and cisterns] . . . [You should pay] a little attention to wot will GROW in yr/ so picturesque woptoMandolinia/ and new means of making poor earth into SOIL . . . certain things would GROW and FEED yr/ damwopulation."[22]

We might also consider in passing that, although Americans decisively withdrew their support for Mussolini at the time of the invasion of Ethiopia (or, in the case of many Italian-Americans, at the time of Italy's attack on France in the summer of 1940), there was considerable enthusiasm for the

Duce in America before 1935. John P. Diggins, for example, contends, in *Mussolini and Fascism: The View from America,* that "from the time of the March on Rome to the beginning of the Ethiopian War [Mussolini] was an esteemed figure. Americans in particular saw in [him] certain enduring qualities which enabled him to qualify as a 'great man' not only of his time but of the ages."[23] He was frequently compared with Theodore Roosevelt—which pleased him very much—and credited, paradoxically, with being both a "restorer of conservative tradition" and an innovator, both an "impulsive romantic" and "a redeemer of religion . . . a self-made man of almost superhuman willpower [and] a common man of practical idealism and homely virtue" (72–73).

The change in the direction of Pound's thinking was the direct consequence of a change of direction in Mussolini himself—his decision in 1935 to pursue an imperialist policy and, in contradiction of all his previous assurances, to justify waging war in Ethiopia in the cause of colonial expansion. Unequivocally opposed to war, loath to withdraw his support from Mussolini altogether, Pound tried to take refuge in rationalization. There was plenty of incentive to do this, in addition to the unconscious desire to avoid the pain of giving up all his millennial hopes. There was enormous popular support in Italy for this war against the Abyssinians, who were characterized as brutal, barbaric, and much in need of the "civilizing influence" of Italian culture. Desperately needing to rationalize away his unconscious disapproval of this war, and hence of Mussolini, Pound eagerly embraced this propaganda. James Laughlin, who was with Pound in Italy at this time, remembers how completely Pound became convinced of the necessity for that war after he was sent government propaganda photographs showing atrocities committed by Ethiopians against white settlers. He carried the photographs around with him and showed them to many people in Rapallo.[24]

To take October 1935 as a time of crucial change for Pound is not to suggest that he began to rely on rationalization then for the first time, but rather to understand that from this point on his motives for evading a realistic appraisal of circumstances were now different. He was deluding himself now on issues of moral choice, so the consequences would be much more serious. Before, because of his need to cling to the hope of economic reform despite the odds, he had recourse to a certain kind of evasion of the realities of the situation. He was minimizing or discounting the practical problems of reform, the magnitude of the obstacles facing economic reformers, the unlikeliness of thoroughgoing change. Yet we could say that he had a considerable measure of control over his rationalizations since he had control over his expectations of change and his rationalizations allowed him to continue to hold these expectations. To the extent that his aspirations were morally acceptable—even admirable—his self-delusion was unlikely to be pernicious. But after Abyssinia, although his primary motivation remained unchanged, he now also became involved in rationalizing something over which he had no control—the course of Mussolini's actions. As the Duce became more inconsistent and more blatant in his warmongering, each new piece of evidence of his duplicity made it necessary for Pound to rationalize even more strenuously if he was to continue to block out the rapidly growing accumulation of evidence that his original decision to exculpate the Duce was now wrong.

The invasion of Abyssinia was only the beginning. To rationalize away his strong unconscious aversion to what was to follow—Italian intervention in the Spanish Civil War, the racial laws, the invasion of Albania, the Pact of Steel, Mussolini's declaration of war against England and France, the attack on Greece, and finally the declaration of war against America—would require self-delusion and evasion of reality of such an extreme kind and of so prolonged an extent that his sanity could not help but be threatened. Had Mussolini's intentions been completely clear in 1935 and the nature of the moral decision involved been clear-cut, evasion and rationalization would hardly have been possible. But at this juncture it was apparent to no one, not even to Mussolini himself, into what outrageous courses he would lead Italy.

Pound was in good company in wanting to see Mussolini as the "peacemaker of Europe." This was a possibility that the politicians in what were soon to be the Allied countries clung to as long as they possibly could, even in disregard of evidence to the contrary. In June 1933, Roosevelt wrote to Breckinridge Long, the U.S. ambassador to Italy, that he was "deeply impressed by what [Mussolini] has accomplished and by his evidenced honest purpose in restoring Italy and seeking to prevent general European trouble."[25] And even after Abyssinia, despite Mussolini's intervention in the Spanish Civil War and despite the Rome-Berlin Axis announcement of October 1936, there was a strong desire, even on the part of anti-Fascists, to believe that, if forced to choose, Mussolini would align himself with the democracies. When Mussolini persuaded Hitler against his will to postpone the "liberation" of the Sudetenland by a German invasion and to submit the matter to arbitration at the Munich Conference, the Duce was gratefully acclaimed as the peacemaker of Europe.

From early on, Pound had received criticisms of Mussolini, even from his associates who were most unequivocally committed to Social Credit.

Since Pound's support for the Duce was almost entirely based on his belief that the Fascist regime offered the only immediate hope for the instituting of a Social Credit program on a national scale, it was clearly necessary for him to deal, in some way, with the skepticism of Social Credit's leading theorists. That he did so with no qualms or misgivings is a good indication both of his complete self-assurance on the issue of Mussolini's intentions and of his habit of closing his mind to ideas or evidence that he did not wish to consider. As early as January 21, 1931, Douglas had written: "I can quite believe that a number of most excellent things are being done in Italy but I doubt the value of the organisation" (EPA). By May 29, 1934, Douglas was skeptical also of Mussolini's commitment to the freedom of the individual and to preventing war: "What I should like to hear from you is a statement as to the increasing, or otherwise freedom, of the Italian subject, of all classes, to get up and crow upon his own dunghill, no matter whether his views are official or otherwise. The better housing and feeding of the animals does not appear to me either a matter of difficulty, nor as likely to affect the eventual catastrophe for any considerable length of time" (EPA). Pound's response was one he came to use habitually whenever lack of individual freedom under Mussolini's regime was at issue. On June 2, 1934, he wrote back to Douglas not undertaking any serious discussion of political censorship and repression but offering instead a "luminous detail" intended as conclusive evidence that the irrepressible Italian insistence on self-expression would make any fears of government interference with personal freedoms unnecessary: "In a shop the shop keeper will just have to finish remarks, his rounded paragraph to former customer. . . . BEFORE he will sell you 4d. worth of cheese" (EPA). We see Pound making the same point, decked out in the eccentric rhetoric of the radio speeches, in a broadcast of April 20, 1942:

Every peasant in Italy knows where to go and KICK if something ain't done to suit'em. And my Gawd they DO kick . . . . The Italians are the greatest kickers on earth. Started back in the Quattrocento. Eyetalian individualism, development of the personality, raised to point of exaggeration, but enlightened the world.
    Nothing less than the Fascist system would keep these people together. Some of the kickin' is aimless, but the mass of it keeps things movin' forward. [EPS, 103]

Orage's reservations, both about the value of Fascist economics and about Pound's effectiveness as Social Credit propagandist, were even more searching than Douglas's. We have already noted his skepticism about the

Gesellist theory of stamp script, and his skepticism extended, as with Douglas, to Pound's most fundamental belief that Mussolini's Fascist economics were an authentic, even though as yet embryonic, form of Social Credit. On March 6, 1934, Orage wrote to Pound: "Por is here, but I can't get any sense out of him,—only propaganda for the Corporate State. My death-bed conviction is that sans National Credit control there ain't nothing doing worth more than [an] ant's attention; it's all only a re-arrangement within the limits prescribed by the Money-Church. And this goes for B[enito] M[ussolini] as well as for Franklin D[elano]" (*EPA*). On July 3, 1932, Orage put his finger on precisely those rhetorical idiosyncracies in Pound's propaganda which would eventually—in the radio broadcasts—become so pronounced that they would constitute an almost impenetrable barrier to any effective communication of Pound's ideas to his listeners. Orage wrote, "I think your style of writing it is definitely—not intentionally of course—calculated to give the reader the impression that you are condescending to be explicit & explanatory as to bloody fools &, in the process, giving yourself damned little real trouble other than that of spitting it out & getting it off your chest" (*EPA*). On June 18, 1934, Orage wrote to him: "Your style of talking isn't likely to *win* readers, but only to affect them if they *do* read. In other words, *I* collect & hold the audience; and you address 'em. But you couldn't assemble more than an Apostle's dozen yourself!" (*EPA*). By August 22, Orage had apparently given up hope that Pound would ever be an effective propagandist except through his poetry: "Say what you like, I'm the better propagandist. Witness the fact that, without me, Douglas would be still unknown, & that every present-day propagandist was made during the years 1918–22. With submission, again, my dear E.P., your Cantos are your greatest contribution to the cause; & if only you could make *them* the vehicle of your *total being,* their effect would be that of artillery" (*EPA*).

Orage continued, in his frank and decisive way, to offer Pound salutory warnings such as the above, but within two and a half months he would be dead. As it turned out, Orage's death was to be just the first of a series of major blows to the Social Credit movement. The death of Bronson Cutting, the leader of the Social Credit reform movement in the Senate, seemed to Pound a serious setback. In his *New English Weekly* obituary Pound wrote: "Senator Cutting's death at this time is fatal . . . in the sense that it must have results beyond anyone's power to foresee for the moment . . . . The Senate is not rich in men who read the classics for pleasure, in men who have minds sufficiently multifarious to bridge the gap from Huey [Long] to

[Senator William] Borah. Who indeed can NOW get any real economic light into the Kingfish? . . . Who will take over . . . the intellectual economic leadership of the Senate?" (5/16/35).

In March 1935, Pound had a sense of proportion about the likelihood of true Social Credit being put into practice under the leadership of Huey Long or Father Coughlin. He judged Coughlin to be "better as orator than as formulator of programme" and was doubtful whether, even if all the "Radio Priest's" listeners could be recruited to the Social Credit cause, "a ten million enrolment [could] bring on a new idea which it does not yet understand." Pound realized that even though Coughlin attacked many of the same abuses that the Social Creditors did, this did not mean that he was working for an orthodox Social Credit solution. He doubted that Coughlin could "really understand the adjusted price" and thought that a safer bet for "Douglasites" would be to find someone in Washington "who can reach the more serious members of government" (*NEW*, 3/14/35). But on April 11 Pound's attitude was changing. He reminded his readers that "the cry of demagogy against either the Kingfish (Long) or against Father Coughlin don't hold *if measured by* the ballyhoo of their opponents." In fact, in April he was writing to Long himself: "I wish to Xt/ you wd/ get onto Gesell or C.H. Douglas, at least as far as the basic ideas," and on April 13, informing him, "KINGFISH! . . . You is going to need a Sekkertary of the Treasury, THATS ME." On August 18, just three weeks before Long's assassination, he wrote a detailed, lucid letter with no slang in which he told Long about Wörgl and wrote: "It is my impression that Coughlin will stick to F.D.R. for 1936, but if R[oosevelt] double crosses the people, there is still 1940 and we are none of us 70 years of age" (*EPA*).

In the *New English Weekly* for September 12, Pound drew his readers' attention to the closeness of Long's program to Social Credit, noting the proposals for a homestead allowance that would ensure every family "the reasonable COMFORTS of life," a shorter working week, a guaranteed minimum income, and an education allowance and concluding that "if Huey is not for the rigid secretariat version of Douglas, he is most certainly NOT opposed to any Social Credit aim. And he is the NEXT American toward whom U.S. social credit educational effort should be directed." Yet even before this appeared in print, Long had been assassinated. On September 26, Pound wrote of it as a tragedy and must have seen this as yet another instance of the falling away of the prospects for reform: "With Cutting gone, and the Kingfish murdered, the American People will have to do its own saving of itself" (*NEW*).

Yet despite these setbacks, Pound's "castiron faith in life" asserted itself again and, as the prospects for Social Credit dwindled, he called even more emphatically for cooperation among any groups which had any sympathy for the goals of Social Credit, minimizing to a clearly unrealistic degree the differences among them. After Orage's death he had urged the *NEW* readership "to drop idle bickerings, to drop any remnants of personal irritations, and to get on with Orage's work" (12/6/34), and now, after these recent deaths, he insists: "A common program for Coughlin's nine million, the Long group, Cutting's adherents and personal friends in the Senate, can not be beyond the mental grasp of American monetary reformers" (*NEW*, 10/24/35). We see the same impulse to "hope against hope" in Pound's refusal to be discouraged by the way in which Canadian dominion law was invoked to disallow important legislation that Aberhart's Social Credit party wanted to enact when it came to power in Alberta in 1935. On June 30 Pound insisted, "No early political defeat of a movement ever defeated it," and asserted, "The stranger hearing of Social Credit for the first time is more likely to be interested by the fact that a dozen different modes of attack are in progress, than by any one mode itself" (*NEW*). On September 5 he noted that "the light of the world shines from Alberta, with Montague Norman and a lot of obsolete fire-extinguishers praying they can extinguish it" (*NEW*). Even on February 13, 1936, when it was clear that no genuine Social Credit legislation would be enacted, Pound refused to conclude that the cause was lost: "If brother Aberhart is led down the garden pawth . . . by the well-known and unfortunately unjailed Mr. Magor . . . is there any reason to suppose that 50 and more Social Credit members of the Alberta legislature are obliged to follow Ab. into sin?" (*NEW*).

Pound's interest in Father Coughlin as another ally in the battle for Social Credit is no surprise when we consider how many of Coughlin's main concerns were identical to those of the Social Creditors. In *A Series of Lectures on Social Justice,* published in 1935, he insists that the problem is no longer production but distribution and that, since mass production has meant that there cannot be sufficient employment for all, industry can no longer operate according to "a scale of wages, based only on payment while you work and bread lines while you don't work,"[26] but must shorten hours and raise wages so that everyone's income is "commensurate with those annual expenses necessitated for a decent American standard of livelihood" (28). He also rails against the government's decision to finance the public works projects of the National Recovery Act with money borrowed at full interest from private bankers "while $9-billion of gold and silver [lying] idle in the treasury vaults" (203) could be used "as a base against which it could issue its own credit" (216). Until 1934, Coughlin had supported Roosevelt and the New Deal, calling it "Christ's Deal," but in 1934 he became very antisemitic, retitling it the "Jew-deal" and adopting the rhetoric and the conspiracy theories which were the American antisemite's stock in trade. Couglin's reference to "Bernard Manassas Baruch whose full name has seldom been mentioned . . . the Rothschilds in Europe, the Lazzeres in France, the Warburgs, the Kuhn-Loebs, the Morgans and the rest of that wrecking crew of internationalists whose god is gold" could just as well have been an exerpt from one of Pound's radio speeches of the 1940s, and it is clear that in the case of Coughlin the antisemitism was a panic reaction, not just to economic collapse but to the prospect of war. On the first page of his book Coughlin writes: "It is almost with a cynical smile that we hope for peace when we recognize the feverish efforts of every great nation as they are busy manufacturing cannon and shells, warships and lethal gases. . . . In their laboratories of destruction the chemists of greed and poverty, of hate and of lying propaganda are mingling their poisons of warfare."

Pound had first written to Coughlin on November 30, 1934, and in his *NEW* column for July 4, 1935, notes the publication of Coughlin's *Lectures on Social Justice* and suggests that it is a mistake to underestimate his value to the Social Credit movement just because he is not calling for a national dividend. Pound doubts that "our highbrow orthodox social creditors [have] succeeded in teaching more facts" and credits Coughlin with operating with "the force of starting from a basic demand for righteousness" and expressing his ideas with much more clarity than most Social Creditors. He concludes the "if [Coughlin] leads his hearers just *up to* social credit, the said creditors would be better advised in carrying them over the last stile than in carping at Father Coughlin." On August 29, 1935, he writes to Couglin: "For God's sake get to a radio and help our Canadian brethren. After the Alberta sweep the Dominion election COULD be swung." And then, in a flush of completely unrealistic optimism, "given the dominions, and the passage of the holding company bill we COULD get [Social Credit] into the elections for 1936. Thousand to one chance, but it would be living." On December 5, 1935, after Abyssinia, Pound passes on to Coughlin from a "French author of some standing" the information that "BOTH Hoare and Eden are Masons" (*EPA*) and by March 12, 1936, is hailing without reservation the national importance of "The New Coughlin" (*NEW*). In a broadcast of January 12, Coughlin had drawn his listeners' attention to Senator Robert L. Owen's proposed Federal Reserve Banking Act, which would have given Congress power over the nation's money and was proposing a suit to the Supreme Court challenging the constitutionality of the current Federal Reserve Act. Pound assured his readers: "It will make the greatest case perhaps since the 1830's. It means a demand at law for Social Credit as originally written into the U.S. Constitution" and suggested that "January 12, the date of that broadcast, is in the running for an annual holiday" (*NEW*, 3/12/36).

As Coughlin's stock rises in Pound's opinion through this period, Roosevelt's suffers an equal but opposite decline. As was the case in Pound's evaluation of all politicians, his judgment of Roosevelt was almost exclu- sively determined by his assessment of how compatible his policies were with Social Credit. Once it was evident that Roosevelt would not include provisions for a national credit account and interest-free debt in his New Deal innovations, Pound renounced him—and with even more bitterness because he had allowed his hopes to be raised so high. Yet the common accusation, made without qualification, that Pound hated and villified FDR seriously misrepresents the truth of the case. It completely leaves out of account the fact that Pound clung to his optimistic view of the president and continued to give him "the benefit of the doubt" as long as he could.

On May 2, 1933, Pound wrote to Roosevelt, drawing his attention to a typesetter's error in the president's *Looking Forward,* persuading him to read Douglas and offering "as a mark of respect" to dedicate to him his *Jefferson and/or Mussolini,* which Pound suggests was written "from motives which seem very [*sic*] to me very like those which moved you to write yr./ own bo[o]k, though at that time I had no hope that you wd/ act upon such lines, or any reason to suppose that you were to be anything but just another damn president" (*EPA*). This comment makes clear that Pound genuinely in- tended the writing of this book to be a gesture of American patriotism but also shows his grandiose and disoriented state of mind. If the version of the letter which went to the president was the one whose carbon is preserved in the archive, it is worth noting that it contained both the misprint in "To The President of the Untied States" and, as salutation, "YOUR EXCEL- LENCY," which he used for his letters to Mussolini.

In Pound's comments on Roosevelt in his contributions to the *New English Weekly* for 1935 and 1936 we can see clearly how his attitude toward the president swings back and forth—sometimes dramatically— according to the latest "evidence" of Roosevelt's economic intentions. He is alert for any encouraging sign, but in early 1935 his ability to be realistic shows in his impulse to be mainly skeptical about the likelihood of Roosevelt's being committed to the thoroughgoing changes that would be necessary to break the bankers' control of the nation's finances. Yet Pound does find it encouraging that under this administration, politicians whose views he does approve of—such as Governor Eccles of the Federal Reserve Board, Representative Goldsborough, Senator Hiram Johnson, Senator Black of Alabama, Senator Ickes, and even Henry Wallace, secretary of agriculture—are having their say.

On June 27, he wrote: "[This] has come so near to being a good administration, yet is not" but concedes that "at any rate it is immeasurably superior to what the U.S. wished on itself with Wilson, Harding, Coolidge and Hoover" (*NEW*). Yet after this we see an increasing tendency to overreaction in Pound. On July 4, after the news that the banking house of N. M. Rothschild and Sons had agreed to "cooperate with the new Silver Market, and to issue warrants against fine silver deposited," Pound concludes that "Roosevelt is fundamentally the usurer's champion." But on October 10 Pound seizes upon "the passage of the utilities holding co. bill" as such a significant advance that he writes: "For this victory alone Roosevelt deserved re-election" (*NEW*).

As evidence of the significant reforms he had hoped to see fails to materialize, Pound seems to feel a mounting sense of desperation which leads him to attribute to isolated incidents unrealistically optimistic implica-tions. By January 9, 1936, he is crediting Roosevelt with "some good intentions" and with being " 'sincere' . . . in collecting his 'brain trust' from the available MATERIAL." Even though this has meant having to choose among "half baked, jejeune ideologues from fresh water beaneries." But on January 16 Pound's effusive overreaction to one of Roosevelt's speeches shows clearly his desperation to read into a situation the encouraging implications which he needed to find: "AT LAST the President has made a very astute speech at Atlanta. AT LAST, after three years social credit hammering the Great White Father has TOLD the flock that Americans are 'LIVING on a THIRD CLASS DIET. For the very simple reason that the masses of the American people have not the purchasing power to eat more and better food. The Atlanta Speech is a high tribute to the achievement of the administration . . . . the reason WHY the American people don't get better food is AT last OFFICIAL." On March 5 he is still willing out of this incident the significance he wants it to have: "Estimable reports reach us that President Roosevelt's remarks in Atlanta were not isolated, and that he knows the U.S. needs Social Credit." On October 26 he writes to Father Coughlin, "I suppose Rossevelt [sic] is being elected. Landon wd. be worse . . . . Frankie is the clerver [sic] man" (*EPA*).

By December 17 he found more encouragement for his optimism. When Roosevelt attended the Inter-American Conference for Peace in Buenos Aires in 1936 and reconfirmed United States commitment to the principle that states within the Americas have no right to intervene in one another's internal or external affairs, and promised to consult with these states when mutual safety was at issue, Pound hailed this with a *New English Weekly* article called "Bravo; Roosevelt!" Calling it a "definite step toward peace, economic continentalism . . . a step onward and not a step away from economic nationalism, the HISTORIC PROCESS observed," Pound asserted that this "affirmation of the Monroe doctrine in Buenos Aires . . . will go far to tranquilize and really content a whole faction of anti-Roosevelt Americans who saw the American Führer about to drag his country into the World Court and out where the pimps of Basel could tempt the simple upstate perpetually Peter-Panish Morgenthaus and their incompetent and incult successors . . . a definite move toward such enlightenment of international relations as will permanently make it more difficult for the Morgans, Niemeyers, etc., to entangle one nation in the affairs and munition deals of any other" (12/17/36).

Yet, as hopeful as such an event seems to him, for Pound, the absolutely reliable guarantee of international peace is thoroughgoing economic reform, and we can see, in this same article, how strongly he wants to believe that this is imminent. He claims to have some inside information to this effect, but his mannered rhetoric bespeaks a tentativeness which betrays his underlying awareness that he is dealing more in wishful thinking than in hard evidence: "A roseate whisper has reached us that F.D.R. has murmured something about 'reversal of interest,' that is (according to unconfirmed report) a drift toward the Gesellite system to be applied somewhere in the interstices of Morgenthau's 'department.'"

For FDR to establish himself conclusively in Pound's eyes as worthy of the confidence he wanted to place in him, the president would have to show that he was prepared to make a complete separation between the value of the American dollar and the price of gold. The sine qua non of Pound's economic philosophy was that the value of the dollar and the amount of money in circulation could legitimately be determined only by the productive capacity of the country—that to tie it to gold in any way was to serve the interests of international speculators and bankers at the expense of the American people. America had gone off the gold standard in 1933, but the value of the dollar continued to be tied indirectly to the price of gold, and Pound was afraid that "restoring the gold standard is a war aim" for Roosevelt's administration (*NEW*, 4/4/40). In February 1940 Pound had complained that, by devaluing the dollar, the president had raised the value of gold.

By this point, of course, Pound can no longer be considered to be campaigning as an economic reformer, even though in his own eyes he was. When he insisted that economic reform was the crucial issue, his primary concern was not to face the truth of the economic situation but to evade the truth of the international political situation. He insisted that Roosevelt had got America into the war to protect the interests of the usurers because this saved him from admitting to himself the real nature of the menace that the Allies were fighting. It is not surprising that, as he began increasingly to use his economic propaganda as a personal strategy of evasion, a gulf widened between him and bona fide Social Creditors who kept their original altruistic commitment to the cause intact. In this context we can see the eventual breaking off of Pound's relationship with John Hargrave as marking a point of no return in Pound's decline.

Hargrave knew Pound to be sincere in his commitment to Social Credit, but from the first he believed that Pound's faith in Mussolini was misplaced. On January 6, 1935, he wrote: "In spite of what you have told me about Ital. Fascism, I am not at all sure that your outlook is sound in this matter. I could also quote Mussolini 'of the Right' in utter contradiction of your Mussolini 'of the Left.' . . . If Mussolini had implemented the *mechanism* of Douglas S.C. he would be able to avoid that 'Left-Right' swing, which is the flaw of the Corp. State, & arises from the idea 'that the State is more important than the individual' " (EPA). At first, Pound, like Hargrave, was wary of Mosley and wrote on December 26, 1935, of "the travesties of Fascism presented . . . by the antics of Sir O. Moseley" (NEW), but by December 30, 1937, Pound had begun to dissociate himself from the Social Credit movements in England and America. In a letter to NEW he accused its readership and Social Creditors in general of failure to read key works such as Butchart's *Money* and failing to heed Pound's own "demand for a definition of economic terminology," and he concluded that "Mosley's party has been more alert to this necessity and by that much at least has shown its superiority, in a sort of literacy test. The fight has gone on in 'Rassegna Monetaria' and the 'British Union Quarterly,' not in Social Credit organs."

On September 8, 1939, Hargrave wrote a final letter to Pound, making clear how irrevocably Pound had lost touch, not only with the spirit of the Social Credit movement in England but with the perspective of the British people in general: "Neither Fascism nor Communism is a step towards my objective . . . Both Left and Right are sunk, over here; . . . They lost their way, not only in economics—but in the Left-Right conflict. And I feel that you did too. . . . You have backed a wrong horse . . . but you don't know it yet." He described Mosley as a "mugg" for backing Hitler and as "a feeble opportunist who has squandered two whole fortunes with practically no result at all," and pointed out to Pound: "You just have not got the internal position in these islands sized up correctly. . . . You wanted me to 'go in with' Mosley. And you were quite sincere. That makes it worse. Proves you didn't know the ropes in these tricky affairs . . . . Had I taken your advice there would be no S[ocial] C[redit] P[arty] at all . . . . Mosley is lost, I tell you . . . and fascism is lost." Hargrave makes it clear that he has known for some time how out of touch Pound has been but has postponed confronting him with this, out of respect for his sincerity: "Your propaganda hasn't helped me much the last 12 months or more . . . . I don't forget it, because it was (damn it) honest—you actually *believed* you were right, and that Mosley and the poor pimpy fascists over here actually *meant* something" (EPA).

It was evident to Hargrave that it was beside the point to blame him. As illogical as his thinking was, it was ("damn it") sincere. Before we can judge Pound's thinking, we must first understand the pseudologic that generated it. To do this, we need to be able to follow the sequence of steps in the line of reasoning that he was forced to adopt if he was to preserve his rationalization of Mussolini's intentions and accommodate this to the major new developments in the Duce's policies. Once we see the extent to which, to be able to persist in his rationalization, he was forced to misrepresent to himself all the most basic facts about the motives of Mussolini, Hitler, Roosevelt, and Churchill, we realize that we have no choice but to judge him "of unsound mind." His perception of the wartime situation was so drastically at odds with its reality that his thinking on this subject was clearly psychotic.

His initial premises were logical enough: that Social Credit reform was necessary both to establish social justice and to help break the cycle of recurrent war; that the only Western leader who was actively implementing reforms of a Social Credit nature was Mussolini; that a leader with a genuine commitment to Social Credit would inevitably be strongly opposed to war out of the same moral conviction that made him a champion of social justice. This meant that, once Mussolini changed to a policy of belligerence, it was a double blow for Pound, not only discrediting the Duce as a peacemaker but also throwing serious doubt on the sincerity of his commitment to Social Credit. The fact of the Abyssinian invasion left Pound with only two choices: to face the truth and renounce Mussolini, or to continue to have faith in Mussolini's moral integrity and to deny the truth of the situation. Flying in the face of all the evidence he insisted, to himself as well as to others, that Mussolini was opposed to war. This explains his comments on the conquest of Abyssinia, for example his assertion to John Buchan in a letter of September 1, 1935, that "Mussolini has GOT WAR *OUT of* Europe, [at] the one safety valve under Comité des Forges pressure. All the fools, slithering liberal apes in England are crying for pan european war in the name of peace."[27] The "logic" of this, based upon a complete inversion of the facts, is that Mussolini only seems to be warmongering in attacking Abyssinia; that he is really doing this to preserve peace and as a way of peventing a war in Europe, frustrating the attempts of the munitions makers to put on pressure for a major war by providing the "safety valve" of a small war that will not escalate. A similar inversion is needed to explain the British opposition to Mussolini's militarism, and Pound takes care of that with the assertion that, though the British are saying they want peace, they really mean that they want a "pan european war." From here on he relies heavily on a process of transference. In this same letter he transfers to Britain and Abyssinia the policy of oppression which Mussolini has adopted by invading Abyssinia: "England claiming universal dominion in the name of no right, no honesty, no JUSTICE, with a record for ill treating the people of England that perhaps only her sister Abyssinia can equal??"

To rationalize away Mussolini's turn to belligerence required an evasion of reality which in itself was drastic enough, but once Mussolini abandoned his anti-German stand and allied himself with Hitler, Pound had to be able to rationalize away Hitler's warmongering also to be able to continue to whitewash Mussolini. This required a denial of reality so extreme as to be clearly psychotic. By the time of the Rome Radio broadcasts, we can see that his strategy of evasion was simply to assert that it was not Germany but Britain which was pushing for war. The underlying thesis of the broadcasts is the following: Neither Hitler nor Mussolini is responsible for World War II; responsiblity for the war lies first with Churchill, then with Roosevelt, both of whom are serving as fronts for the international conspiracy of usurers and munitions makers.

Pound makes this all a matter of economics. He begins with the reasonable position that wars can have economic causes, but his need to exculpate Hitler and Mussolini leads him to assertions which have the implicit premise that there are no causes of war *except for* economic ones. His position in his broadcasts is that Hitler is not making a war of conquest, that both Hitler and Mussolini are primarily concerned to set up, in their own countries, new, "usury-proof" economic systems. Churchill and Roosevelt, acting as agents of the usurers' conspiracy, are determined to prevent this, which is why they are fighting the Axis. When Hitler invades the Soviet Union it is to crush communism with its pernicious economic system. Britain, the United States, and the Soviet Union are allies because their leaders are all "pro-usury" and sworn enemies of economic justice. Once we can see how the "logic" of his rationalization runs, we can see that he was speaking in complete sincerity and in the belief that he was offering an entirely reasonable propositon when he said: "The day Hitler went into Russia, England had her chance to pull out. She had her chance to let bygones be bygones. If you can stop the Muscovite horror, we will let bygones be bygones. We will try to see at least HALF of your argument" (*EPA*, 27). He offers with equal sincerity the claim that the Allied leaders have involved their countries in war not only knowing that they will be defeated but counting on this because it will be to the advantage of the usurers:

USE people in war UNPREPARED. That is called destroying the people . . . . Roosevelt and Churchill, for instance, . . . have pushed the American and English into the war . . . . KNOWN in England in 1938 that England would LOSE. . . . DAMN it all, every man that dies in McArthur's army is sacrificed to Frankfurter's friends. But NOT to WIN. To destroy himself, to destroy any nation, one after another. Not that the Russian empire should survive, that the Austrians should survive, that England or the British Empire should survive, but to pull down the mighty . . . . France hurled against the unbeatable Germans, England pushed unprepared, and the climax of unpreparedness, the Lehman, Frankfurter, Morgenthau SUCCESS, [or] SUC/Cess in hurling America into the conflict, and now yelling for MORE disasters. [*EPS*, 78–79]

A statement such as the above, made as it clearly was in all sincerity, seems to me to make the strongest possible case that we are dealing here not with deliberate treason but with genuine psychosis.

Once the decision to rationalize was made and the crucial false premises were adopted, the rules of logic were observed. Pound's outrageous assertions followed logically, even though the premises were false. To make any appraisal of what he said and wrote after 1935, one must be aware of the premises from which he was operating, especially because his comments tended to become increasingly cryptic and "telegraphic." To determine his position on the Spanish Civil War, for example, we have to decipher his statement, in answer to a questionnaire circulated by Nancy Cunard, that it was a "sham conflict." Noel Stock, Pound's biographer, suggests that Pound called this a sham conflict because "the real forces behind it were the international usurers and the manufacturers of armaments"; yet, by this point, Pound believed that this was the case with all wars, so, according to this reading, his comment would be a redundancy. It seems more likely that this comment reflects his determination to insist to himself that there would be no European war. He must have sensed that this war in Spain was the harbinger of the larger war that he had been warning against for twenty years, but, rather than admit this painful conclusion to himself, he seems to have felt that, by claiming that this was not a "real war," he could continue to reassure himself that the cause of peace was not yet lost. This strategy of avoidance is entirely of a piece with his way of evading the painful facts about Mussolini that he could not bear to face and, if we accept it as the explanation of his reaction to the Spanish Civil War, we are bound to judge his attitude considerably less harshly than if we believed that he called it a sham conflict out of a calculated callousness and deliberate indifference to the plight of a suffering people.

We see a striking example of his desperate need to believe that war could still be averted and to suppress any intimations that Mussolini was bent on war in his *NEW* article of November 3, 1938, on the Munich Conference of the previous month. This article begins: "Within two days of the Munich Agreement the gun-and-usury people were up and out with new war scares. The total Italian press was out for peace. Italy, where there had been no hysteria, was all set up for a new Europe of cooperation." Chamberlain, described by Pound as recently as December 3, 1936, as a "black infamy," now, as the apparent architect of "peace with honour," is metamorphosed in Pound's estimation: "Chamberlain is the FIRST British statesman to inspire any respect on the continent since 1918." Pound then assures his readers that Hjalmar Schacht, Hitler's finance minister, talks sense about money, that the usurers are using every lie they can to blind the public to "the growing monetary clarity in Italy and in Germany," and concludes his analysis with an assertion made in all sincerity: "War against Germany would have meant war against a clean concept of money." He persists in this delusion throughout the war, clinging to the outrageous idea that Hitler is a fiscal reformer, misrepresented by a usurers' conspiracy as a warmonger.

In fact, Pound had no interest in Hitler and turned his attention to him at all only because he was forced to extend the reach of his rationalization to include him also once Mussolini had allied himself with the führer. In May 24, 1934, for example, Pound had written: "Adolphe is, an almost, pathetic hysteric. . . . He is, so far as I can work out, a tool of *almost* the worst Huns" (*NEW*). To defend the reliability of Mussolini's judgment after October 1936 meant becoming an apologist for Hitler. Since Pound's conscience would not allow him to justify what Hitler was doing in reality, he was driven to delude himself into believing that Hitler was only doing what he, Pound, *could* approve of.

In his radio broadcast for May 18, 1942, Pound explained: "I almost never talk of Germany because I have seen very little of Germany. . . . Apart from Von der Vogelweide . . . I didn't much cotton to German literature. . . . And then philology, ERROR of old German university system got my goat. . . . Also being in England 12 years, I certainly saw the last war from the London angle." In his explanation of how he came to pay some attention to Hitler's Germany, he shows clearly the real reason—his need to justify Mussolini: "NOT till the time of Sanctions did I begin to consider Germany from a new angle. . . . I was behindhand in readin' *Mein Kampf*. . . . Hitler in 1924 saying that Germany ought to lay off the Tyrol, ought to SEE Italy. See Italy Fascist as the ONE ray of light in a world that was going to sunset, sinking. Just as I saw it as the ONE inch of SOLID basis" (*EPS*, 137–139). Pound projects his own refusal to face the whole truth about Hitler onto Hitler's adversaries. Germany, as perceived by the Allies, is, Pound claims, "the German PHANTOM, NOT the reality. And that phantom has been built out of lies, till the pious and kindly American, and simple hearted British boob BY the million believe it, see it, hear it. And FAIL to grasp or face the reality. . . . And as to LYING I reckon Hitler has been lied about more than any man livin' except Mussolini" (137, 138). By this point we notice that, on secondary points, he is not necessarily consistent from broadcast to broadcast. His point here, for example, that millions of Americans and Britons have been taken in by lies about Hitler, contradicts the assertion he had made only a month before that "as for the English, nine of 'em out of ten do NOT believe they ought to be fighting the Germans" (*EPS*, 96).

Perhaps the most striking volte face in Pound's estimation of Germany occurs in his pronouncements on Nazi economists. On January 15, 1935, he wrote to Hargrave of the need to "bigod can [get rid of] that bastard Schacht," and on January 26 Hargrave wrote back agreeing that "Schacht has got Adolf where he wants him. Hitlerism is banker-fascism" (*EPA*). Pound's attitude toward Hitler and his economists was entirely determined by Mussolini's policy of the moment toward Germany. At the time of the Conference of Stresa, when Italy was collaborating with Britain and France to oppose any unilateral repudiation of treaties with the particular intention of protecting Austria against German aggression, Pound included in a "five-point program" he sent to Hargrave the resolutions "We will fight AGAINST militarism and Dr. Schacht. . . . The only germans who we will treat with are the FREIWIRTSCHAFT people, and organizations, which have been suppressed," and the assertion that "Adolf at beginning promised reforms that so far as one knows are completely OUT of program now" (*EPA,* "After Stresa"). In "The Individual in His Milieu" of October 1935, Pound described Germany as "under the heel of Dr. Schacht" and as "the betrayer of herself from within" (*SP* 278), and in a letter to John Buchan of September 1, 1935, he had called Schacht a "dirty jew," a comment which he qualified with the observation "Usurers are raceless. Shylock betrayed his race by hinding [*sic*] behind it."[28] But by October 1936, once the Italian press had been ordered to take a pro-German line and after establishment of the Rome-Berlin axis, Pound's estimation of Schacht changes accordingly. When he writes to Wyndham Lewis to accuse Germany of being "fairly ignorant. just IGNORANT," he makes an exception of Schacht.[29] By April 1939 he considered the words of economic wisdom of Schacht and Hitler worthy to stand alongside those of his American heroes of economic justice. In an article for the *Townsman,* he followed the four brief quotations from Adams, Jefferson, Lincoln, and the Constitution that together constituted his "Introductory Text-Book in Four Chapters" with a section called "The Nazi Movement in Germany," which consisted of the following:

> War on international finance and LOAN CAPITAL
> becomes the most weighty etc. in the struggle towards
> freedom.   *Adolf Hitler, Mein Kampf,* 1924

> Money that is not issued against needed goods is mere
> printed paper.   *Hjalmar Horace Greely Schacht,* 1938

> The position of a country abroad depends *exclusively* on
> its organization and INTERNAL coherence.
>   *Der Führer,* 1939

By the time of the radio broadcasts, he has taken the most extreme position possible and has elevated Hitler and Gottfried Feder, the economic expert of the early days of the Nazi movement, above even Douglas. On the strength of just one sentence of Feder's—"A great deal of purchasing power is allocated for reasons other than the performance of useful labor"—Pound proclaims him the forerunner of Social Credit thinking and, on the strength of Hitler's appreciation of the wisdom of Feder's sentence, decides that the führer "went to a deeper root" than Douglas himself. Douglas is credited with having "practical experience" and "a sense of justice" but could not be as effective a reformer as Hitler because he had "no faith in the goodness of man" (*EPS,* 280, 281). "Feder's sentence . . . contains about all mankind needs to know about economics. . . . Feder got it into one sentence and Germany rose from her ashes, ran from her miseries and her chaos. Douglas (C. H.) found it out. But he said it with more wrappings and trappin's; and

England went further and FURTHER into the discard. However, that sentence of Feder's gives about all you need as a basis for Social Credit?" (*EPS*, 213). Feder, Pound claims, opened Hitler's eyes to the fact that a great deal of purchasing power comes not from labor but from "speculation, rigging stock markets and by method of issuing so much of the nation's money as interest payin' . . . debt." By speaking out on this, Hitler made himself "like Mussolini . . . [the] target for repeated attempts at assassi- nation" (*EPS*, 281). Or, as Pound told his American listeners in an earlier broadcast, they went to war with Germany merely "on the pretense that you don't like Hitler's municipal government" (*EPS*, 95).

For a while Pound was further encouraged to think that his new positive opinion of Hitler was justified when he discovered what Wyndham Lewis had written in praise of the führer. On November 4, 1938, Pound wrote to Lewis that he had just read Lewis's *Hitler*. Lewis had published this in 1931 as his evaluation of nazism, based on what he had seen in a visit to Germany the previous year. He described nazism and German commu- nism as "rival rackets"[30] but saw the Nazis as far preferable to the Communists in being less violent, less materialistic, and with a much sounder economic understanding. Here was Lewis saying, in 1931, exactly what Pound himself had come to believe now: "The heart of the economic doctrine of the National socialist [is] . . . the absolute distinction between concrete and *productive* capital (great or small) upon the one hand, and Loan-capital . . . upon the other. The arch-enemy is not *Das Kapital* pure and simple, as with Marx, but *Das Leihkapital* or Loan-Capital" (147–48). In his conclusion Lewis describes Hitler as "the Expression of current german manhood—resolved, with that admirable tenacity, hardihood, and intellectual acumen of the Teuton . . . to seize the big bull of Finance by the horns, and to take a chance for the sake of freedom" (201–02).

Lewis also had decided in 1930 that the antisemitism of the Nazis presented no serious danger and suggested that his reader "allow a little Blutsgefüll to have its way (a blood-feeling towards this other mind and body like your own)—in favour of this brave and very unhappy impover- ished kinsman. Do not allow a mere bagatelle of a *Judenfrage* to stand in the way of that!" Feeling that this little injunction effectively removes all need for misplaced anxiety on this issue, he is now comfortable in his assurance that he can "proceed without interference from this particular racial red-herring" (42). He continued to be strongly sympathetic to Hitler through 1937, and in 1936 his *Left Wings Over Europe* was another defense of Hitler and of Mussolini's invasion of Abyssinia. But in 1939 Lewis finally saw nazism and Hitler for what they were and in *The Jews, Are They*

Human? and *The Hitler Cult* recanted, reversed his earlier views, and decided that the Nazis were vulgar, warlike, and nihilistic. Pound, writing to Lewis in 1939, is unaware of his reversal, and in two of his letters modifies his usual signature EZ to $\overline{E}_2$. This is in March, when he is making plans to visit America, and he writes in the first letter: "sig. chur fer use in Murka ? or not" and, in the second, "az fer Murka/ I have something much more unpleasant/ something that will rile 'em a lot more than Littoria [the Italian emblem of the fasces] or hackenkreuz [the swastika]/ I.E. and namely the CONSTITUTION of the U.S. which they have never read."[31]

By February 7, 1940, Pound has read *The Hitler Cult,* and the four-page letter (and one-page addendum in the later post) that he sent Lewis on this day clearly shows his genuine perplexity and bewilderment at discovering that Lewis no longer sees Hitler and Mussolini as Pound himself does. He begins by wondering if Lewis is attacking Hitler in this way "89% to get [his] boat fare OUT of judaea [England]," but, realizing that Lewis is hardly the kind of person to write the opposite of what he thinks for any reason, let alone for money, Pound has to face the fact that Lewis's attack on Hitler is sincere. The anxiety occasioned by this realization takes the same form in this letter to a close friend as it does in the radio speeches:

War for usury, for gold monopoly/ for unutterable stink/ with the poor b[loo]dy/ brit/ told he is fightin fer the rose covered cottage and tennis on Sat. p;M.
  Rothschild vengeance running for 150 years/ Sas/ bloody/ shitten soon [Sassoon]; silver, and mass murder in China/ the cunt of all arseholes [Alfred M.] Mond [British financier and Zionist] being nickel; the Times; Hamboro [British banking family]/ Manshitster Stinkereen [Manchester Guardian]/ 60% interest; god save and so forth. . . . The mond sassoon rothschild set up is cert/ worse than anything you have adduced vs/ Adolph. and, on the interlexchul plane, I begin to doubt that the yidd/ fluence has ever been anything but a stinking curse to Europe. < from A.D. 1 to 1940 . . . >" [P/L, 217–18]

The tone of this registers Pound's distress at finding himself deserted by a former supporter whom he admired as much as he did Lewis, but he knows that simple diatribe will not be persuasive to his friend and tries various other approaches in the hope of carrying his point. He makes a systematic commentary on specific passages from *The Hitler Cult* which shows at every point the sincerity of his conviction that the war was not caused by Hitler but by international bankers. He ends the first part of the letter:

You hide from monetary question for the whole book/ O.K. only way to be printed in a usuriocracy with Astor at the top/ BUT this federation poop [League of Nations] is just the same old Bank of Basil [Zaharoff]/ secret committee of shit, bleeding the world thru a money system/// it is NO go.

god damn it have you got down to Wells' level?? . . . It is war for money lending and a few metal monopolies. Can you print that? Why all this slap stick about Adolf . . . ? wot you need is a bit of economic background.

Blessings on yr muzzy ole top
yrz
EZ [220]

Although he thinks that Lewis overdoes his satirizing of the Germans, Pound points out, as he does in the radio speeches, that his own real interest has always been Italy rather than Germany:

Havin', as you know, plugged for latin clarity and the mediterannean [*sic*] ambience I am not going to tell the world what happens north of the alps; apart from some lucid and coherent argument, and the Geheimrat Frobenius who was a man and a brother. I can't agree that all huns are comics, as seen by the british bombadeer [Lewis].
. . . Certainly HERE (Italy) is more freedom to print than under the shitten arse of the Times in London/ and more goddam chance for any man who wants to paint or carve anything of ANY merit . . . . Say the best fancy writer here is Malaparte/ YES they took away his badge, and sent him off to think in the Confino [jail]/ but LET HIM go on writing newspaper articles from villiagature ["vacation"], and have now set him up with a big fancy magazine to talk about Breton and Elouard [Eluard]. [218–19]

It seems worth emphasizing, in passing, that to find Pound in this letter to a close friend giving exactly the same reasons for defending Hitler and Mussolini that he gives in his radio speeches, is very persuasive evidence that they were reasons which he himself believed to be valid.

This letter is also like the radio speeches in showing Pound censoring some of his own antisemitic comments as he goes along. Presumably concerned that his letter has not put his case persuasively enough, he begins his addendum with an attempt to appeal to Lewis's self-interest, only to find that he has gone off on a particularly unpersuasive antisemitic tangent:

Later post sets me off again/ considering how bloodily bothered you are for money/ why the hell dont it occur to you that the lousy jews who run yr/ fahrt of an empire steal 7 bob to the quid from a mans royalties/ naturally loathing the idea that one shd/ produce literature in a language not yittisch/ Waaal it was a scotch louse [William Paterson] that started the bank/ and didn't profit/ and the brits are as bad as the yitts when it comes to theft and oppression/ so keep it economic. [221]

As Timothy Materer notes, Pound in his letters to Lewis was not always so "economic." In the correspondence before 1936, Pound's "many enthusiasms are subordinated to his passion for the arts," but when he begins writing to Lewis in 1936 "after more than three years in which there seems to have been little or no correspondence between them," there is a "disturbing change" in the tone of his letters (181). Now all the emphasis is on the economic and political, and Pound is now writing *at* Lewis more than writing *to* him. His letter of October 29, 1936, takes the form of a seven-point manifesto which he wants Lewis to round up signatures for. The letter ends: "You will probably think up ten (invalid) reasons against a third issue of Blast. From my pt/ of view it wd. be useful" (186). Mainly he is projecting *Blast III* as a "big gun" in his assault against the "forces of usury," but we sense also in this impractical suggestion a nostalgic impulse—the forlorn hope that it might be possible to recapture the devil-may-care, antiestablishment camaraderie of that now irrevocably lost world before the Great War. Lewis, the last person to be beguiled by such nostalgic wishful thinking and, moreover, clearly wary of Pound's new frenetic mind-set, replies with a short letter designed to disabuse Pound of any expectations of support from the "bombadeer" for this new campaign:

Thank you for the 2 notes. . . . You cannot "kill John Bull" with economics any more than you can with art. Besides why kill John Bull? A debauched & rather decrepid police-dog! You might with advantage kill the masters of J.B. but I doubt if you can do that with economic theory. . . . However, I will write you again in a day or two. This just to wish you un petit bonjour & start in a mild way a correspondence! [187]

After receiving Pound's anguished response to *The Hitler Cult*, Lewis breaks off this correspondence, not resuming it until July 1946, when Pound is in St. Elizabeths. Lewis's letters then are intriguing in that they reveal to us such an unfamiliar side of this writer and artist who seemed before to have opted for "hardness" in all things and to have done all he could to earn for himself the public persona of the "Enemy." Here we see him feeling his way, trying to be solicitous and reassuring without sounding so out of character that Pound will feel that he is being humored. In his first letter he opens on just the right note: "I am told that you believe yourself to be Napoleon—or is it Mussolini? What a pity you did not choose Buddha while you were about it, instead of a politician!" (230). Then he moves quickly to try to allay some of Pound's money worries by telling him how well Pound's books are selling in London and how many more he could sell if the publishers would ship them.

Pound's letters by now have become scattershot in approach and cryptic in the extreme, and keeping up his side of the correspondence was something of a strain for someone as inclined to impatience as Lewis was. We see this very clearly in a letter drafted in May 1948 but "probably not sent."

Your letter, tortuous comme d'habitude, but a few clear spots . . . . Just for the record let me say that you have not especially afforded me your support in the past, except during the recent war when you wrote about me, with a view some might think to drag me into the silly mess where you had landed yourself. . . . And in writing me do understand that I am politically a complete agnostic. No theory of the State interests me in the slightest. It is a waste of time talking to me about social credit, because I take no interest in it. If you would take my advice you would throw any books you possess dealing with economics out of the window. . . . You are in a chaos. Why not face the fact and sing the chaos, songbird that you are? [247]

Pound's two closest writer friends, Eliot and Williams, take rather different approaches in their wartime correspondence with him. Eliot's reserve makes him much less likely than Williams to take Pound to task for his increasing lack of control. In addition, Pound's letters to Eliot are much less intemperate than they might otherwise be because they are so focused on the practical task of getting the Chinese History Cantos ready for Faber to publish. In a letter of July 15, 1939, in which Eliot's main object is to persuade Pound to omit Rothschild's name from Canto 52, Eliot does admonish Pound in closing, "Concentrate Ez, conconcentriate,"[32] but in general their editor/author relationship keeps Pound on nonproblematic subjects. In letters written between 1939 and June 1940, he talks lucidly and calmly about their Appleplex/Eeldrop causeries from the *Little Review,* John Adams, Santayana, Erigena, Cavalcanti, Dante, St. Ambrose, Mencius, Frazer, Frobenius, and even Petroleum V. Nasby. He is even on guard against Brooks Adams's determinism and fatalism, advising Eliot "better read Brooks Adams (omitting the perlite despair)" (6/1/40).

The angry, paranoid mood surfaces only once, in a letter of March 15, 1940, when, in the course of explaining to Eliot that he is anxious to get his own accurate translation of Mencius out to counteract the dangerous influence of "false versions," he makes an assault on Arthur Waley. "As you may remember, I found Waley's Taoism the SHIT, and more so/ possibly all semitic activity is evil, I mean unconsciously and without their meaning it. Anyhow that book spread the principle of evil/ it was, whether intended or not a mass of infection? so much so that I sacrificed the chq/ I wd have had for reviewing it, thinking the fewer readers it had the better."

All in all, Pound was probably closer to Eliot than to any of his other friends, and even when their views and priorities seemed very different, Pound continued to respect Eliot more highly than anyone else for his intelligence and his poetic gift. Even when Pound's sense of proportion was as shaky as it was during these years, he was still capable of the old bantering give and take of the London years; this also helped to keep the mood of his letters to Eliot stable. Eliot, in a letter of July 15, 1939, playing up to Pound's habitual disparagement of his overly "episcopal" ways, writes: "And Ez you shouldn't allow yourself to be so credulous; don't believe anything you read about me unless it's in the Osservatore Romano." Eliot writes to let Pound know that he is considering stopping in Rapallo for two nights and to inquire about appropriate clothing. Pound, in a letter of April 12, 1940, addresses the question of whether his friend will find the evenings cold and then, remembering "Ash Wednesday," "But mebbe you iz TOUGH. the leopards done tried to ate you and then bent their goddam tin teeth."

Compared to Williams, Eliot makes little attempt to call Pound on his unreason; yet we feel that Eliot understood Pound's psychology a good deal better than Williams did. Part of Eliot's hesitance to confront Pound may have come from his habitual reserve, but it was also likely that he realized that whatever he said was not likely to change Pound's headstrong and headlong course. He could have seen, for example, from Pound's reactions to Basil Bunting's criticisms, how little Pound was disposed or able, at this stage, to take the advice of friends. In a letter of January 18, 1940, Pound writes that Bunting "ought to be employed. got good mind. Disgusted with my politics, but that no reason he shouldn't contribute to civilization." On April 1, writing to urge Eliot to publish Bunting, he adds, "DON'T mention ole EZ as Buntn DISapproves of my pollytix." Characteristically, Pound is completely non-egotistic in his reaction to Bunting's disgust with his views. Believing that Bunting can "contribute to civilization," Pound wants to protect not himself but Bunting from the consequences of this disgust. He saves Bunting from having to turn down his support by offering it anonymously. Although consciously he has not given Bunting's criticism serious consideration, the fact that he mentions it in both letters suggests that it has made an impact at the unconscious level, where it has become another of the clamoring voices in the increasingly strident argument between conscience and rationalization.

Unlike Eliot, Williams does keep trying to convince Pound of how wrong his views are, but he finds it impossible to change these views. Even in 1935 he tries to warn Pound of the danger of pontificating on economics and writes: "After all[,] the greatest things Orage might have instructed you in, the things that made him GO, have never entered your consciousness. Why don't you quit writing for a year and look around a bit. It'll do you good" (3/25/35). In his impatience with Pound's refusal to take his advice he attempts to wash his hands of Pound: "Thanks to you old Tomcat: For the rest. Go to hell. We just wasn't born to work together. I can respect you—even love you which I do—but from hence forth unto the boundaries of senility, aufwiedersehn" (6/5/35). In fact, he cannot bring himself to cast Pound off and continues to write to him through 1941. His warnings were entirely to the point:

[April 6, 1938] You belong in this country. . . . I detest your bastardly Italy today . . . . I think that if anyone needs a change, a new viewpoint its you. You can't even smell the stink you're in any more . . . . Perhaps this letter will convince you that I still admire you and love you but—GEZUS CHRRRRIST!—you're missing your strokes Comerado! This ain't the old Ez I used to know. You're in the wrong bin. Your arse is congealed. Your cock fell in the jell*o. . . . Wake up!

[April 29, 1938] I think you're wrong about Spain. I think you're letting yourself be played for a sucker by the party in power in the country in which you happen to be living . . . . It is you, not Hemingway, in this case who is playing directly into the hands of the International Bankers.

[May 18, 1938] Your principal value is your lack of reason which might permit you to jump the track in time to prevent you from going over the precipice. . . . You are so completely wrong in what you say of the Spanish situation that you have to build up a myth to support yourself that you only get inside information on what is going on and that nobody else knows anything . . . . I only agree with you when you tell me of all the concession seekers who are following Franco around and what that signifies. And what concessions are you seeking from Mussolini and Hitler? God help you. Anyhow, you're my Ezra and you ain't the worst vice I own to. I have my trouble defending you in America these days but I still do it. Go on farting. I'm tough.

[April 6, 1940] You leave yourself too many loop-holes for mental escape the way you write now . . . . I think you're slipping badly both in your mentality and in the force of your attacks. It comes from babying yourself and hiding behind a philosophy you know damned well is contrary to everything you stand for, really . . . . Why, for instance, try to tell me that your whole initiative hasn't been anti-semitic of recent years? You know damned well it has been so.

When Pound not only failed to correct his outrageous views but actually broadcast them across the Atlantic and referred to Williams in the broadcasts, Williams became understandably angry and attacked Pound publicly on several occasions. Although Williams was accurate in his descripton of *how* Pound's views were wrong, he did not understand Pound's motivation. Not realizing how psychotic Pound had become, Williams felt that Pound had willfully disregarded his advice out of arrogance. As a result, Pound's attitude seemed to him a double insult, not just a dismissal of William's perception of the international situation but also a rejection of the respect and affection that Williams had openly expressed in his attempts to impress upon his friend the genuineness of his concern to help him. It was hardly surprising that Williams's wartime comments on Pound often registered an angry sense of betrayal.

Pound's radio speech for July 20, 1943, stands out as a particularly dramatic illustration of the psychotic nature of the distortions in his perception of the current situation (*EPS*, 370–72). He is writing here in the immediate political context of recent Allied successes in the North African campaign, Guadalcanal, the Solomon Islands, and New Guinea. His commentary shows that his premises about Allied war aims were an exact inversion of these aims in reality. Pound's view of the situation is as follows: World War II is a war of aggression on the part of the Allies, whose real aims are the enrichment of international financiers and Allied domination of world markets. Roosevelt's aim is to conquer whatever territory is necessary to provide America with uninterrupted trade routes to the orient, both westward across the Pacific and eastward across Europe, North Africa, and the Soviet Union. In North Africa, American troops are fighting against Arabs, whose lands they intend to seize. (His omission of any reference to the Germans here suggests a bizarre displacement onto Roosevelt of Mussolini's guilt for the invasion of Abyssinia.) In Europe, British and American forces are fighting as invaders of (presumably pro-Hitler) France, Spain, Portugal, Germany, and Scandanavia with the intention of acting as an army of occupation. To maintain these trade routes, Pound adds, Allied troops will even have to be prepared to "hold down" not only the countries of Europe but also numbers of Russians who are turning against Stalin. Instead of an Allied war effort to free the conquered countries of Europe from German occupation, we have this vision of an Allied blitzkrieg to take over a European community which realizes that their best hope for economic justice and cultural freedom lies with Hitler and Mussolini.

In addition, Pound came to have less and less control over the direction of his thoughts. In "The British Imperium," his broadcast for June 14, 1942, for example, we find him trying to convince the people of the United Kingdom first that their situation is analogous to that of Austria before Hitler "took over," then that it really is not, then that Britain should not have the United States as an ally because this will mean "to drop into the melting pot," then that America should not have Britain for an ally because the British want to use U.S. troops as mercenaries, then that the "abysmal, unfathomable IGNORANCE" of the United States makes it "unqualified for intervention" in Europe.

As it becomes harder and harder for Pound to keep a line of argument going without swerving off at a tangent, we notice that increasingly his own inability to concentrate and to see the facts straight becomes itself the indirect focus of his comments. He projects onto his listeners his own shortcomings so that his injunctions and warnings to them are more applicable as warnings to himself. "You are in black darkness and confusion. You have been hugger-muggared, and carom-shotted into a war, and you know NOTHING about it. You know NOTHING about the forces that caused it, or you know next to nothing . . . . You have got to learn some things or die, got to learn some things or perish" (*EPS,* 202).

In several instances it is his fear of insanity that he is projecting. "[Vice President] Hank Wallace comes out—no peace till the world accepts the gold standard. *Quem Deus vult perdere.* Does look like there was a weakness of mind in some quarters. Whom God would destroy, he first sends to the bug house" (*EPS,* 27). His anxiety about insanity is particularly noticeable in the speech in which he claims that what the *Protocols of Zion* said about an international Jewish conspiracy should be taken seriously even though the *Protocols* are a forgery. "Certainly they are a forgery" he argues, "and that is the one proof we have of their authenticity. The Jews have worked with forged documents for the past 24 hundred years . . . . The interest in the [*Protocols*] does not lie in [the] question of their having been, or NOT been concocted by a legislative assembly of Rabbis, democratically elected, or secretly chosen by the Mysterious Order of Seven Branched Antlers or the Bowling Society of Milwaukee. Their interest lies in the type of mind, or state of mind of their author. That was their interest for the psychologist the day they first appeared" (283). "Either there is and was a plot to ruin all goyim, all nations of Europe," he claims, "or some people are stark raving crazy." In the state of mind that this speech reveals him to be in, even crossword puzzles become a threat: "Is it possible to persuade more than six or eight people to consider the scope of crossword puzzles and other devices for looking at words for something that is NOT their meaning? Cabala, for example, anything to make the word mean something it does NOT say" (284).

In some speeches, Pound's anxiety about his loss of control is not only projected but also to some extent acknowledged openly. In a speech which he calls "Continuity" and which turns out to be a perfect model of discontinuousness, he begins by acknowledging the impossibility of ensuring that his listeners will see the unity in his talks even though, he argues, they do have a unity. Part of the fault, he suggests, lies with the broadcast form since it allows the listeners no opportunity to turn back and find connections that escaped them on a first hearing:

Nevertheless you may as well make the effort to grasp at least the fact that there IS a sequence in what I am saying. . . . And if you . . . DON'T make the effort . . . and TRY to get [the] main threads and cables of what I am telling you, you will lose time.

Just as the writers who did NOT read the Little Review lost time . . . I hear a million Americans have taken advantage of Mr. Hemmingway's [sic] last production, and so they ought to. TWO million ought to read it (probably . . . I haven't yet seen a copy but that is due to conditions of Atlantic transport).

PITY is that there is so much else, so much essential else that they are unblissfully UNaware of. And I honestly do not know where they can get essential parts of that else, except from my broadcasts. And out of them, out of these talks, the young men in England and America will have to build their souls, or at least their minds for tomorrow, or LOSE time, never get into life at all. [*EPS,* 191]

This is followed by Pound's most direct acknowledgment of his present mental confusion and problems with maintaining continuity:

And after a hundred broadcasts it is STILL hard to know where to begin. There is so MUCH that the United States does not know. This war is [the] fruit of such vast incomprehensions, such tangled ignorance, so many strains of unknowing.

I am held up, enraged, by the delay needed to change a typing ribbon, so much is there that OUGHT to be put into the young American head. Don't know which, what to put down, can't write two scripts at once. NECESSARY facts, ideas, come in pell-mell. I try to get too much into ten minutes. Condensed form O.K. in book, saves eyesight, reader can turn back, can look at a summary. Mebbe if I had more sense of form, legal training, God knows what, could get the matter across the Atlantic, or the bally old channel. Art, economics, pathology. You need to know MORE about all of 'em. Need to GIT out of this war, need to stay out of, or prevent the next one, need to change the stinkin' old system.

ROT in art, art as pathology, university delays. How come class war? What is it the professors don't know? Got to choose between two or four subjects or I will git nothing over in any one talk. Very well. I will start on: How come. Two bits of ignorance that have recently been rubbed into me by a mob or congress of professorial persons. NO . . . let's start on something that HAS been discussed IN America for twenty years, 30 years, Doctor looks at literature. All this quite silly stuff about the diseased mind back of modern painting. [192]

Yet the impression we receive of Pound from his radio speeches is necessarily an incomplete one. Romano Bilenchi's recollections of Pound in 1942 help to fill out this impression to the extent that they show how, in Pound's personal interactions, his fixations and evasions coexisted with a spontaneous and un-self-conscious considerateness and kindliness. Bilenchi's account shows how "locked in" to his evasions Pound was by then and describes what had become a habitual dismissive gesture of Pound's—as of "swatting a fly or mosquito"—which was a sign that he was "brushing aside" any information that would threaten his rationalizations. Bilenchi recalls:

Pound often talked about the war. He was sure that the Italian people had wanted the war and wanted to win it. I responded that no war had even been less popular in Italy, that we were drawing near to a terrible catastrophe, and I asked him where in the world he had picked up such absurd information and impressions. I recounted all the things I was seeing and hearing in the streets that proved the opposite of what he believed . . . . Pound listened to these stories, was shocked, and then pensive for a moment, as if he were weighing the amount of veracity to accord me. Then he rocked back on his chair and made the motion of waving away a bothersome insect with his hand. "All of these complaints and lamentations can be heard in every country in the world, and they will stop after we've won the war. The Axis is stronger than the Anglo-Americans in armaments and military skill. The only thing that might cause us to lose the war in the long run is the scarcity of butter. But I've found the answer: sow peanuts in the Alps. . . . One of these days after I've talked it over with Pea at Viareggio, I'll go to Rome to explain the problem to Mussolini." After the war Pea confirmed Pound's visit and his intentions. "The fellow is crazy, crazy, completely crazy," said Pea, shaking his head.[33]

On another occasion, Bilenchi recalls, "I observed that if he failed to escape after the war, the Americans would send him to the gas chamber. Pound made his usual gesture of shooing an insect away from his face. 'The Americans are used to it,' he said. 'They've known for years what I think of them.' "[34]

Despite its evocations of the Mad Hatter's tea party, Pound's comments on the strategic importance of finding a substitute for butter was not merely a passing observation but an idea which he took seriously and so, as was characteristic of him, acted upon. Chilanti tells how, shortly before he and his group of Fascist dissidents were arrested, Pound introduced this idea during one of their meetings: "He took my daughter Tati on his knees and stroked her hair [which] curled around her face, which was always pale. 'You ought to eat a lot of butter,' he said. And my wife, and all of the others: 'You can't get any butter. Italy is out of oil and butter. They are all used up by the war industry.' " Pound, returning unexpectedly to the apartment the next afternoon "set his cane in the usual corner, took off his wide hat, and handed Tati a small jar full of peanut butter. . . . Tati liked it. Then we went up to the terrace of my home, a large terrace *alla Romana*. Up there, at that hour just before evening, Ezra Pound suggested we plant peanuts on the terrace, and that we convince everyone living in the center of Rome to transform their terraces into peanut plantations. . . . He had one hand on his hair, and with the other he pointed to the terraces all round, from the Pincio to the Tiber. He moved his arm as if he were spreading seeds." Chilanti reflects: "We were a little surprised to take part in that strange, imaginary sowing. But planting peanuts on the terraces was, after all, one subject in the larger program to give the world a government of poetry, and ransom men from need and from the tyranny of usury."[35]

Ezra Pound as young child [no date available].
Beinecke Rare Book and Manuscript Library, Yale University.

Ezra Pound in 1893. Photograph by
the Gilbert Studios. Courtesy of
Mary de Rachewiltz.

Ezra Pound at school
[no date available].
Courtesy of Mary
de Rachewiltz.

Ezra Pound, London 1909.
Photograph by Elliot and Fry.
Beinecke Library, Yale University.

Ezra Pound in 1929.
Beinecke Library, Yale University.

Ezra Pound on the liner *Rex*, April 20, 1939. © *New York Post*.

Ezra Pound in Rome, 1959. Courtesy of Omar Pound.

Ezra Pound at Sant' Ambrogio, October 1965. Courtesy of Omar Pound.

a hero at peace

2 XI 72

Frumi

Lotte Frumi's sketch of Pound after his death. November 2, 1972.
Courtesy of Lotte Frumi.

Ezra Pound in the garden of the Maneras. Venice, 1972.
Courtesy of Olga Rudge.

The Antisemitism
of the
Rome Radio Broadcasts

4

The critic who wishes to arrive at and to present a considered commentary upon Pound's antisemitism faces several major challenges. To begin with, there is considerable resistance to the idea that further discussion of Pound's case is even necessary. Many readers have already made up their minds about the nature of his guilt and see no particular reason for a reexamination of the issue. Some arrived at a judgment of Pound—at the time of his arrest for treason in 1945 or at the time of the Bollingen Award controversy in 1947—which has remained essentially unchanged over the years. As a result, he continues to be thought of by many people, albeit in a rather unspecified way, as essentially some kind of war criminal. In 1945, critics were considering whether he should be hanged and some decided that he should. One can even find that view expressed today.[1] Hence the inclusion in this chapter of a comparison of the cases and states of mind of Pound and Adolf Eichmann.

Before it is possible to make such a comparison, or even to make an informed analysis of Pound's antisemitism, it is necessary to take on the further challenge of arriving at some sound theoretical hypotheses about the dynamics and patterns of antisemitic thinking. In most studies which treat antisemitism in the context of World War II, accountability is a matter to be established on the basis of factual evidence of criminal acts either committed by, facilitated by, or ordered by the individual. Such works are usually written by historians whose primary concern is adding to the historical record. In the case of Pound, however, there is no such evidence, since his broadcasts apparently led to no actions of any kind having been taken. Here our concern is exclusively with the moral accountability of the artist and intellectual and specifically with what Pound's antisemitism indicates about his personality and implies about his aesthetic and ideological positions.

Pound's case requires us to discuss the issue of antisemitism from a perspective less often taken—as an issue of individual moral choice considered in the context of the psychological predispositions of the average person. Much postwar philosophy has tended to problematize the whole issue of moral choice so radically as to effectively remove it from the province of philosophical discussion altogether. Varieties of Freudian psychology have tended, by directing inquiry back toward childhood influences, to direct it away from the act of choice itself. Even more immediately relevant to the present study's concern with commonly held views of Pound is the fact that most people's thinking about antisemitism tends to be highly impressionistic and unsystematic.

In my own case, what the fact of the Holocaust might imply about human nature and the nature of moral choice had been a preoccupation of long standing. Before it was possible to arrive at some reliable sense of Pound's state of mind at the time of the radio broadcasts, it became necessary to formulate, in a systematic way, hypotheses about types and patterns of antisemitic thinking. The analysis of an issue of such complexity is necessarily an ongoing project, but I have published some of the preliminary conclusions of this analysis in "The Psychology of Antisemitism: ConscienceFree Rationalization and the Deferring of Moral Choice."[2] This paper treats in somewhat more detail the general observations on antisemitic thinking which follow here.

A close examination of antisemitic patterns of thought quickly shows that common assumptions about the nature of antisemitism are often mistaken. A frequent recourse is to make a separation between ordinary or "normal" people and the "real antisemite" who is assumed to be an extreme case: the pathological bigot who suffers from a deeply rooted fear of inadequacy that dates from childhood, is independent of present circumstances and impervious to reason or logic. The appeal of this assumption is that it establishes a safe distance between the real antisemite and normal people. The problem is that it overlooks the fundamental fact that normal people have a predisposition toward prejudice—that prejudice, including antisemitism, is not an aberration but an instinctive reaction that can be corrected only by effort and by choice.

The assumption that the real antisemite is different from normal people is often implicit in attempts to explain Pound's antisemitism by looking back to childhood influences. A typical explanation of this kind is one that points to a latent grudge or anger which, we are told, surfaced during the Mussolini years and took its particular coloration from Fascist or even Nazi hate propaganda. This childhood anger is attributed either to Pound's envy of the greater affluence of the families of his Wyncote friends, and hence anger with his father for not being more of a moneymaker, or to his frustration at the stifling influence of the rather claustrophobic upbringing that he received from his very proper and straightlaced mother. Yet, rather than finding any evidence of veiled hatreds and grudges toward others or an injured sense of a wounded ego, we find Pound before the 1930s to be generous toward others, free from hatred, and unselfregarding to a sufficiently unusual degree to be the cause for particular comment on the part of many people who knew him. The anger that we see from the mid-1930s on was not the welling up of resentments repressed from childhood but the direct, immediate, and documentable consequence of unconscious decisions made at this later period.

It is important to realize that we cannot assume an equation between the expression of hysterical or virulent antisemitic sentiments and murderous intent. In almost all cases, as Hannah Arendt discovered in her study of Eichmann, as Robert Jay Lifton shows in *The Nazi Doctors,* and as Claude Lanzmann's *Shoah* reveals throughout, those directly responsible for the systematic murder of Jews under Hitler were not rabid or ranting but, in Arendt's words, "terrifyingly normal."[3] As the implementation of the Final Solution shows, for prejudice to become active persecution on a large scale, the majority of "normal people" within the society must give either their direct services or their tacit acquiescence.

To compare the cases of Pound and of Eichmann is to be made aware that the most dangerous moral recourse is to delegate to others the responsibility of moral choice. In the most important ways the behavior and states of mind of Pound and of Eichmann are opposite. Eichmann was calm and unemotional and was directly involved in activities that led to the killing of Jews. Pound was frenetic, angry, irrational, and obsessive and did nothing that led either directly or indirectly to the taking of any action against Jews whatsoever. It is of the utmost importance to be aware that Eichmann's calm is symptomatic of a moral irresponsibility that is not only far greater but also, in a way that is made clear by its lethal consequences, qualitatively different from Pound's.

As paradoxical as it might seem, Pound's frenetic and disoriented state of mind was, in fact, symptomatic of the continuing influence over him of his sense of moral responsibility. The crucial difference was that, whereas Eichmann was prepared to delegate the responsibility of moral choice to his superiors, Pound, even when his ability to make conscious choices logically was seriously impaired, continued to act on his own authority. This meant that a margin of lucidity and rationality continued to be left open within which his unconscious aversion to hatred, coercion, and murder could still exercise a restraining influence. The profound and disorienting anxiety generated by Pound's attempt to evade the responsibility of moral choice influenced the radio speeches in two ways. On one hand the anxiety gave rise to anger which vented itself in the isolated passages of antisemitic ranting. On the other hand the anxiety acted as a dismantling force, causing the various parts of the speech to work against one another and the internal structure of the argument of the speech as a whole to self-destruct.

The connection between lack of anxiety at wrongdoing and the voluntary abdication of the responsibility for moral choice is illustrated dramatically by Eichmann's account of his feelings at the Wannsee Conference of January 1942. Here, undersecretaries of state, legal experts from all the government ministries, and high-ranking members of the civil service met to discuss how best to exterminate the Jews. Reinhard Heydrich, who called the meeting knowing that many of those present were not even party members, "expected the greatest difficulties"; but rather than arousing objections, "the Final Solution was greeted with 'extraordinary enthusiasm' by all present." Eichmann, who originally had misgivings about "such a bloody solution through violence," found these misgivings recede: "Now he could see with his own eyes and hear with his own ears that not only Hitler, not only Heydrich . . . , not just the S.S. or the Party, but the élite of the good old Civil Service were vying and fighting with each other for the honor of taking the lead in these 'bloody' matters. 'At that moment [he reported], I sensed a kind of Pontius Pilate feeling for I felt free of all guilt.' "[4]

Pound's earnest and jeremiac moralism made it impossible for him to abdicate his own responsibility for moral choice in this way. He refused to avail himself of this "Pontius Pilate feeling" and to become a Fascist functionary. The completely independent—and highly idiosyncratic— nature of his radio "campaign" meant that he cannot be thought of as a "follower of Mussolini." The Fascists' attitude toward him was a combination of bewilderment and suspicion. On one hand they doubted his sanity: to one of his 1934 letters to Mussolini a memorandum was attached in Ciano's office, noting how "incomprehensible" Pound's Italian was and commenting that it is "clear . . . that the author is mentally unbalanced."[5] On the other hand, they suspected that he might be an Allied spy. Pellizzi recalls how, in Rome:

more than once influential members of the regime asked me these kinds of questions: "But what is this man up to? Are we really sure that there might not be some 'code' in his speeches? Could you give any guarantee that Ezra Pound is not a spy?" They credited me . . . with a particular ability to understand Anglo-Saxon people and how their minds work; and since they could not begin to understand this phenomenon, this famous American man of letters, who in the midst of war carried on a polemic on Rome Radio against Roosevelt and against usury, who was acting in an obviously disinterested way, who was exalting the traditions and classical principles of American democracy, and would not allow even a comma to be changed in the texts he had prepared for broadcasting, for all these reasons then, they wanted from me some kind of proof that Pound was not a spy! I would shrug my shoulders, saying that, in my opinion, Pound was no spy; but added that it would take a whole university course, given by a person far more learned than I, to explain to the Italian mind the fact that a man such as Pound, undeniably an American patriot, animated by a rigorous conscience, should feel the irresistible impulse to give such talks on the radio.[6]

Before we concentrate upon a close examination of the texts of the radio speeches for the evidence they provide of Pound's state of mind at that time, we might briefly consider how and in what ways he was antisemitic before the 1930s. To do so, we need to be aware that, in any individual case, we are dealing not with a unitary kind of antisemitism but with several "antisemitisms" overlayering one another. The bedrock is the fundamental psychological predisposition toward prejudice that all people have; above this lies the particular variety of antisemitic stereotyping that is current in the local culture; superimposed on this is the national climate of prejudice at any one time, which is influenced by the state of the national economy, patterns of social change, and the extent to which national leaders are perceived to censor, tolerate, or condone prejudice. Uppermost and by far the most decisive in those cases when antisemitism has real animus behind it is the concatenation of personal anxieties of the individual, which may be related to anxieties on the national level but are bound to be determined primarily by his or her personal situation.

When we turn to the pre-1930s to determine how antisemitic Pound was from childhood on, we must take into account the kinds of antisemitic attitudes that were standard both locally, during his childhood, and then nationally, as he moved from America to England, to France, and to Italy. Since I have written at some length on this subject in "The Pound Problem,"[7] I will recur here only briefly to some of the main points made in that article.

In the Wyncote of Pound's childhood, antisemitism, like anti-Italian prejudice, was a matter of course among the WASP population. To a considerable extent it was a manifestation of the snobbery of those not sufficiently confident of their own social status. Homer and Isabel Pound were bound to have shared at least some of the antisemitic snobbery of their neighbors, but more important to our understanding of the attitudes they instilled in their son was the very public protest against anti-Jewish discrimination that they made by renting their home, in 1902 and 1903, to Dr. Hackenburg, president of the Jewish Hospital Association.[8]

Neither Pound nor his parents held the offensively condescending and hostile attitudes toward the immigrant that were common in the WASP establishment. We see this from their work with Italian immigrants in Philadelphia and in Pound's enthusiastic optimism in *Patria Mia* about the contribution that he believes immigrants from all countries will make to the vitality of American society. Upon his arrival in England, Pound was exposed to the particular variety of supercilious and spiteful antisemitism that was de rigeur among both the British upper class and the marginally upper class to which the Shakespears and Wyndham Lewis belonged. Lewis describes, for example, how, when he first saw Pound, the group had been informed in advance that Pound was Jewish and all, including Lewis, snubbed him.[9]

It is possible that on those rare occasions during his London years when Pound made an antisemitic observation in writing, he was attempting to affect the manner of those around him. This may well be the case with his 1912 serialized version of *Patria Mia* in the *New Age*.[10] Here, having insisted that "the Englishman" is wrong in assuming that "the United States . . . is by race Anglo-Saxon," he points out that "Philadelphia is farther south than Rome" and that the characteristics of Americans are determined more by the climate than by their "ethnology." He then adds: "The Jew alone can retain his detestable qualities, despite climatic conditions. That is, perhaps, an overstatement." While it is the offensiveness of the comment that makes the strongest impression, that he himself was uncomfortable with this offensiveness is suggested both by his qualification of it and also by his decision to omit the passage in his 1913 revision.

By the 1920s in America antisemitism was rampant, and discriminatory measures against Jews in universities and medical schools, in hiring, in housing, and even in clubs, hotels, and resorts had become institutionalized. There was widespread support for the eugenic movement and for the restriction of immigration. In 1924 Pound was living in Italy, the least antisemitic of all the European countries. This same year, E. Digby Baltzell writes, "President Coolidge, who had previously written an article on the dangers of race-pollution for *Good Housekeeping* magazine, called for some final and permanent restrictive [immigration] legislation in his annual message to Congress." Later that year he signed into law such a bill. This bill "ended the dream of America as a land of hope and opportunity for the toiling and oppressed masses of the Old World. It was indeed the end of an optimistic and humanitarian epoch in American history. Yet this so-called Nordic victory was . . . a popular triumph, supported by the vast majority of the American people of all classes and various economic interests."[11]

Pound's anger with Roosevelt in the radio speeches is often referred to as particularly strong evidence of his anti-American spirit, but always with no mention of the virulence of opposition to Roosevelt in America itself. As we have seen, Pound was not initially hostile to Roosevelt and became so only in response to what he saw as the president's readiness to involve America in war. In contrast, Baltzell sees as the reason for "the hatred of Roosevelt, shared by the majority of the WASP establishment" in America, "an irrational fear, if not horror, of social and racial equality."[12] He cites George Wolfskill's judgment that this hatred "had far deeper origins than economics, as anyone who dined out in polite society at that time knows—anyone, that is, who remembers being called a Jew- or nigger-lover for making even a mildly favorable comment on 'That Man, Rosenfelt.' "[13]

Pound himself is never guilty of this antisemitism of the privileged. His commitment to reform, no matter how impractical it came to seem, was always thoroughly sincere; this, together with his natural optimism, altruism, and generosity of spirit, made him incapable of the selfish and self-righteous commitment to repression found in the new class of American establishment antisemites of the 1920s. When he does finally give in to antisemitic rhetoric when war comes, he recurs to the slogans of the old-style, populist antisemitism of the thwarted agrarian reformers of the 1890s, which centers on the theme of Jewish control of international finance.

Pound's antisemitism is usually assumed to be of a piece with his enthusiasm for Mussolini; yet Pound developed this enthusiasm in the 1920s, when Italy, unlike America, was virtually without antisemitism in any form. Not only was Italy the least antisemitic of all the countries in Europe, but until 1938 Mussolini himself, in his public pronouncements, was actively philosemitic. In *Mussolini and the Jews*, Meir Michaelis points out that "after a decade of Fascist rule, Italy was still a model of tolerance as far as treatment of her Jewish minority was concerned. Relations between the authorities and the Jews had never been better."[14]

Until the early 1930s, "Italian antisemitism was still only an oddity" (51) and it was not until Mussolini decided to conquer an empire for Italy that race became an issue for him (115). Despite his "unfeigned repugnance" at Hitler's theories of race, Mussolini, once he had chosen opportunistically to ally himself with the führer, realized that this rapprochement would "automatically bring him into conflict with Jews all over the world, despite his tolerant attitude to the Jews of Italy" (119). He produced the "Manifesto of the Race" and from August 1938 introduced a series of racial laws severely limiting the freedom of Jews in Italy. Dismayed by his reverses in Africa and angry with Hitler's treatment of him, Mussolini lashed out at his generals, the Church, and the Italian middle classes. Nevertheless, instead of trying to blame the Jews, "his references to his Jewish subjects became increasingly philo-Semitic" (302), and he continued steadfast in his resistance to the murder of Jews. As long as he was in power, no Jews were deported from Italy to the death camps. Despite the best efforts of the Nazi SS, Jews were also safe in the Italian-occupied areas of Croatia, France, and Greece, which became havens or escape routes for Jewish refugees from German or Bulgarian zones of occupation thanks to the inventiveness of the Italian consular authorities and full cooperation of Italian soldiers of all ranks (304–11). It was only after the Duce's overthrow that the Germans were able to begin the deportation of Italian Jews. As Michaelis says, "If the 'Jew-lovers' of Salò [Giovanni Preziosi's term for Mussolini and his cabinet] had been masters in their own house, no Italian Jew would have perished in the Holocaust" (352).

An anecdote usually referred to to prove Pound's moral degeneracy is interesting for the evidence it provides of the way in which people who came into contact with him, even at the time when he was most strongly in the grips of his antisemitic delusions, recognized and trusted the fundamental decency and humaneness that persisted independently of his anti-Jewish theories. In his memoir, *Amici: Vittorini, Rosai, e altri incontri*, Romano Bilenchi recalls how in 1941 he told Pound about a young German Jew who was a frequent visitor at the house of Bilenchi's friend Carlo Bo, who lived about ten miles outside Rapallo.[15] The young Jew had escaped to Italy after the SS had massacred the rest of his family and, Bilenchi writes, "was living in continual fear of being arrested and deported, the more so because he had to travel in the course of his work." Pound's reaction to hearing about the young man certainly showed how much of a reflex action his recurrence to the idea of an international Jewish conspiracy had by now become, but Bilenchi's decision to confide to Pound the young man's situation and whereabouts demonstrates particularly eloquently how clear it was to

Bilenchi that the fact that Pound subscribed, at this stage, to the theory of an international Jewish conspiracy had nothing to do with his attitude or behavior toward Jews as individuals. Had he not been completely confident of Pound's moral integrity and his compassion, he would obviously not have entrusted him with this information. Bilenchi writes:

I recounted the story of the young German Jew to Pound, knowing that I could count on his trustworthiness, his readiness to keep this secret, and his sense of humanity. Pound was shaken by my story; he said that he understood my grief at seeing a man reduced to desperation as this young German was. He said that, from my point of view, I was maybe right: that considered individually, Jews, especially the poor ones, were human beings just like us, but as a group controlled by the capitalists, they had organized a relentless conspiracy against humanity, a conspiracy which should be denounced, fought against and broken, but by presenting the case politically [con argomenti politici] and certainly not by murders and massacres.[16]

As this anecdote shows, the unconscious compulsion to maintain his rationalization intact was an urgent one and yet it coexisted with his strong moral sense in such a way that it left uncontaminated his temperamental predisposition to react kindly and humanely toward those with whom he came in contact. This was made possible by his strong tendency to compartmentalize the concatenation of delusional allegations that went to make up his rationalization, to keep it sealed off from contact with the world of action. It was, in fact, necessary to the preservation of the plausibility of the rationalization that he do so, since the prospect or intention of action would hold the serious risk of exposing the untenability of the rationaliza-tions and the impossibility of aligning them with "things as they are." In the most fundamental way, the whole project of the radio broadcasts was backward looking rather than forward looking. The purpose of his "elucida-tions" was not to dispense with objections to something which he wanted to happen but to persist in the self-defeating project of justifying something unjustifiable that had already happened. This is certainly in keeping with the extremely retrospective nature of the greater part of the broadcasts. His impulse to recur repeatedly to the past in fact reflects his desire to maintain contact with his uncompromised moral self.

To determine Pound's intentions in making the radio broadcasts, we must register the complete directness, openness, and forthrightness with which he spoke. To the extent that he acted consciously he was entirely frank and honest and made no use of the indirect and calculating arts of persuasion that are the stock in trade of the deliberate demagogue. It was this complete directness and absence of deviousness in Pound's approach which guaranteed that the broadcasts would have no dangerous consequences for anyone other than Pound himself. His conscious intentions were frequently overridden by his unconscious motives, which were of such a nature as to guarantee that the speeches would have no destructive effect on others.

Consciously, Pound believed that his purpose and his effect in the broadcasts was to convince others of the truth of what he was saying. His strongest motivation, we realize when we respond to the speeches, was to convince himself. Through his commentary we hear the two conflicting voices of the opposed unconscious drives which generate it. There is a war going on in his own mind between the strong drive to rationalize his decision to evade the truth about Mussolini and the equally strong contrary impulse to acknowledge that these rationalizations are lies. He could neither renounce the rationalizations nor be convinced by them, and the discontinuous nature of his commentary is the consequence of this conflict. The "line of argument" in the speeches is the continuous movement back and forth of advances toward a position which is untenable and retreats from it. These retreats are not orderly but headlong and usually involve such complete changes of subject as to seem random. At the two extremes we have the retreat to nostalgia and the retreat to vituperation. The speeches are full of passages of highly personal reminiscence which are frequently so cryptic in their allusions that they would mean nothing to a listener who did not already know a great deal about Pound's past. There is no doubt that in these passages he is absolutely talking to himself.

And Mr. Fouquet, and pop Quackenbush, all that generation that remembered the Civil War. All gone with the ash barrels. Think of swell ballroom, right where my Great Uncle used to keep his bunch of bananas, and I used to play chequers with him; my old Great Aunt's black man of general all work, or rather any work, some work, that he used to dodge to play chequers on top of the apple barrel, before the days of the Windsor fire, Two Hotels, Windsor and Buckingham, ornament of Fifth Avenue, back before you kids remember. [EPS, 99]

The retreat to vituperation—against politicians, "usurers," the Jews— is an indication that the tension generated by this mental conflict is becoming unbearable. The fear of loss of mental control is projected as anger, but it is important to realize that this never involves any call to action. This anger, generated by Pound's panic at his mental confusion, is always expressed in the context of injunctions to the reader to think, analyze, diagnose—to see through confusing surfaces to the underlying truth. Commonly, also, allegations about the death-dealing influence of the "usurers," their "accomplices," and the Jews include specific injunctions against action:

Don't shoot him. Don't shoot him. Don't shoot the president. I dare say he deserves worse, but don't shoot him. Assassination only makes more mess. . . . What you can do is to understand just how the President is an imbecile. I mean that, learn JUST how, in what way he is a dumb cluck, a goof, a two fisted double-time liar (oh well, you know THAT already, and lyin' is NOT a sign of intelligence) but don't shoot him. Di/ag/nose him. Diagnose him. It is not your only out, but it is your bounden duty as an American citizen. DUTY begins at home. [*EPS*, 221]

Or we can consider, in the following passage, how the injunction against action is followed by the idea of safe containment, of the need for inquiry and research and then by the oblique revelation of his own anxiety about the loss of the ability to make connections and to contribute and, finally, of his fear of being cut off from communication and "vital relation" with humanity altogether:

Don't start a pogrom. That is, not an old style killing of small Jews. That system is no good whatsoever. Of course if some man had a stroke of genius and could start a pogrom UP AT THE top, there might be something to say for it.

But on the whole legal measures are preferable. The sixty Kikes who started the war might be sent to St. Helena as a measure of world prophylaxis. And some hyper-kike[s] or non-Jewish kikes along with 'em. I shall be content if I contribute my buffalo nickel to arouse a little sane CURIOSITY, a little healthy inquiry as to what causes the whichness.

Goethe was gittin' at something when he wrote his play "Faust." I can't do ALL the researchin' but thaaar . . . is a field for proficuous research. . . .

. . . I am an authority on Arnaut Daniel . . . any post graduate student can become an authority. . . . If he don't lose all capacity to incorporate what he knows, if he don't see that it . . . may have connections—may IMPLY something or other.

Just as the LOSS, the absolute loss of craftsmanship [both of nineteenth-century London and colonial America] . . . IMPLIED something or other. . . . When do such things synchronize with other phenomena such as usury tolerance? There is WORK for all sorts and kinds of humans as long as [each artist and craftsman] . . . carries his mind deep enough into it, he will find that he is not alone, not isolated, solitary, has something to do; some revelation, VITAL relation with the rest of humanity.

Enough for this evening. [*EPS*, 115–16]

This is not demagoguery, but rather its opposite. This fails to be a rabble-rouser's call to action, not through ineptitude or by chance, but because it is specifically and deliberately not a call to action to all. Pound's conscious aim is to get his listeners to understand the international political situation more clearly and to see that the causes of the war are economic, but his unconscious compulsion was to rehearse his rationalizations in the forlorn hope of silencing his misgivings about them. The forlornness of the hope shows itself in his swervings from the topic of discussion, in his bursts of anger, and in the frequency with which he presents his listeners with questions instead of assertions. In the pursuit of reassurance, Pound can often do no more than register his confusion.

A look at the endings of the speeches will show how far they are from calls to action. He calls on his readers to think, investigate, even to study evidence past and present which would validate his argument that wars, the present one included, occur only because they are deliberately engineered by financiers and could be kept from occurring if the American people would return to the principles of the Constitution and of the Founding Fathers. "I hope to God you will start asking some day," he writes (54); "Ask yourselves why . . . the real thought of the American founders was hidden, stuffed into corners" (65); "Well think it over" (96); "You have not yet started thinking" (216); "When are you going to look into this?" (270).

The broadcasts often end with injunctions to the listener to study by reading, most often the work of the Founding Fathers, but also of Brooks Adams, of the British historian Christopher Hollis, of Cummings (144), of the American historian W. E. Woodward (243), and of Mary Butts (239). He even ends one broadcast by suggesting, "It is perhaps time for young Americans to start reading the classics, Plutarch, or Cicero against Verres" (174) and another by regretting that if his American listeners follow his advice to investigate the ways in which they have failed to "make use of the machinery" of the Constitution, "the worst of it is that . . . it will prevent you from filling your mind with the light of the classics, and may tend to distract you from inheriting our cultural heritage" (331). His call for the listener to work at "retooling" the Constitution would be hard to use as a point of departure for concrete action: "Lots of folks want to keep [the Constitution] rusty and inefficient, so'z it won't interfere with their various rackets.

I am tellin' you how to oil up the machine, and change a few gadgets so that it would work as the founders intended" (205).

It is incontrovertible that his conception of his role as broadcaster is that of teacher and elucidator. His authority to speak, he believes, comes primarily from the fact that he has been studying the relationship between wars and debt for so long—that he has been investigating this ever since the last war and feels, moreover, that the advent of World War II has proved his theories right. Even as the war is raging around him, he gravitates at times toward the theoretical perspective and the overview. His broadcast for May 23, 1943, ends: "The moment is serious. The moment is also confusing . . . because there are two sets of concurrent phenomena, namely, those connected with fighting this war, and those which sow seeds for the next one. Your leading men ought to *see* that. You ought to see it. It should constitute food for reflection. For YOUR reflection. You are between two very rough millstones" (319). And again, on June 5, 1943: "It is not, and has not been my purpose in these talks to speak of this war as an isolated phenomenon, a bit of meteorite fallen from some other planet. My function is to arouse a little curiosity about a PROCESS. War is PART of a process. Some men would want to know what part of a process it is, and what process it is part OF" (334).

In a very real sense, Pound in the radio broadcasts remains Gertrude Stein's "village explainer," although, with benefit of radio, the village is now a global village. Interestingly, Pound himself is exactly aware of this as we see in his final speech, made on July 25, 1943, the day of Mussolini's fall, in which he describes his series of broadcasts as "the debating club, the international, mondial world wide, etc, academy of the air" (377). His use of the radio gives him a misleading sense of participation in the world of political action around him, but it allows him to remain, in reality and from anyone's viewpoint other than his, completely insulated from the world of events. He is the single inhabitant of a "homemade world" of theoretical speculation and explanation having direct contact with reality at almost no point.

A particularly striking example of this is the 1941 speech in which he presents with complete seriousness his plan for "PEACE in the Pacific," which would involve giving "Guam to the Japanese in return for one set of color and sound films of the 300 best Noh dramas." The Japanese, he argues, "would be truly grateful to us, not for Guam, but for prodding 'em on to make a complete high grade record of these plays before the tradition gets damaged" (384–85). He reassures his listeners twice that he is entirely serious in presenting this as a peace plan, and that he was so is only too clear from his delusion, when he was flown from Pisa to Washington to stand trial, that the United States government had finally realized that his knowledge of Japanese culture would make him diplomatically useful to his country. James Laughlin reports Pound's distress and confusion when, finding himself confined in Gallagher Mental Hospital, Pound asked why he was being kept there when he thought that the government's intention was to send him on to Tokyo to convert the Japanese from Shintoism to Confucianism.

It is hard to see, in the light of such extreme instances as this—and there are several—why there is such resistance to the idea that Pound was "of unsound mind." James Laughlin also tells how, in St. Elizabeths, Pound paid another inmate to be his food taster and, in explanation claimed, "Berny Baruch is trying to have me poisoned. I can't understand why the Jews are after me because I sent them the plans to rebuild the Temple in Jerusalem."[17] Williams, recounting in his *Autobiography* a visit to St. Elizabeths, writes: "Ezra is convinced that after twenty minutes' instruction in the Georgian dialect, if at the beginning of our difficulties, with Russia, Stalin would have given him a five-minute interview, he could have shown the man the error in his thinking, made him see, comprehend, and act on it, and all the subsequent confusion and disaster could have been avoided.[18]

While it is clear, as these examples show, that Pound's perceptions of the political world and his relationship to it were so at odds with the real situation as to be genuinely psychotic, in matters not directly connected to economics and war—particularly matters of literature, culture, and his own past—he was capable of being reasonable and logical. Also, an intuitive sense of moral responsibility and moral decency seems to have been preserved intact beneath and despite the completely morally irresponsible anti-semitic generalizations he was making.

We see this, in fact, even in those instances which are most frequently offered as evidence of Pound's moral degeneracy. Of late, the most frequently cited example of Pound's "evil" is his reference to "dead meat" on the Russian steppes. He is gloating, we are told, over the spectacle of war dead or even of slaughtered Jews. If we look at what Pound actually wrote we receive a different impression. On October 18, 1941, Pound wrote to Williams: "I assume that yr/ article is full of meat (date of demise not yet ascertainable). . . . There is a lot of meat lying round on the Steppes at this moment" (EPA). In a letter of November 26, Williams refers to this comment as "your brutal and sufficiently stupid reference to meat lying around on the Steppes,"[19] but some familiarity with Pound's other expressions of his reaction to the idea of young men killed to no end in a war that need never have happened suggests that the comment was made in a far from brutal spirit.

In a radio speech made on May 4, 1943, for example, when his mental state was even less stable than it had been in 1941, he had written : "*Dulce et decorum est*. Lovely to die for the Prudential Insurance Co. which has the strength of Gibraltar. To be exported as so much dead meat in order to extend the Russian or Semitic control from Moscow down to the Persian

Gulph?" (296). On March 19, 1943, he had said, "I take it I sometimes do display some sort of indignation . . . . And when a man comes out and says: NO American boy shall be sent out to fight outside the country. Then a few months or a year later, you hear him holler: Millyums of American soldiers are in all parts of the globe, ain't it wunnerfuuuulll! Am I expected to display moral indignation! Two hundred corpses floatin' about in the sea off the harbor of Cadiz? Whaaaa, only 200, why in a year or so there'll be thousands and thaaaaousans of corpses floatin' all over the ocean. Ain't it wunnnnnerful! (254). Shifting the weight of the blame from FDR to the usurers, whose tool Pound claims the president to be, he reiterates the same outrage against death in war as he has registered in these other broadcasts: "And now I hear New York meat is slaughtered by chewish butchers, or was a decade ago. Mebbe now there is [word missing] of it to slaughter [that is, after the Depression, which was itself, he claims, caused by the usurers.] Mebbe all American meat [war dead] is slaughtered by Jewish butchers. [the international financiers who caused the war.] Beef as wuz. Long pig as may be. (Yaaas, long pig is what the cannibals call it.) But their preparation of it is for consumption, not merely as carnage" (331). Morally, it is no small step from deluding oneself into believing in a conspiracy of predominantly Jewish "Usurers" to gloating over the spectacle of mass deaths and, fortunately, this was a step that Pound never took.

If there were evidence that Pound was guilty of espousing antisemitic views of a Nazi variety and specifically of advocating or condoning the mass murder of Jews, we would be most likely to find it in his comments on race and "racial purity." An examination of such comments in his writings between May 1934 and June 1943 shows that, disturbing and distressing as these ideas are, they are not genocidal but rather, in line with the arguments of the American eugenicists which were widely accepted throughout America and even publicly advocated in a matter-of-course way, as we have seen, by President Coolidge.

Pound's motives, however, were essentially different from those of the American eugenicists in that they stemmed from his personal, and hence unique, psychosis. As *Patria Mia* shows, he had always considered that the mixing of racial strains led to social vitality and nowhere is his lack of enthusiasm for "racial purity" clearer than in his assertion to Williams in a letter of September 11, 1920: "You have the advantage of arriving in the milieu [in America] with a fresh flood of Europe in your veins, Spanish, French, English, Danish. You had not the thin milk of New York and New England from the pap" (*LEP*, 158). His recourse after 1935 to comments about a "racial problem" is, of course, directly linked to the deterioration of his mental state. Unaware of this deterioration, and that it was the result of suppressed guilt at having failed to condemn Mussolini's belligerence, the only cause for anxiety Pound can identify is the failure of his attempts at economic reform propaganda to get results: "Hitherto the best United States thought has not been racial. The majority, 99.9% of the serious thought in both England and America has been economic. And it has NOT brought reform into being. We may have been ALL of us wrong, except Lothrop Stoddard, and a half dozen writers: Better known abroad than in either England or in America" (168). As this comment makes clear, Pound is aware that a eugenicist line of thinking is a completely new departure for him and one that he adopts as a last resort out of frustration at failure. It also shows him associating himself with the American eugenicists through his reference to Stoddard.

Nazi scapegoating of the Jews was to a radically different end than Pound's. The Nazis displaced their own guilt onto the Jews and committed themselves to destroy them. All their energy was directed toward domination and killing in a way that was entirely consonant with their whole political and military program. Pound, on the other hand, had always been committed to the opposite program of eliminating oppression, both "economic oppression" and in particular the wars which he claimed it was bound to lead to. Now that he had lost emotional control, he wanted to exteriorize the threat of personal, psychological disorder by blaming "the Jews" as the cause of chaos and danger, but he wanted to stop at blaming them. He wanted to avoid, as far as he could, following through from blaming to suggestions about what should be done as a consequence of their "guilt." He sensed that it was dangerous even to begin to consider seriously what measures should be taken against these "fomenters of disorder" because to specify measures would mean having to be specific about what their "crimes" consisted of, and this he could not do. A great deal of the self-dismantling nature of the radio speeches results directly from the way in which the momentum created by his accusations is derailed by the equal and opposite resistance to thinking about what the implications of these accusations might be.

Even in the grips of psychosis, Pound's innate moral sense was tenacious enough to interfere with any attempt to move beyond accusation to suggestions of coercion. The most striking instances of this show the mind veering abruptly away from what threatens to be a dangerous direction of thought. Two particularly interesting examples of this occur in a talk called, inappropriately enough, "Disbursement of Wisdom" (187–90), which is so comprehensive in including his major dilemmas that it is worth considering as a whole. Early in the talk we find the typical accusation: "You have an ORGANIZED minority of a different race amongst you. A race that never tires, a race possessed of subcrocodilian vitality." What we do not find is any talk of measures to be taken *against* this sinister race. His first recommendation is addressed to those who would save the "victims" and is typically unspecific and even odd. "Against an organized force of . . . probably EIGHT million, a hundred individuals can NOT prevail until ORGANIZED. . . . The inhabitants of the United States can organize on ONE basis only, namely, that on which Europe has finally been constrained to organize its rebellion against the pervasive, the ubiquitous Yidd. Pacts may be signed between the Pennsylvania Deitsch [*sic*] and the scrawny New Englander of British or Anglo-Scotch origin, but on no basis save that of race, and of allied more or less consanguineous races can you cohere."

He then rules out "organization" on a "religious base" as a way of eliminating the Jewish threat, claiming that this has always been used in the past as a ploy "to stir up war." Similarly he rules out the adoption of communism as a solution. He also laments the fact that attempts at economic reform must now be admitted to have failed to provide a solution as well:

religious basis NO use. What CAN you organize on?
    Can't move 'em with a cold thing like economics. Marx advised fighting on an economic basis. I still meet people who fall for that bit of eminently semitic strategy. For ONE HUNDRED years, simpletons and inexperienced young men have tried AS, damn it . . . I tried ever since my kitten of a mind got its eyes half open. And what came of it? Five thousand in prison. Worgl, Alberta.
    Yes, yes, we lily-livered humanitarians fussed 'round wantin' to cure the evil by honest accountancy; and we did NOT prevent this war.

Here and in the first of the "veering away" passages which follows it, we can clearly see the struggle in his mind between the temptation to abandon his former humanitarian perspective and his resistance to this. Here he condemns his humanitarianism for having failed and is torn between self-criticism for cowardice, calling it "lily-livered," and self-pity at vulnerability, comparing it to a half-blind kitten. To "move beyond" humanitarianism, though, means to move toward violence, and his mind will simply not let him follow through with the idea of violent measures against the Jews:

    The Talmud announced destruction of 75% of the goy. Yes, brother you have an OPPONENT. And what CAN you rely on? Dan Boone out shootin' squirrels. Hit 'em in the eye every time, but the Boone era . . . has gone forever. The Boone era seems to have got mislaid for the moment. Prosperity has went, it has vamoosed. We wipp, nichishin, chippewa language has vanished with the pure injun dialects. Even the mixed idiom, such as *"que voulex vou buju, nicichin"* is no longer current on the Canadian frontier. And Henry James already noticed a change in New York phonetics.

On the seventh day gawd rested. I noted THAT even in [the] days of the Little Review.

We could hardly ask for a more telling revelation of Pound's state of mind. He attempts to talk himself into thinking about violent opposition to the "Jewish threat," even trying to stir himself up with antisemitic propaganda about the Jewish mission to destroy the Gentiles. The most violent thought he can bring himself to entertain is the idea of Daniel Boone shooting squirrels and he cannot even hold this. Boone, killer of squirrels and pioneer, suggests Thaddeus Pound as pioneer and his son, Homer, the first white child born in northern Wisconsin with a Chippewa Indian as a nurse. This leads Pound to thoughts of the corruption of the Chippewa language and to Henry James's and Pound's own concern with threats to the integrity of the English language. By then he is safely back in the days of his editorship of the *Little Review*.

He tries once more in this speech to make himself consider measures that might be taken and with a similar lack of success:

One of these days you will have to start thinking about the problem of race, BREED, preservation.

I do NOT like to think of my race as going toward total extinction, NOR into absolute bondage.

The Cincinnati etc. erred from snobbery. They did not in George Washington's time organize on a racial basis. No one . . . could have then thought of it. There WAS a racially homogeneous population in the newly freed colonies. Certain privileges were dear to the privileged. Snobbism is NOT conservative. Fashion is not conservative. *La Mode,* etc. is a ramp. Cf. with Hungarian and Roumanian peasant linen, one shirt or blouse lasts a life time, indestructable as real Chinese silk, "no can tear."

That is what the advertising trade diddles you out of and you will have to think about Race.

What is ostensibly undertaken here as a commitment to argue the need for "racial measures" to be taken reveals itself for what it really is: a testimony to Pound's unconscious determination to deflect all thoughts about such measures. First he displaces the responsibility for thinking about the subject from himself onto his reader. Then he focuses on the time of the Founding Fathers in saying that then it was not even possible to have thought about this. Finally he attacks "Fashion" as a kind of snobbism through which consumers are tricked into sacrificing quality of materials through their vulnerability to being brainwashed by advertising, which makes a fetish of conformity to styles which constantly change. He waits to remind his listeners that they "will have to think about Race" until after he has shown that he is incapable of doing this himself and after his broadcast time is used up.

As we would expect, the few direct comments that he does make on racial measures are minimal and very generalized. On a few occasions he raises the issue of deportation, but hardly in a considered or serious way. Speaking not to Americans but to the British—in itself a distancing strategy—he asks when they are going to "see to it that the ENGLISH remain and the Yiddish go forth to Bolivia or wherever," and suggests that they "will have to give back their naturalization papers to the sweepings of Europe." He adds: "Let the Jews BUY a national homeland somewhere in your ruins. They have sold a good deal of Africa into serfdom" (186). In a later broadcast to the United Kingdom he says, "Don't start a pogrom; SELL 'em Australia . . . and give 'em Cripps for High Commissar, and Eden to be their Prime Minister; and fatty Temple [Archbishop of Canterbury], clothed in an ephod to serve in the synagogue, or to be high priest of his new synthetic religion" (255). These "throwaway comments" hardly seem intended as serious recommendations for an anti-Jewish policy, especially since elsewhere he questions the need for any anti-Jewish policy at all: "If you would run your own government properly. If you would think out a clean code of ethics. If you would make use of the machinery our respectable forebears bequeathed us, you wouldn't need to be bothered with Jewry . . . and its peculiar, oh VERY, organization" (330).

On the subject of eugenics itself, he is predictably vague and general. Instead of talking about doing anything to Jews, he focuses on what Gentiles should avoid doing on their own account. Apart from advising that "mixed marriages" should be avoided, his other main suggestions are the obvious one, to avoid inbreeding, and the paranoid one, to ensure against "race suicide" by not using contraception and by ignoring "propaganda" for the small family. Again, these comments tend to be descriptive rather than prescriptive: "[The British]'ve been suicidin' their race for some time. Even openly gloryin' in the small family, gloryin' in not breedin'. That is NOT aimed at survival." Revealingly, he alludes, albeit euphemistically, to his own emotional instability on this issue when he adds, "My fight from bad temper and natural kussedness, that also is understandable, but not admirable" (203).

When he tries to raise the issue of measures other than "preventative" ones that might be taken to "improve the breed," he predictably reaches an impasse. At first he avoids the problem by stopping short of even considering the implications of the comparison he starts to set up between the breeding of animals and of humans. "England has chosen birth control INSTEAD of Eugenics. You could see that 30 years ago, and then they went to breeding fool-blooded [fullblooded?] grey hounds and *whiffets* [whippets], not even edible farm stock, INSTEAD of trying to make human thoroughbreds. The so-called example of the race course, horsebreedin' would have served the English race as a paradigm, but they didn't use it. Contraception, killin' the native stock before it was hatched, instead of BREEDING a population. Good evening" (126).

In a speech made three weeks later, on May 31, 1942, he tries to pursue the implications of this idea and finds that he cannot do it. His only recourse is evasion and angry frustration.

One of your brain . . . trustees remarked . . . if you could, breed human beings like cattle. That is perhaps a good sample . . . of brain trustees' methods. It hides the crux [of] the issue. You possibly can not breed human beings "like cattle" but you can or could at least bend as much human intelligence on the problem of human breeding as you do on breeding cattle or wiffets. And on that BASIS Hitler is also YOUR leader. . . . It is mere evasion to say you can not breed humans like cattle. Some things you can do. You can, but DID NOT take proper measures against syphylis, tuberculosis, malnutrition NOR breeding itself, whereof RACE is a component. You have encouraged the most fatal admixtures, you have not run [wode? that is, mad] as in the U.S. of A, because you had not the same opportunity. But you have bandaged your eyes. You have not squared up to the problem. [154–55]

Of course, as is so often the case in these speeches, Pound is talking not only to himself but also of himself. His real subject here is his discovery of the impossibility of "squaring up to" this "problem." He has been forced to realize that the Brains Trust commentator was correct, that human beings cannot be "bred like cattle," certainly not under any regime compatible with the standards he has hitherto strenuously upheld with his consistent condemnation of any governmental or institutional attempts to interfere with the individual's private life. As late as *Guide to Kulchur* he had reiterated this theme: "The word puritan has become a term of reproach, made so by the 'stinking puritan' who is a pseudo. Comstockery is a variant on the failure to distinguish between public and private affairs. The stinking pseudo fusses about the private lives of others, as distinct from and often as an avoidance of trying to ameliorate public affairs, such as monetary abuses" (GK, 194).

The closest Pound comes to squaring up to the issue of institutionalized eugenics is when, on one occasion, he makes reference to the theories of Louis-Ferdinand Céline and the French eugenicist Albert Londres.[20] This passage manages to sound thoroughly repulsive despite the fact that it avoids all reference to specific measures:

You make a race by homogeneity and avoiding INbreeding. . . . The next move, the next world movement is a move toward the production of thoroughbreds. Think it over. The idea is a risin'. Means no hardship to anyone. It is eugenic. No argument has ever been sprouted against it. You like it in dogs and horses. One would think the human was worth as much attention as the British fanciers give to whiffets.

Albert Londres had a hunch that the French ought to try it on blacks in their Africa. He hated to see the Africans going rotten, covered with scabs in French colonies. Céline thinks it would be useful to use that much sense on Frenchmen. [132]

The fact that he insists that such measures produce "no hardship to anyone" means that he is not thinking in terms of enforced sterilization, but what he does have in mind is never specified.

The transition from an inadvertent to a deliberate antisemitism was one that Pound made not readily and with relief, but reluctantly and only after having put up considerable resistance. We can see this when we consider his comments between 1934 and 1943 chronologically. In a letter of May 1, 1934, to John Buchan, he writes: "The filthy London School of pseudo-conomy is mainly middle/europa yidtisch. (Not that that proves anything—and jewish destructivity may be left out of the discussion or lumped into the general abstract of destructivity at large.)"[21] On July 5 of that year he writes in a similar vein in a letter to W. E. Woodward on the advantages of stamp scrip: "Has been tried and WORKED, blocked only by rage of bank sharks. (to hell with [talk of] jew conspiracies and all that irrelevant tosh.)"[22] In his "American Notes" feature of the *New English Weekly* for November 21, 1935, he is also consciously on guard against the temptation to scapegoat the Jews when he writes: "Usurers have no race. How long the whole Jewish people is to be sacrificial goat for the usurer, I know not. . . . Whenever a usurer is spotted he scuttles down under the ghetto and leaves the plain man Jew to take the bullets and beatings. There are always the ten thousand Cohens in the Bronx phone book, very few of 'em millionaires, very few of 'em getting pushed up stairs by benevolent despotism. . . . All hostilities are grist to the usurer, all racial hates wear down sales resistance on cannon." Yet the inadvertent antisemitism is clearly in evidence in this piece, as when he relays "the one witticism that shows us (outside Germany) why [Hitler] is Führer" and quotes: "A Jew doctor is a Jew, A Jew Lawyer is a Jew, but a Jew Banker is a banker."

In "Race," a *New English Weekly* article for October 15, 1936, he contends that different systems of government are appropriate for different races. He argues that "Communism is Muscovite, Socialism is German and embodies . . . ALL the WORST features of German stupidity" and that the "squadrismo," or "love of military drill" dear to the Italians, would never appeal to the British and the Americans, who are "racially" suited to parliamentary government. His commentary on this point shows that although he has already begun to entertain dangerous racist ideas, he is also sufficiently in control to be able to sense the dangers of following that line of thinking, even though he registers this unsatisfactorily in the form of a misplaced assurance. "There was never any talk of decline of parliamentary government until imitations of it were set up in countries whereto it was RACIALLY alien. There would be no talk of it now in America, had America not been flooded first by German and then by Muscovite and Semitic populations. The support of racially alien trends in American politics need NOT give rise to religious furies, pogroms or discrimination against any man because of religion or colour. The creators of darkness and obfuscation of the Press can be damned or shot without any bitterness between one race and another."

We realize that he has arrived at a new stage in the deterioration of his mental state when we find him saying, "I think you lose by not thinking about this problem as RACIAL" (3/23/42), but it is significant that, having said this, he feels compelled to try to reassure himself that, in consider-ing racial theories, he is not condoning prejudice:

Yes, I know I went at it from the economic part of the picture. Brought up on American principles; no prejudice against any man for race, creed, or color.

Waaal, the chemist is not supposed to have prejudice against any particular chemical; in the laboratory some stink and some do not. Some explode and some do not . . . the . . . chemical engineer is supposed to look at different chemical elements with a fair eye and mind.

So I don't reckon to go along my road as with prejudice. I have tried to see the thing straight. *EPS,* [71]

Although this is obviously not persuasive as a disclaimer of prejudice, it is interesting in several ways as an index to Pound's thinking at this point. It shows that he feels resistance to and anxiety about the idea of being prejudiced. It indicates that, despite his strong unconscious compulsion to prejudiced thinking, he is still also in touch with his unconscious impulse to disapprove of and resist prejudice and can register this verbally at the conscious level. It also shows that his thinking on the connection between holding "racial theories" and being prejudiced is very vague and illogical. We have already seen that he never does, in fact, follow through on his racial ideas to the point of advocating or even being able to formulate actual "racial" measures.

The inchoate nature of his thinking on this topic is the direct result of the fact that he never, finally, moves beyond his original theoretical base. His point of reference continues to be the original one, which sees the underlying "crime" as the economic one and the villain as the "Big Jew"/"Usurer," even when his psychotic and paranoid state reduces him to rantings which are unfocused and uncontrolled outbursts of anger. When he says, as late as May 1942, "I don't reckon to go along my road as with prejudice," he is showing that he does not consider his attacks on Jews as instances of prejudice, as long as he makes them in the context of his exposé of usurious conspiracies and "monetary crimes."

Usually, even when Pound's comments seem closest to being denunciations of the Jews as a race, he does circle back to the theme of the enemy as "Big Jew"/"Usurer. "The Jews" in the speeches are not "the Jew as person." It is as though these "Jews" exist on another level of reality from the actual Jews that Pound knew personally, such as his friend Louis Zukofsky, or his wife's protegé, the pianist Lonny Mayer—as, in a sense they did. These "Jews" were almost like allegorical figures who would have been at home in a mystery play or in the pages of Spenser or Bunyan. They seemed to be members of a group that was almost feudal in its social structure, being either overlords wielding irresistible power, albeit clandestinely, or else serfs. Pound also seemed to believe that his lack of any animus against this "underclass" was further proof that he was not antisemitic, but he was, at least, sincere in his repeated denunciations of any persecution of Jews. His speech for June 1, 1943, was called "Big Jew" and begins, "Don't go for the little Jews, go for the big Jews, and study KAHAL organization," and repeats, "Don't go for the poor Jews. Don't pick on the amhaarez. Look into the system" (*EPS*, 329–30).

What is probably the most distressing of the antisemitic comments, and Pound's only reference to torture, occurs in a context which particularly emphasizes the "Big Jew/villain; small Jew/victim" paradigm:

The Jew is behind you, but you cannot blame it all on the Jew, though you are the Jew's most damned accomplice. Above all you can not blame it all on the small Jew; for he is in most cases as damned a fool and as witless a victim as you are, [he is] the shock troop, below the starvation line; . . . below which there is NO morality. Only the instinct for survival at the cost of whatever baseness, more often heedlessness than planned iniquity; milked by his damned kahal just as you are. Truly you had great possessions.

And while the BBC was evoking or reconstructing Carlyle, for propaganda purposes they might have included the item from Froude's life of their hero. Carlyle stood opposite the Rothschild great house at Hyde Park Corner, looked at it a little and said: "I do not mean that I want King John back again, but if you ask me which mode of treating these people was nearest to the will of the Almighty about them, to build them palaces like that or to take the pincers for them, I declare for the pincers." [311]

By reporting Carlyle's comment that it would be more appropriate to imprison and torture "Big Jews" than to allow them to accumulate fortunes so great that they could build palaces, Pound is at least implying that there is some truth to it. He introduces this reference at the end of the speech but he does add his own conclusion: "Carlyle was a historian. Never till you kill off your Churchills and Edens will you get your history without bandages" (311).

It is worth considering at this point how far he is prepared to go in advocating violence as a solution to "economic oppression." We notice that, although he does say that the wholesale slaughter of young men in this war occurred because of the failure to eliminate key figures in the conspiracy of the "Central Staff," he consistently backs away from the idea of doing this in any way other than by due legal process:

I think it might be a good thing to hang Roosevelt and a few hundred yidds IF you can do it by due legal process, NOT otherwise. Law must be preserved. I know that this may sound tame, but so is it. It is sometimes hard to think so. Hard to think that the 35 ex-army subalterns or whatever who wanted to bump off all the kike congressmen weren't just a bit crude and *simpliste*. Sometimes one feels that it would be better to get the job done somehow, ANY how, than to delay execution.

. . . . I don't think there is any American law that permits you to shoot Nic. Butler. It is a pity but so it is. No *ex post facto* laws are to be dreamt of. Not that Frankfurter or any other damn Jews care a hoot for law or for the American Consitution. But we are not here to uphold Frankfurter or the Jewish vendetta. In the midst of which YOU jolly well are. And every American boy that gets drowned owes it to Roosevelt and Baruch, and to Roosevelt's VIOLATION of the duties of office.

It is on the ground of those violations, those that occurred before Pearl Harbor, that you should impeach him. It is time that the matter was studied. [289]

He had mentioned this alleged plot to assassinate Jewish congressmen in an earlier speech and in a way that shows very strikingly the struggle within himself between attraction to and aversion from violence; his habitual inversion of American and Italian responsibility for belligerence in this war; and the extent of his identification of his own best moral impulses with Italian decency and hatred of violence:

Only England dare not mention the expulsion of Jews by Maria Theresa, nor England's blackmail of Maria Theresa, nor the Jews' relations with Cromwell. American radio is silent, partly from ignorance, the poor hicks just don't know any history, though a gang of foolish young men had the exuberance to get jailed for plotting to bump off all the Jew members of Congress. Had they succeeded, such is the American gangster and anarchist psychology that the only comment inside the United States would have been "and a damn good thing too." (With echos [sic] in unspeaking England.) The only place where anyone would have been shocked is in Italy, where there is a millennial conservatism and a prejudice against . . . [text indecipherable]. [186]

It is no coincidence that those passages in which Pound's antisemitism is most objectionable, such as the allusion to the plot against the Jewish congressmen and the references to the views of Carlyle, Céline, and Albert Londres, are also those in which he recurs to the antisemitic acts or the expression of antisemitic views of other people. Yet this is as close as Pound comes to delegating moral responsibility and, even when his thinking was psychotic, his fundamental moral decency was insistent enough to cut through the clamor of rationalizations and to continue to exercise a restraining influence. Even when the hold that his antisemitic delusions had over him was too strong to break, his moral conscience could still act to interject caveats and responsible qualifications of irresponsible assertions; to make him veer abruptly away from dangerous subjects into irrelevancies, nostalgic reminiscences, and unidentifiable allusions; and, in general, to stir up such mental confusion that finally the only victim of the effects of these broadcasts was Pound himself.

Saint Elizabeths: Confucius against Confusion

5

" 'Did you get a square deal?' To this question the patient made no reply, but continued to talk about his extreme fatigue, to make deep sighs, hold his head, and to assume a very worried and anxious appearance. He then became rather angry, raised his voice to a shout: 'I want quiet. If this is a hospital, you have got to cure me.' 'Cure you of what?' 'Whatever the hell is the matter with me—you must decide whether I am to be cured or punished.' "[1] If, having looked carefully through the hospital's records of the twelve and one half years that Pound spent there, we turn again to this glimpse of him as he was when he first arrived, we can see these words as a painfully eloquent commentary on his dilemma. Yet they were eloquent in a way that none of the large number of people who came into contact with Pound during his years in St. Elizabeths was able to appreciate. "You have got to cure me" was a cry for help that went unanswered, not because of indifference or callousness but because of a fundamental lack of understanding for which no amount of concern for his welfare could be a substitute.

It was very much out of character for Pound to ask for help, and the fact that he did on this occasion is an indication of the directness and sincerity with which he was speaking. Under the pressure of fear and confusion, his unconscious thoughts revealed themselves and we see that, no matter what he might contend later, he believed that there was a simple alternative. Either he could be cured at St. Elizabeths or he would have to be punished. He was not cured—the psychiatrists could not even arrive at an accurate or adequate diagnosis—and so, once he was a free man again and fully responsible for himself, he proceeded to undertake his own punishment.

There was nothing devious about Pound—he was direct and he was always consistent. He could not knowingly and willingly evade the truth, so that, when the implications of the truth became too painful for him to bear—as they did in the mid-1930s—his only recourse was to convince himself that what he wanted to be true in fact was. It is of the utmost importance to realize that his mental illness entailed genuine self-delusion, since this fact has such a direct bearing upon the question of his treason. If he consciously believed what he said in his broadcasts over Rome Radio, his intention was (as he claimed) not to betray the United States but to save it.

The fact that Pound was declared unfit to stand trial for treason angered many people, and there was concern that he was being treated more leniently than was just, solely because he was a well-known poet. Clearly, the fact that he was a poet should have no bearing on his punishment if his guilt was established beyond doubt. But this fact should have been taken into account more—and also more carefully—than it was by the psychiatrists whose professional opinions determined the courts' decisions in Pound's case.

The psychiatric diagnosis of Pound's mental illness was imprecise and therefore inadequate as a basis for treatment. Winfred Overholser's reports show that he was aware of this imprecision and of the inability of the St. Elizabeths staff to arrive at a conclusive diagnosis, and yet the reports that he made and the decisions he took indicate that he had an intuitive understanding of Pound's state of mind even though he could not identify its causes. The contention that Overholser willingly perjured himself and obstructed justice to win for himself the reputation of protector of a great poet is completely unjustified.[2] Overholser was wise enough to know that diagnostic categories are often rather clumsy attempts at systematization of complex patterns of mental activity, that they are subsequent to the intuitive insights that lead to their formulation, and that their authority is often tentative and provisional—viable only until a more profound intuitive insight requires that they be refined, revised, or rejected altogether.

Dr. Overholser's general sense of Pound's mental condition can now be seen to have been correct. That Pound was in a paranoid state is obvious enough, as we have seen from his delusions about a conspiracy of international bankers and a Jewish "central committee" and about Bernard Baruch's attempts to poison him. Overholser's reservations about the degree to which Pound was genuinely psychotic are a comment not upon the psychotic nature of Pound's symptoms but upon the guidelines for diagnosis of psychosis which obtained in the 1940s and 1950s. These guidelines, as they have been standardized and updated, now leave no doubt that paranoia of the kind from which Pound was suffering qualifies as a psychosis. The 1980, third edition of the *Diagnostic and Statistical Manual of Mental Disorders* of the American Psychiatric Association states categorically that "psychotic disorders include . . . Paranoid Disorders."[3] This study considers a psychotic condition to exist when there is "gross impairment in reality testing [and] the individual incorrectly evaluates the accuracy of his or her perceptions and thoughts and makes incorrect inferences about external reality, even in the face of contrary evidence." Direct evidence of such a state is "the presence of . . . delusions . . . without insight into their pathological nature."

The *Manual*'s section "Paranoid Disorders" states that paranoid persecutory delusions "usually involve a single theme or series of connected themes, such as being conspired against . . . poisoned . . . or obstructed in the pursuit of long-term goals." It notes, as common associated features, "resentment and anger," "grandiosity," "suspiciousness," and "letter writing [and] complaining about various injustices." While social functioning is often severaly impaired, "impairment in daily functioning is rare [and] intellectual and occupational functioning are usually preserved, even when the disorder is chronic" (195). The commentary on "Paranoia" gives as the essential feature of this condition "the insidious development of a Paranoid Disorder with a permanent and unshakable delusional system accompanied by preservation of clear and orderly thinking." It notes that "frequently the individual considers himself or herself endowed with unique and superior abilities" (197).

The fact that Pound was a poet, a social reformer, and an idealist is of the utmost importance for anyone attempting a diagnosis of his mental state from the mid-1930s. It was impossible to understand how his mind was working in 1945 and 1946 without taking into account what a very large percentage of his mental activity over the past thirty years had been devoted to researching, thinking, and writing about the literary, cultural, social, and economic ideals to which he had dedicated himself. The intensity of his commitment to these ideals and the degree to which he became absorbed in his self-elected role of reformer meant that he lived more in the world of his own ideas than in any objective reality. Any accurate diagnosis of his disturbed mental state must take these facts as its point of departure. It is for this reason that his writings provide a much more complete and accurate picture of his state of mind in the 1930s than any study of his activities and relationships or the events of the time could do. Without the insight into his thinking that a study of his writings provides, the psychiatrists at St. Elizabeths were bound to be at a loss in making a definitive diagnosis.

The difficulty of arriving at a satisfactory diagnosis prompted several of the psychiatrists who examined Pound to take a defensive position. Noticing how obviously he evaded any examination of crucial personal questions by pleading fatigue and exhaustion, they implied in their reports that he was simply faking tiredness to protect himself from painful self-examination. By overestimating the extent of his conscious control over his feelings of physical exhaustion, they passed up the chance to treat it as a symptom which might provide a valuable clue to the source of his mental problems. Although they assumed the contrary, there is evidence that Pound knew that he needed psychiatric help, wanted to be helped, and believed that he could be helped: "If this is a hospital, you have got to cure me . . . . you must decide whether I am to be cured or punished." And again, in the course of providing information for a lengthy family history, Pound volunteered for the record: "Whatever diagnosis they put on me, I have an internal conflict. If they would treat me for something I have, rather than what they think I have, I would solve my conflicts."[4]

Since it was so difficult for him to bring himself to ask for help, he probably did not make many or very direct overtures, and when they were not responded to quickly and helpfully, he withdrew. Unwittingly, one of the doctors who interviewed him offers a very clear instance of this in his report. He describes how Pound "first came into the interviewing room stripped to the waist, appeared slightly distractible and ill at ease and, since it was cold in the room, he invited me to his own room, where he is usually interviewed by the doctors, so that he could lie in bed and speak more freely as he is so much more relaxed in that position. I declined the invitation and suggested that he put on a shirt and return."[5]

As an afterthought, when he is already halfway through his description of the interview, the doctor remembers that, at the beginning of the interview proper, Pound "made a gesture to extend his hand in handshake which, when it was not immediately accepted, was withdrawn." Following this he "took out his close reading glasses, and scrutinized the interviewer's face, asked questions about his name and attempted generally to take over the interview and do the interviewing himself. When this wasn't permitted, it was then that he began his histrionic poses, beating the air [and vituperations]." Yet even having been kept at a distance by the doctor's professional formality, Pound continued to be self-revealing and conciliatory toward the doctor: "He described himself as a watch caught in a cement mixer as he complained against the cruel injustice of a man of his sensibilities being subjected to such treatment. He is utterly fatigued by interviews and it just takes him about three months to recuperate from such torture when another interview comes up. He aplogizes to the interviewer, indicating that there is nothing personal, etc., etc. . . . He indicates that it is impossible for anybody in this stupid country to be able to understand him because we have not had the truth and only the propaganda from our newspapers; we have not been familiar with the 40 years of his work and he has lost the knack of communicating with simple people because for the past 40 years he has associated only with men of genius." When, as Pound continues to complain, the psychiatrist reminds him that it was not he but Pound who had introduced his painful subject and "voluntarily begun talking about it." Pound responded, "Oh, I'm not blaming you, I know you have your job to do and I was just trying to give you some of the information."

We see here two contradictory impulses and it is important to identify both of them. Most immediately noticeable is the apparently obstructive complaint about the strain and injustice of the interviews and yet, as the interviewer reminded him, Pound himself raised the very subjects that he found so painful; in other words, his initial impulse was to cooperate and to bring his problems into the open for discussion. As we see from later interviews, had he decided to obstruct this one altogether, he could have done so.[6] In this interview, although he must be losing faith that he can be helped by the psychiatrists, he has not given up hope entirely. The overwhelming exhaustion that these interviews produce is certainly a significant symptom that should be investigated. He has "lost the knack of communicating with simple people," and it would, in fact, enable the psychiatrists to explain his problem to him had they been familiar with "the 40 years of his work."

Pound's stream of compliants was more than a self-defeating indulgence in self-pity, and he was speaking in good faith when he said: "I know you have your job to do and I was just trying to give you some of the information." In the course of the interview, Pound spells out exactly what he believes: that his intention was to help people develop a civic sense, that the Italian corporate state was truly democratic, that his broadcasts "were directed towards peace," and that the BBC deliberately cut off the "interchange of ideas" that could have averted World War II. These provide ample evidence of his self-delusion, but rather than looking for the specifics which would show when and why the delusion originated, the interviewed opted for misleading generalities: "Although some of his ideas might be considered paranoid and delusioned, this is true only for our particular culture as other cultures have not found these trends paranoid or delusional. . . . The ideational activity of this man and his particular distortion seem related to other socially destructive philosophies such as that of Wagner, Hitler and Mussolini and perhaps Machiavelli. It seems to this observer, therefore, that this patient might be understood in terms of a social illness or of a mild illness in the broader sense of the term."

It was evident that no help would be forthcoming: "Since he has been in this Hospital, it has not been possible to make a diagnosis in this case, as it appears he does not fit into any of the categories in our present system of classification of mental illness" (1398b). Here the psychiatrist is echoing the position taken by Dr. Overholser. On December 14, 1945, in their statement to the District Court of Columbia as government witnesses in their capacity as psychiatrists, Overholser, Marion King, and Joseph Gilbert gave their professional opinion that Pound was "suffering from a paranoid state which renders him mentally unfit to advise properly with counsel or to participate intelligently and reasonably in his own defense."[7] In light of the evidence, this is a completely accurate statement and focuses on the most crucial issue in the case. No matter how logical and lucid he was on other matters, on the one subject upon which his trial would exclusively focus—his motives for making the broadcasts from Rome—he was in the grips of a full-fledged delusion, so thoroughgoing as to be classified as psychotic.

With benefit of hindsight, we can see why differences of opinion about the exact nature of Pound's mental state should have focused on the matter of psychosis. Clearly a psychosis in someone like Pound would be likely to take an idiosyncratic form. To begin with, psychosis which is psychogenic rather than organic—which involves a "thought disorder"—will manifest itself much more selectively than one which is the result of a disorder of perception, of consciousness, or of affectivity and mood. But in Pound's case, his "thought disorder" itself was bound to be different in significant ways from that of a person of common or average mental activity. Not just his high level of intelligence—about which the psychiatrists were in agreement—but also the highly unusual intensity and sustained exercise of his intellect were very likely to produce a configuration of mental activity which was out of the ordinary. It is hardly to be expected that he would fit the textbook definition of psychotic behavior.

Once he had made the unconscious decision to exclude all the evidence that would, if confronted, force him to reject his faith in Mussolini as a man of goodwill, his strength of will and his unusual creativity and powers of imagination became weapons to be used against himself. His creative imagination, which had shaped and given substance to his visionary idealism, now gave a spurious vitality to his delusions; the strength of will which had kept him working at his program of cultural and social reform now became an obsessive insistence on the validity of his self-delusion. And yet he was able to an unusual degree to confine his psychotic thinking to the one topic around which it had grown up in the first place. On any subject other than his theory that World War II was "made to create debt . . . [by] the persons behind Hitler and Mussolini who were only fronts" he was entirely lucid and reasonable.[8] Yet on this one subject his thinking was genuinely psychotic. His fantasy of a "bankers' conspiracy" which had ultimate power over the governments of the world had become for him a reality and one with which he was so preoccupied that it dictated all his professional activities and influenced almost all his personal relationships.

The evidence for this is available to us now but would not have been, for the most part, for the psychiatrists of St. Elizabeths, even had they had the time to investigate it. Now we can examine the texts of the typescripts of many of the radio speeches, and read *Jefferson and/or Mussolini, Guide to Kulchur,* and much of the enormous body of Pound's economic writings from his London years on. We can see also from his private correspondence of the 1930s how totally he had bought into the fantasy.

When we are dealing with escape into a fantasy world, we expect to find evidence of paranoia and narcissism and, predictably enough, Pound is described as paranoid and narcissistic by the psychiatrists; yet no one stops to consider that paranoia and narcissism are likely to be rather different from usual in a case like Pound's. There is likely to be a considerable difference between narcissism which is a dedication to one's self-gratification and personal whims and that of a poet and social reformer who has subordinated the satisfying of immediate personal needs to a preoccupation with and commitment to a body of intensely held civic and cultural ideals and a far-ranging utopian scheme of social reform.

The same considerations apply in the matter of his paranoia. We look differently upon paranoia which springs from a fear of personal harm than we do upon a paranoia which springs from and continues to refer to a fear of the consequences of war for the people of the Western world. Finding it hard to imagine ourselves "reversing priorities" in this way, we may wish to be skeptical toward the suggestion that such an "altruistic paranoia" is even possible, and yet, when we think of Pound as a poet first and foremost, we remember that Keats is not alone in reserving the highest poetic elevation for "those to whom the miseries of the world / Are misery, and will not let them rest."[9]

An accurate diagnosis would have to take into account the fact that

Pound was a poet, but even more crucially the fact that he was psychotic—
that since the mid-1930s he had suffered from a delusion which had made
him unable to grasp the nature of reality on the one subject which, more
than any other, determined his professional activities. He felt that his duty
as a responsible artist required him to educate the public to the truth as he
saw it and to speak out against the war, but his perception of the war bore
no relation to reality. We are faced with a simple alternative. Either his
rhetoric in the radio broadcasts and in his comments during the St. Elizabeth
years on the causes of the war were the consequence of genuine delusion, or
he was, in his normal state, full of anger, hatred, and destructive feelings.
Many people have tried to suggest the latter. He is commonly described as a
"rabid" and "vicious" antisemite by those who see the Pound of the radio
broadcasts as the "real Pound," and yet those who knew him personally are
likely to insist that the Pound they knew was incapable of being "rabid" or
"vicious."

To date, defenses of Pound have usually been rationalizations of what
he said, and it is hardly surprising that these have not persuaded those who
see Pound as vicious to change their minds. Another well-intentioned but
equally limited approach is to search Pound's childhood for clues to a buried
resentment at the low ebb of the financial fortunes of the Pound family, a
resentment which, fueled by frustration with his inability to earn more than
a doubtful existence through his writings, finally blazed out in a spiteful
rage. Although his childhood certainly provides clues to temperamental
traits that left him vulnerable to the psychosis which overcame him in the
1930s, it is important to see the psychosis itself as the direct consequence of
the unconscious decision which he took at the time of the invasion of
Abyssinia to deny the fact of Mussolini's belligerence and to rationalize
away all evidence of it. Once he had taken the fatal first step of suppressing
what he knew to be the truth, the very qualities of intelligence and
imagination which had made him a great poet now became the means of his
undoing. They made it all too easy for him to find facts which, taken in
isolation from their true context, seemed to support his delusion of
conspiracy. What might in a less inventive mind have remained merely an
eccentric or cranky theory became for him a complete vision of the
orchestration of all important world affairs by a malign cabal whose hidden
power would remain virtually irresistible unless it could be exposed to
public view.

Nor is his notion of the dubious involvement of business in political
affairs a complete chimera. There is some truth to many of the allegations
that he makes. But the evidence was compromised or vitiated altogether by

the fact that it was being used in the service of a lie. Nothing could change the fact that Hitler was a warmonger or that Mussolini, by allying himself with him, had taken the side of the aggressor. Hitler stood for everything that Pound despised and detested, but, by deciding not to question Mussolini's good faith, Pound had put himself in a position from which to denounce Hitler would be to expose Mussolini's motives to question.

A fair and accurate account of Pound's motives and attitudes must recognize that he was acting not destructively toward others but self-destructively. His state of mind at the time of the radio broadcasts was one into which he had trapped himself. He was not expressing freely what he deeply felt but desperately attempting to rationalize a set of opinions which he was unconsciously aware were wrong. And this was self-destructive rather than destructive, not just in terms of his own psychology but in fact. There is no evidence that anyone other than Pound himself—and his immediate family—suffered as a result of his broadcasts. The very idea that what he said would have incited anyone on the Allied side to go over to the enemy is clearly beyond belief, as is the idea that his broadcasts gave "aid and comfort" to the enemy. Nor is this merely a testimony to his incompetence as a rabble-rouser. As we have already seen, the transcripts of the broadcasts show that they are not intended as incitements to destruction or to betrayal of the Allied cause. In the main they are a call to question the Allied version of the causes of the war. As Leonard Doob notices in the second appendix to his edition of the radio speeches, although "48% of the speeches contained a call for action . . . the specific actions Pound advocated appear . . . to be somewhat mild" (*EPS,* 419). He gives as examples passages focusing on the following injunctions: "You have got to talk to each other, you have got to write letters one to another." (2/3/42); "It is time to get together and think" (2/26/42); "There is NO time like the present to stop being such asses" (4/9/42); "You ought to organize against . . . sabotage of everything that makes life worth living . . . and for a sense of justice" (7/13/42); "As nobody is likely to believe me, I suggest that they start thinking it out for themselves" (3/16/43); "Let your wishes be known to your senators" (3/30/43); "Diagnoze [the 'Roosevelt-Frankfurter government'], don't shoot 'em, analyze their . . . behavior, and tell us whether their policy is due to bad heartedness or caries of the cerebellum" (2/23/43); "I think it is time you opened Kipling's memoirs" (4/27/43).

The broadcasts are so idiosyncratic and their content is so completely determined by his own psychological needs that they cannot possibly be thought of as broadcasts *made for* Mussolini or the Fascist party or at the instigation of anyone other than Pound himself. We can see, as he could not, how far they served the purpose of rationalizing his evasions of the truth about Mussolini, but it is also true that his conscious intention was to benefit not just Italy or the Rome-Berlin Axis but the whole of Europe and America (and also Japan) and their culture. It is for this reason that anyone who knows anything at all about Pound's writings is likely to find so outrageous the accusations that he embraced a Nazi philosophy.

In view of the highly idiosyncratic nature of his thought, it is not surprising that most people, having neither the time nor the inclination to familiarize themselves with its complexities, would assume that a man who broadcast on Rome Radio at that time would be preaching Fascist propaganda. Yet to leave such as assumption uninvestigated is an act of irresponsibility in anyone claiming to be speaking about Pound in an official capacity—either as a literary critic or a psychiatrist. Since it was proving impossible to fit Pound's case neatly into any of the standard diagnostic categories, there was a temptation for his psychiatrists to take an easy way out. We have already seen how one of them assumed that he shared the "socially destructive philosophies [of] . . . Hitler and Mussolini," and six years later in 1953 we find another psychiatrist noting that "an official diagnosis has not been made in this case," and venturing a long and impressionistic "Recommendation For Diagnosis" in which he refers to what he describes as the poet's "destructive philosophy with its sadistic overtones" and offers an opinion of Pound's motives which runs directly counter to all the very considerable evidence of his generosity: "It is my impression that his 'giving' was a masochistic pseudo-giving with the solid expectation of a forth-coming reward and when the reward did not rapidly appear, all Hell would break loose."[10]

As we would expect, this psychiatrist finds "no evidence of psychosis," and this reminds us of what is entailed in the assumption that Pound was not psychotic. If he was in the grips of thoroughgoing delusion, then his assertions that Hitler and Mussolini were only "fronts," that Churchill's aim was "the betrayal of Europe" (*EPS*, 292), that Hitler was a great champion of human rights (*EPS*, 316) were an aberration, part of a fantasy which had usurped the place of reality in his mind and perverted his perceptions. If, on the other hand, he was not in the grips of delusion to a psychotic degree, then the Pound of the radio speeches was the "real Pound." But for this to be the case, we would have to believe that when he described Hitler and Mussolini as men of goodwill and humane ideals, he either knew this to be a lie and so was a monster of cynicism and viciousness, or believed it be the truth and was unbelievably stupid.

The psychiatrist's summary of the "findings" of a Rorschach test, administered to Pound, shows very clearly how limited a diagnostic tool the test can be unless the psychiatrist is able to refine the generalized impressions that such a test indicates in the light of very specific information about the patient's particular preoccupations and past history. This is even more important in the case of someone like Pound for reasons that have already been indicated. The relevant "past history" for him is the "history" of his intellectual activity, and the considerable difficulties confronting a psychiatrist who is trying to arrive at some overview of a creative mind are further compounded in the case of Pound by the unusual intensity and complexity—not to mention the idiosyncracy—of his thought. The psychiatrist has not made sufficient allowances either for the force of the poet's will—here used to subvert the test procedure as far as possible—or for the separation between his basic personality (the "real" Pound) and the psychotic state of mind into which he falls when the subject is his support of Mussolini. This state of mind takes over, in St. Elizabeths, whenever he is examined by the psychiatrists, because he knows that they will raise the very questions about his motives for supporting Mussolini which he wants to avoid because they threaten to force him to confront his self-deception. For the same reason he was adamant in giving people permission to visit him only on the condition that they did not interview him or want to question him on his wartime activities.

That he was determined to sabotage the Rorschach test was clear enough, and yet the tester underestimated the extent to which Pound's responses were deliberately perverse rather than involuntary. The psychiatrist reports that "despite the brilliance of [Pound's] mind . . . very accurate form perception . . . , abstract and theoretical intelligence of a high order and unusual creative gifts, [h]is whole responses are cheap and popular and he gives no original interpretations at all." In his opinion the responses suggest "in part indifference and contempt for the test procedure (very apparent throughout) but probably also certain retrogressive changes accompanying his advancing years since he must certainly have had the capacity for more original synthesis." But it was the tester's failure to appreciate the effect of Pound's open hostility on his responses that made his interpretations of the responses so inadequate.

There was no question of Pound's extreme anger at being subjected to the test or of his open hostility toward the tester, who noted: "His interpretations and his comments as the test progressed were critical, hostile and sarcastic [and] occasionally vitriolic, revealing great hostility"; however, the psychiatrist sees this as evidence of "marked aggression in interpersonal relations" in general. He gives as one piece of evidence of this generalized aggression Pound's interpretation of one figure as "people moving in opposite directions 'making snouts at each other looking over their shoulders, I don't know whether kicking each other or not.'" Yet despite the fact that the tester adds, "The last impulsively illustrated by pushing out his own foot toward the examiner," he does not consider that Pound's interpretation is much more illustrative of his immediate hostility toward the doctor as tester than an indication of his habitual reaction to people in general.

The psychiatrist's failure to take into account the fact of his patient's vocation leads him to miss the main point with a gravity which it is hard not to find amusing: "This hostility, emphasis on order and symmetry, and his meticulous regard for detail . . . suggest an anal-erotic personality make-up, and it is perhaps significant that apparently the only serious illness he ever had was an anal fistula." Surely it is even more significant that he was the founder of Imagism.

The most significant of the clues to Pound's state of mind that his responses provided was passed over without comment. If, as I have suggested, the event that precipitated the crisis of confidence in Mussolini which led him into self-destructive delusion was the invasion of Abyssinia, then it is no coincidence that he characterized plate III of the test "first as representative of 'twenty-five years of surrealist imbecility,'" then interpreted it as "'a couple of degenerate blacks,'" which he subsequently defined as "'Abyssinians with Whiskers.'" Yet again the possibility of psychosis is rejected in favor of the idea of Pound as Fascist: "There is no evidence of psychosis. . . . His hatred of women and of other races, implied in his interpretations, is in line with Fascist ideology" (1385a,b).

Pound was not a moral degenerate who admired what Mussolini really stood for, but the victim of a delusion who had convinced himself that Mussolini really stood for what Pound himself admired. The psychiatrists at St. Elizabeths simply did not have access to the evidence that this was so—that his perception of reality and not his humaneness was defective. In the absence of this evidence and of the precise understanding of his case that the evidence would make possible, Winfred Overholser took the most reasonable course. By refusing to shoehorn the poet into a category that he only partly fitted, the psychiatrist was able to leave the matter of diagnosis open-ended and to modify it where necessary in light of his increasing insight into the nature of Pound's mental state.

In a letter to the medical director of the Bureau of Prisons, Stanley E. Krumbiegel, on August 18, 1953, the superintendent was still hesitating to call Pound definitely psychotic: "The exact category in which he should be classified diagnostically is difficult to ascertain. There is no doubt that he is medically unsound to a degree which renders him mentally incompetent yet he does not fit well into any of the psychiatric categories." He believes that the closest category would be Personality Trait Disturbance, Narcissistic Personality, but this is not considered psychotic even though it does "constitute mental incompetence." At this stage, Overholser sees some resolution to this discrepancy in the fact that "one may be incompetent without being technically psychotic" (499).

In a letter of October 13, 1954, to the assistant attorney general, William F. Tompkins, Overholser notes that Pound "suffers from numerous paranoid delusions. His mental processes are considerably disorganized, particularly when it comes to discussing any of his own problems" (590). By March 26, 1957, in a letter to the assistant director of the Bureau of Prisons, Frank Loveland, he has accepted the diagnosis of psychosis with a proviso: "The exact diagnosis in his case has not been easy because he does not fit too accurately into any of the regular diagnostic categories. We have therefore classified him as "Psychotic Disorder, Undifferentiated" (929). In the text of the dismissal of the indictment of Pound on April 18, 1958, we read: "There is available to the defense psychiatric testimony to the effect that there is a strong probability that the commission of crimes charged was the result of insanity, and it appear[s] that the Government is not in a position to challenge the medical testimony" (1395b).

When most of the psychiatrists at St. Elizabeths resist the idea that Pound's delusion is genuinely psychotic, it is necessary for them to pass off one of the most pronounced symptoms of the psychosis, his attacks of extreme fatigue, as merely a pretense. Although these bouts of exhaustion are abnormal for the suddenness with which they seem to come and go, it becomes clear, if we take an overview of his behavior, that although psychosomatic rather than physiological in origin, they are not, for the most part, under his conscious control. It is clear that they are the physiological manifestation of the impulse to evasion of a painful reality that, in its intellectual form, became the paranoid elaborations of his theories of a worldwide bankers' conspiracy to encourage wars. Of course the bouts of fatigue are intended to discourage others and even himself from analyzing the painful matter of his self-delusion, but they are no more under his conscious control than his comments on Mussolini and Roosevelt were. The exaggerated display of fatigue was there from the beginning. The "Admission Note" for Pound (Dec. 22, 1945) records: "He showed considerable reluctance to discuss the case at all, on the pretense that he was so weary and fatigued that it would be beyond the endurance of his strength to enter into such discussion."

Of an interview on March 31, 1946, another psychiatrist writes: "When he is questioned about his earlier poetic works . . . his memory appears perfectly intact as he expatiates at length on this and on other neutral subjects. But when queried about his scurrilous and anti-Semitic broadcasts in Italy . . . he protests that his memory fails him. On one occasion when he was asked if he wishes to stand trial, he effected an elaborate caricature of fatigue, and the interview had to be terminated" (1397f). This behavior remains consistent from interview to interview. One doctor notes, on April 13, 1946, that although at the beginning of the interview Pound was "a picture of complete and utter exhaustion," speaking in "low tones and with sighing gasps, . . . when the question of publishers was innocently mentioned by the examiner . . . the patient suddenly became excited and bolted upright from his relaxed position" (1397g).

Perhaps it is not surprising that most of the psychiatrists assumed that their patient was faking. One doctor, for example, concluded (March 18, 1949) that "his weakness is certainly periodic and can be turned off and on at will (1399c), and another (July 20, 1953) that: "There is considerable about him of the poseur and his professed neurasthenia is theatrically dramatized, only to be frequently discarded as he forgets himself and becomes animated in discussion" (1411a). Yet they had access to information which could have prompted them to see the bouts of fatigue as a clue to the cause of his psychosis. It was common knowledge that he did not suffer from fatigue only during interviews. Included in his file is the observation, dated June 27, 1947, that "on the ward he is stated by the attendants to be suffering from sleeping sickness, is always lying down, even when he has visitors." Before he had a reclining lawn chair, he would take a blanket out onto the grounds with him and would lie on that while the other patients were sitting on benches (1397n). When this information was included in a letter to Olga Rudge, she received the mistaken impression that he was required to do this. In her letter to Dr. Overholser she expressed her concern that Pound would very much dislike this since he "has always strongly objected to sitting or lying out of doors," even on the beach.

It seems unlikely on two counts that Pound's waves of fatigue were a pretense. First, had he been fully in control of them and intended to convince the doctors that they were genuine, he would surely have made them less histrionic, less sudden, and generally more "plausible." Second, if he did not bother to "act out" his periods of exhaustion more convincingly, why would he act so consistently on the ward as to be thought of as suffering from "sleeping sickness."

We can prove conclusively that he was not just putting on a show for his doctors when we consider his behavior once he had returned to Italy, but there is also a possibility that the psychosomatic fatigue dated back to the pre-St. Elizabeths period. Although one of his psychiatrists assumes that Pound had more conscious control over the fatigue than he really had, he does seem to have given this symptom more careful thought than the other doctors and to have been more open to the possibility that it might be the result of something more complex than blatant deception on Pound's part. He notes how, in an interview on April 13, 1946, Pound told him that "while in Italy for many, many years he spent a good part of the day reclining before getting up to the typewriter to work. He claims he required a good many hours of rest to build up enough energy for a few minutes' work" (1397g). Although the doctor assumes that this is a "carefully cultivated eccentricity," it seems more likely, especially in the light of Pound's behavior after his return to Italy, that it was the consequence of the psychological strain of having to repress such profound unconscious misgivings about the self-deception he was involved in.

Several of those who visited Pound at St. Elizabeths have recorded their memories of his behavior and comments on their impressions of his state of mind.[11] Those who had most contact with him and so were in a position to provide most details were, or course, those whom he wanted to have as visitors and so theirs is the testimony of welcome guests. We do not have much evidence of how he would have behaved toward those for whom he would have felt impatience or hostility since these were either refused permission to visit or were promptly turned away. For this reason, most of the accounts of him present a very positive picture of what was, in fact, Pound's essential nature, uncontaminated by his psychotic reactions. Marcella Spann Booth's reminiscence, "Through the Smoke Hole," gives us a sensitive and intimate portrait of Pound as he was in 1957–58, when he was with the person with whom he felt most at his ease and most disposed to be positive and hopeful.[12] Many visitors concur in being struck by his genuine friendliness, interest in them, generosity, and gratitude to them for their visits. They emphasize his refusal to dwell on his own situation, his disapproval of self-pity, and his insistence on the importance of selflessness in intellectual and literary undertakings.[13]

They often mention the swiftness of his thought also. David Gordon says of him, "He had a great deal of natural affection and understanding that he immediately showed. It was overwhelming. . . . And magnetism. Yes. And geniality: a great sense of warmth. As if immediately knowing one's own purpose; catching on, was the sense of it. . . . He used the term 'twig' very frequently and it meant a great deal to him. He used the term 'mental velocity' in reference to writing a letter or about the difference in mental velocity among people. He would be so far ahead . . . in seeing everything, the whole football field, before you would even see anything. This was always the way he was. He always knew. 'Oh, this is what you were talking about;' or 'this is wonderful' or 'is this what you mean?' " (Gordon, p. 347).

Yet, as Carroll Terrell, having surveyed many of the reminiscences of Pound's visitors, writes, "He was a man of many moods: at times mean, irritable, nasty-tempered, angry, hostile and outraged with frustrations [even though] the bad tempers passed quickly [and] most of the time he was patient, enthusiastic, understanding, involved, and dedicated to his own work and the work of as many others as he could foster and support."[14]

The reason for proceeding now to give particular attention to those moments when his psychotic patterns of thought reasserted themselves is not that these moments were prevalent or showed how Pound "really was"—neither of which was the case—but because it was in these fixations that his problems lay. Free from them he would not have made the Rome Radio broadcasts and so would not be in the asylum. These were the source of his mental imbalance, and they would continue to assert themselves in the form of intense anxieties and angry irritability until he could allow himself to acknowledge their delusory nature.

We can see the persistence of his wartime mind-set most accessibly in the volume of his correspondence with John Theobald.[15] Writing to Theobald in 1957, for example, he quotes Douglas on the *Protocols of Zion*: "If not the outline of a conspiracy, must have been written by someone with gift of prophecy never claimed for the prophets of old. all yu got do is correlate events AFTER 1919" (45). He is also anxious to pass on the information, found in one of Elizabeth Dilling's books on the "communist menace," that the name Calvin is a variant of Cohen: "Calvin, Cauvin, Cohen, sez Liz. useful item" (80). He also reiterates his belief that his imprisonment itself is the result of a Jewish conspiracy: "What is keeping me in here is JEWS/ B. Baruch/ [Walter] Winchell 'E.P. out over my [Winchell's] dead body.' [Jacob] Javitz Ike's latest confessor and light/ who set up howl over Bubblegum [Bollingen] award AFTER the kike commies in S. America howled/ None but commies had zense to observe that *Cantos* are a POLITICAL implement like the *div. Com.* (vs. temporal power)" (44). "JEWS" were keeping him in St. Elizabeths all right, but not actual Jews, only the fantasy Jews that people the antisemite's delusions. In response to Theobald's suggestions that this antisemitism was unworthy of him, that Henry James would have disapproved of it and that "some angel in authority ought to prod you to knock it off" (81), Pound responds predictably enough by displacing his own self-delusion onto others: "Yu an the gt/ Mariannah [M. Moore] and even O. R. A. [Olivia Rossetti Agresti] marVElous for overlooking historic facts when they don't fit yr/ pattern. and erecting exceptions into laws. the PRINCIPLE of DEGRADATION of bastardization and *mélange*" (84).

Now Pound's anger toward psychiatry as a "Jewish science" adds a new dimension to his antisemitism. He had always been very negative about psychiatry and dismissed any self-scrutinizing attitude as an unhealthy obsession with negative emotions which would incapacitate the individual for constructive interaction with the outside world. His mistrust of psychiatry was clearly rooted in his temperamental aversion to introspection, but at St. Elizabeths there was an additional incentive for it. He was imprisoned here because he had been judged to be of unsound mind and so he would see the psychiatrists as his accusers. When he said to one of them on his arrival there, "You must decide whether I am to be cured or punished," he was pointing out the two options for his relationship with them, both of which made the psychiatrists a threat. If he was to be cured, they became the embodiment of the accusation that he was of unsound mind; if he was to be punished, of the accusation that he was guilty of wrongdoing. Either option was threatening, both because it was an accusation of inadequacy and because it pointed to the necessity for self-analysis, the one thing of which he was most afraid, both consciously, because he claimed to despise it, and unconsciously, because it would lead to the tearing away of the mask from his self-deceptions and his spurious rationalizations of them.

One of his most egregious violations of the truth was his acceptance of the theory of a Jewish conspiracy against the health of Western culture and so against those who, like himself, were particularly committed to keeping this culture healthy. To continue to believe in this conspiracy was crucial to sustaining the psychotic mind-set upon which he still relied, since to be unable to blame the Jewish "Kahal" would mean having to blame Mussolini and Pound's own blindness. It is easy to see how the fact that many of the psychiatrists were Jewish only served to strengthen his perception of them as a threat—as yet another, even if unwitting, arm of the conspiracy—and as evidence that the conspiracy was, in fact, operating. "Connect ALL psychiatry with Beria program [Russian secret police] and get a census of russo kike origin of employees," he writes to Theobald (83), suggesting that he consider "the statistics of russian immigration and the number of immigrant kikiatrists now drawing pay from the boobarican taxpayer??" (104). If, as I would argue, his most fundamental unconscious drive was the impulse to psychic health, he would have welcomed and even invested his hopes in the possibility of "being cured." The fact that no help toward such a cure was forthcoming from his psychiatrists would have given him an additional, albeit not conscious, motive for a feeling of betrayal and so of even further hostility toward them.

THE CONFUCIAN AGENDA OF THE LATER CANTOS

Because no cure was forthcoming, Pound had to rely upon his own efforts to protect himself as far as possible against the onslaughts of his psychotic confusion and anger. That he recognized the need to do so is clear from his repetition of "And not to lose life for bad temper" (98/693)" and from repeated references to King Kati as a reminder of this pharoah's maxim, "A man's paradise is his good nature" (93/623, 626, 627, 631, 98/690). He focuses his energies upon his best stays against confusion, the writing of cantos, the researches which this entails, and his translations of Sophocles' plays and of the *Confucian Odes*. He cannot exclude altogether the issue which is the root of all his anxieties—the guilt of Mussolini and the consequences of Pound's own blinding of himself to this guilt—but it is only allowed to enter his St. Elizabeths writings obliquely.

The Confucianism upon which Pound is so heavily relying by this point insists that such a fate as Mussolini's is likely to be the just consequence of having flouted "the mandate of Heaven," and, in private conversation at St. Elizabeths, Pound could concede this. He quoted as an explanation of the Duce's destruction, "To love what the people hate, to hate what they love is called doing violence to man's inborn nature. Calamities will come to him who does this [definite physical calamities], the wild grass will grow over his dead body."[16] Yet, in his cantos he falls back upon the evasion that the cause of the Duce's problems was his reliance on unfit ministers, that he did not "know whom to trust" (89/590; see 77/470 & 86/570), and continues to displace, onto FDR, Mussolini's and Pound's own most serious flaw: a refusal or an inability to listen to the truth (85/568). He is trying to deny his own intimations of Mussolini's responsibility for his own destruction when he writes: "What has been, should have" (87/572), alluding to the Duce's reputed comment," *Tutto quello che è accaduto, doveva accadere.*

In 1949 Pound translated Sophocles' *Elektra* and by 1953 had finished *Women of Trachis,* his version of the *Trachiniae.* He chose as the most important words in the latter play,"λαμπρὰ ςυμβαίνει," from the speech in which the dying Herakles realizes and acknowledges that his present agony does fulfill the oracle's prediction of his fate. Pound singles out these words typographically: "Come at it that way, my boy what / SPLENDOUR, / IT ALL COHERES," and also in a footnote which is very revealing about the way in which the fates of Herakles and of Mussolini are linked in his own mind. The footnote reads: "This is the key phrase, for which the play exists, as in the Elektra: 'Need we add cowardice to all the rest of these ills? . . . And later: 'Tutto quello che è accaduto, doveva accadere.' "[17] This deliberate linking of the fates of Herakles and Mussolini shows how Pound's evasive attitude toward Mussolini's guilt persists. Sophocles does intend us to think of Herakles as a great hero whose death by treachery was truly tragic and whose acceptance of his fate was the culminating proof of his stoicism in the face of unmerited trials and suffering. To imply that Mussolini's "Tutto quello che è accaduto" was in any way comparable either in heroism or in its implications is to attempt to deny the fact that the fate of Mussolini and the fate of Italy under Mussolini were the direct result of the dangerous political choices he willfully made.

Inevitably Pound sees in the desperation of Elektra and the agony of Herakles echoes of his own situation, and this is clear from his translations. Elektra, humiliated, ill-treated, obsessively committed to righting a horrible injustice yet deprived of all power to act, speaks for him. He has her call Klytemnestra "the old usurer," has her urge Chrysothemis, "The free born ought not to / sink into slavery," and Chrysothemis warn her to no avail, "Don't go up against the people in power." By adding his own stage direction—"(suddenly perfectly calm)"—Pound attaches particular importance to one of Elektra's responses when Klytemnestra has goaded her to rage: "Well now I think I have got a sense of shame / I distinguish between suitable conduct / and what I am driven to by your hate and your devilments."[18]

Elektra's situation is similar to Pound's own in that she herself has no freedom of action and must wait for someone from outside her own captivity to bring an end to her suffering and restore her to a position of honor. Herakles' situation however is both like and unlike Pound's. Pound obviously feels an affinity with this hero, who was committed perforce to a life of gruelling struggle in which there can be no "release from trouble" short of death itself and whose final destruction follows from having made a mistake whose fatal consequences seem out of all proportion to the nature of his error.

Yet Pound is also tempted to present on his own authority the affirmation of the dying Herakles. In 87/571–72, he writes: λαμπρὰ ϛυμβαίνει / From the dawn blaze to sunset / 'What has been, should have,'" not only equating Mussolini and Herakles but also affirming the appropriateness of accepting what cannot be avoided, the persistence of order behind apparent chaos and the need to become reconciled even to what seems most unfair, outrageous, or haphazard. In fact, Pound has not yet arrived at the self-knowledge which alone would allow him to make such affirmations with real conviction. While consciously he seems unaware that his own state of mind falls short, by a long way, of Herakles' triumphant and unqualified acceptance, that he is unconsciously aware of this is strongly suggested by his jarring use of slang in both his plays. With each instance, our sense of the presence of the characters is temporarily eclipsed by the presence of Pound himself at his most self-caricaturing. These passage of "low speech" assault the poignant, the dignified, and the heroic in the play, just as Pound's own disruptive anxieties and unaddressed sense of guilt war against his attempts at affirmation.

Rather than undertake the frightening and dangerous process of exploring his repressed guilt, Pound realizes that it is safer, given his precarious mental state, to dwell as far as possible upon what is positive and reassuring. We see this opposition between dangerous self-analysis and safe affirmation represented symbolically in the St. Elizabeths cantos by the imagery of the sea-surface, associated with the sun, safety, and healing; and sea-depths imagery, associated with darkness, danger, and death. After the visionary Canto 90 with its materialization of the altar in the grove and its celebration of οἱ χθόνιοί—those of the earth—Canto 91 is a sea canto. Here the sea-depths are associated with the depths of a woman's eye, and both can offer either healing or destruction. Here "the green deep of an eye" belongs not to the beloved but to the "Reina," an imperious anima whose glance is a call to action of a dangerous and difficult kind. When Sir Francis Drake looks into the eyes of Elizabeth, his queen, he sees both "splendour and wreckage": the chance for fame and political favor but also the failure of his final Caribbean expedition, his death in Her Majesty's service, and his burial at sea "in the Queen's eye the reflection / & sea-wrack— / green deep of the sea-cave."

Significantly, in this context Pound's repressed psychosis briefly emerges. Thoughts of the dead Drake lead him to thoughts of a series of doomed British ancestors from Lazamon's *Brut*. Then this story of the final downfall of the Britons apparently turns Pound's thoughts to the loaded subject of Mussolini's destruction, if one judges from the eruption into the text of "*Democracies electing their sewage / till there is no clear thought about holiness / a dung flow from 1913 / and, in this, their kikery functioned, Marx, Freud / and the american beaneries / Filth under filth.*" Yet he instantly takes refuge from this sudden mood in nostalgic reminiscence and, by the end of the canto, has resolved "that the tone change from elegy."

In this canto, however, as in the St. Elizabeths cantos overall, most of the sea imagery concerns rescue and safety and the reflection of light upon the surface of the water. Here a body of inland water becomes "The GREAT CRYSTAL / doubling the pine, and to cloud," and the "golden sun boat" which moves "by oar, not by sail," and "On river of crystal" is pictured in hieroglyphic form on the page. The sun god, Ra, and Set, a god of evil, the murderer of Osiris, are integrated by Pound into the invented figure of the Princess Ra-Set, who can move safely across the water in the sun boat. Pound's creation of this anima figure clearly expresses a will to integration and "healing." He does not make her a powerful goddess such as Isis but only a princess who is herself vulnerable: "The Princess Ra-Set has climbed / to the great knees of stone, / She enters protection, / the great cloud is about her, / She has entered the protection of crystal."

The main female figure associated with protection from the sea-depths in these cantos is Leucothea, the sea-goddess who saved Odysseus from drowning by giving him her veil, or "kredemnon"—Pound's "bikini"— when his raft was broken up. She appears here, in Canto 91, as "KADMOU THUGATER," Cadmus' daughter, advising Odysseus to "get rid of parapernalia [*sic*]" and telling him, "My bikini is worth your raft." She is referred to many times in the Later Cantos and is given particular prominence by Pound's decision to use her rescue of Odysseus to link the conclusion of *Rock-Drill* to the beginning of *Thrones*.

Above all, in the day-to-day activities, the thoughts, the researches, and the writings of the St. Elizabeths years, Pound's main protection against confusion and provider of stability, order, and calm was Confucianism. This is everywhere apparent in *Rock-Drill* and *Thrones*, beginning with the opening pages of the former, which celebrate *ling²*, Pound's "sensibility" or accurate perception and integrity and provide a digest of Confucian ethics. Here Pound enumerates the indispensable Confucian virtues, the four *tuan¹*, "beginnings" or "foundations." These are *jen²*, "humanity or benevolence" (the sum of all virtues which must begin with love for one's parents), *chih*⁴, "wisdom"; *i*⁴, "righteousness' (right conduct and virtuous thinking); and *li*³, "propriety" (decorous behavior toward others—Pound's "good manners"—and reverential performance of the rites).

The view of human nature which lies behind the Confucian emphasis on these virtues is one that is particularly congenial to Pound. It assumes that all people are born with a reliable moral sense, "the inborn nature," that the moral law which operates infallibly is knowable by every individual and hence that there is good reason to trust to the innate sense of reasonableness and decency in the common people. This is the basis of the democraticizing tendency of Confucianism, of its belief that human nature is fundamentally good and hence that it is appropriate to respect the dignity and intrinsic worth of all individuals and to think of them as all educable to some degree. That Pound had always worked on the assumption of the basic decency of human nature was everywhere implicit in the programs of action he had committed himself to. Yet because of his increasingly obsessive immersion in the theoretical world of his campaigns for reform, "ordinary people" seemed to have lost much of their particularity for him. At Pisa he had reproached himself for not having taken time to "feel for" people sufficiently: "J'ai eu pitié des autres / probablement pas assez, and at moments that suited my own convenience" (76/460). His new and thoroughgoing commitment to Confucian discipline makes him place a much higher value upon benevolence and compassion.

In the past, Pound had shown little patience for religious or moral systems that would require him to modify his thinking or behavior according to their prescriptions. Religion in any institutionalized form had primarily been something to react *against,* and the Eleusinian had mainly interested him to the extent that it provided him with a set of concepts and imagery that would allow him to express his *own* attitude toward sexuality in a formalized and ritual mode. Unlike his celebratory Eleusinianism and Neoplatonism, Confucianism imposed a discipline upon him. It provided him with a set of "instructions for judging and living"—with a comprehensive moral and ethical system and metaphysical orientation that would influence his day-to-day decisions. In his present condition and situation he was well aware of the value of this kind of orderliness and particularity. As he wrote on August 13, 1957, to John Theobald, "Naturally fed UP with all Yeats, Blavat[sky], etc. . . . . no satisfaction till I got to Kung / What you DO about it whicheversodam answer you get to the 7 and 77 jabs at unscrewing the inscrutable" (71).[19]

Now that Pound's own predicament has made clear to him the catastrophic consequences of trying to impose apparently constructive ideas by unrelenting and unreflective force of will, he is ready to consider the Confucian alternative:

The men of old . . . wanting good government in their states, they first established order in their own families; wanting order in the home, they first disciplined themselves; desiring self-discipline, they rectified their own hearts; and wanting to rectify their hearts, they sought precise verbal definitions of their inarticulate thoughts; wishing to attain precise verbal definitions, they set to extend their knowledge to the utmost. [*C,* 31]

Instead of trying to begin with civic order, the Confucian works from study to precision of perception and thought, to self-discipline and benevolence, and to the establishment of order within the family. Upon this basis Pound constructs his own Confucian agenda of study, writing, and reflection.

Throughout the St. Elizabeths cantos we see Pound following the Confucian injunction to "study the histories" and "extend [his] knowledge to the utmost." His attention to "precise verbal definitions" leads him to celebrate the efforts of ancient lexicographers, of the three men responsible for the transmission and elaboration of the Chinese *Sacred Edict,* of the compiler of the Byzantine *Eparch's Book* on fair trading practices, and, most important, of Sir Edward Coke, whose commentaries on the English Charters were a great and necessary safeguard of the liberties of the people and so of order and justice in the state. Pound's Eleusinian enthusiasms are now subordinated to his insistence that "the love of his relatives [is] the true treasure" (*C,* 75),[20] that "energy is near to benevolence" (93/629), and that "Compassion [is] tree's root and water-spring" (99/708).

No longer caught up in grandiose reformist schemes of international scope, Pound is living one day at a time and can find a new applicability in the Confucian *Analects,* of which he had written in 1947: "What the reader can find here is a set of measures whereby, at the end of a day, to learn whether the day has been worth living" (*C,* 194). To the Neoplatonism which had been his habitual celebration of the effortless access of insight and inspiration, he now adds a measure of more effortful Pythagoreanism. Like the Confucian who checks at day's end how constructively he has conducted himself, a Pythagorean, such as Ocellus, was supposed to ask himself each evening the three questions: In what have I failed? What good have I done? What have I omitted to do that I ought to have done? Pound finds here an echo of his favorite "Make it new" injunction, the "hsin jih jih hsin" inscription which, the *Ta Hsio* tells, was written "in letters of gold on

T'ang [Tching's] bathtub" (C, 36) and to which Pound gave a prominent place in Canto 53.

Such reflective attention to the particulars of one's daily actions Pound thinks of as "building light," and we find four "build light" passages in these St. Elizabeths cantos: on 87/571–72, 93/629, 94/642, and 98/684. Each of these constellates some combination of the themes of the "divine light," civic duty, and the "green world" and is built around two constants, the name of Ocellus and the "Make it new" characters. Significantly, all occur in proximity to regretful references to Mussolini.

Trying to "build light" in the harsh environment of the madhouse, his daily activities—apart from his writing—reduced to the most fundamental routines of survival, Pound finds his situation in some ways strangely similar to that of the peasant whose energies are entirely taken up with getting by from day to day. Perhaps for this reason, Pound now focuses more closely than he ever had before upon the figure of the laborer. As a Social Creditor he had always been committed to the principle that the primary considera' tion must be the welfare of the common people, and he was being completely literal and sincere when in *Jefferson and/or Mussolini* he wrote of his conviction that "Mussolini is driven by a vast and deep 'concern' or will for the welfare of Italy, not . . . as a state machinery stuck up on top of the people, but for Italy organic, composed of the last ploughman and the last girl in the olive yards" (34). It is worth noting that, in the opening of the *Pisan Cantos,* the "enormous tragedy of the dream in the peasant's bent shoulders" is given precedence over the image of the corpse of Mussolini hung "by the heels at Milano."

In these later cantos, when he is dealing with the *Sacred Edict,* the *Eparch's Book,* and with Coke's *Institutes,* we find that, from the sources to which we must turn to elucidate the otherwise largely inscrutable frag' mentary quotations, we receive a very particularized and immediate sense of common people engaged in daily activities and occupations that, because they are mundane, are also immemorial. For Pound, these activi' ties take on an important ritual and reverential significance. He insists that work itself is a form of prayer—"Qui laborat, orat" (94/610)—and de' clares: "There is worship in plowing / and equity in the weeding hoe" (99/711).

As far as his circumstances allowed, Pound continued his campaign for economic reform throughout the St. Elizabeths years, urging upon all his visitors the need for the study of key economic texts and building up, through correspondence, a network of contacts to publish economic items in small publications (see *Life,* 424–25, 432–33) and otherwise disseminate economic enlightenment. He was particularly pleased to discover that the *Kuan Tzu,* the economic writings of the Chinese writer, Kuan Chung, to whom Confucius had paid tribute in *The Analects,* were not lost in the "Burning of the Books" as Pound had assumed but were readily available to him in a 1954 English translation.[21]

Pound was understandably fascinated to find in the *Kuan Tzu* a series of observations made twenty-six centuries ago, which are presented as so obviously true that no reasonable person would think to dispute them and which sound like a restatement of Social Credit tenets:

As a result of good and bad years, there may be high or low prices of grain; seasonal demands may be urgent or slack. Hence commodities may be light (cheap) or heavy (expensive). If the sovereign does not know how to control the situation, he virtually permits profiteering merchants to overrun the market, and they, taking advantage of the wants of the people, (sell their goods at prices) one hundred times their outlay.

Though the land were allotted to all men in equal amounts, only the strong would be able to keep their share. The clever can make profits ten times their outlay, but the stupid cannot even retain their capital. If the sovereign cannot regulate (the making of profits), the people's living standards will vary over a range in which one has a hundred times as much as the other.

Today, your Highness, after having had surveyors calculate how much wealth is produced from the land (long) under cultivation and (recently) reclaimed, has been enabled to learn . . . that there should be enough (to feed all). But in fact some people suffer from hunger because grain is hoarded (by the wealthy). Again, Your Highness has minted coins and has established a currency for circulation, so that . . . each person should have hundreds or thousands of coins. However, some people are short of money to finance enterprises or make payments. Why? Because money is hoarded by the wealthy.

It is evident, then, that unless the sovereign puts back into circulation what has been accumulated and hoarded and so redistributes wealth to the people, then even though he . . . encourages farming, and resorts to the endless process of minting coins, he will not save his people from enslaving one another.

The great significance which Pound attached to the widom of Kuan Tzu is clear from his decision to pay tribute to it in Canto 106, one of the most important ritual cantos of *Thrones.* Pound begins by giving the characters of Kuan Tzu's name and by quoting: "The strength of men is in grain." In addition to the character, *kuan*[3] of Kuan Tzu's name, Pound includes *kuan*[1], which means "a frontier pass or gate or the suburbs of a city." Partly he is fascinated by the "architectural" qualities of the character which does indeed look like a gate, and partly he is referring to the source of his opening quotation: "The safety of the country is assured by its (cities') fortresses; the strength of its fortresses lies in its armies; the performance of the arms lies with the men who use them; the strength of the men lies in the grain (which nourishes them.) Therefore if the land is not cultivated, the fortresses will be without strength" (38). The ruler who observes the injunction "Feed the people" will preserve his kingdom so that he can hand it on "Ad posteros," to his posterity. The integrity of the city is preserved both by $kuan^1$—its gates, shutting out would-be usurpers—and by $Kuan^3$—Kuan Tzu and his wise counsel.

For the Confucian, the reverential performance of the rites is an important duty. The exercise of the rites is a very important theme in the Later Cantos and Pound sees many kinds of activities as ritual acts. Bill MacNaughton tells how Pound would burn olibanum on occasion on a small stone on the lawn at St. Elizabeths (*Paideuma* 3.3 (Winter 1974): 323). For Pound, the upward movement of the incense smoke and of the heat waves which form a visible "crystal funnel of air" (97/609) is the "outward and visible sign" of the rising of his spirits: "Out of heaviness where no mind moves at all" (90/607). Yet his translation of the *Confucian Odes,* upon which he spent so much time and energy, and even the painting of the brushstrokes of the individual Chinese characters were just as much ritual acts for him.

By now, certain characters had taken on a particular symbolic, almost mantric significance for Pound. Among these are *hsien,* "the tensile light"; *tan,* the dawn; *ling,* "sincerity," with which the St. Elizabeths cantos begin; *hsin,* the "make it new" character; and the eleven individual characters Pound includes in the "Terminology" section of his *Confucius.* In his painstaking work on the *Odes,* Pound was especially interested in ways in which he might make his translations either echo the rhyming or onomato-poeic sounds of the originals or comment indirectly upon the interre-lationships of radicals within a character. He approached the characters not as the native speaker would, without registering their component radicals, but in the spirit of the etymologist for whom *tan,* [日], does not simply mean "the dawn" but quite clearly shows the sun radical just above the horizon. Pound also thinks of these characters somewhat in the spirit of the master calligrapher who, attentive to the vital energies of the natural world, is trained to conceive of the lines of his characters as a continuation of this current of fluid force.

Pound also sees the ritual forming of characters as comparable to the building of a temple: he thinks of both as the delineation of a "sacred" space, a precinct within which divine energies can symbolically or actually "come to focus." The association of character with temple is suggested particularly immediately and graphically in *Thrones:*

The temple 山 is holy,

because it is not for sale. [97/676]

It also determines Pound's translation of the ending of the final Confucian ode.

The last stanza of Ode 305 describes the building of the temple which commemorates the greatness of King Woo-ting, and its concluding characters are translated by James Legge: "The temple was completed—the tranquil abode [of his tablet]."[22] Pound's version, "to the inner shrine, perfect / that his ray come to point in this quiet," makes an etymological comment upon *ch'ing,* "to complete" or "perfect," which Pound in his "Terminology" section of *Confucius* had isolated as "the righthand half of [the] compound" *ch'eng,* "sincerity." Using his own "creative etymology" he sees in it "pictorially the sun's lance coming to rest on the precise spot." Carrying this etymology into his translation, Pound, with "that his ray come to point in this quiet," links the beneficent effect of the king's virtue with the shining down of the sunlight, his perfecting of his virtue and its enduring influence with the completion of his memorial temple, and even the "carved pillars and rafters" of the temple itself with the brushstrokes of the character *ch'ing.*

In the Later Cantos, when Pound includes one of that group of characters to which he has given a specific ritual significance, it is most often to provide a focal point for a passage of particularly heightened seriousness or emotional intensity. A very important instance of this is the passage in Canto 97 which is built around the giant *ling.*[2] Adding to my previous commentary[23] on this complex passage, I will emphasize here its sea-surface imagery, its linking of the architectural and the calligraphic, its development of the theme of benevolence and the love of relatives, and its anticipation of the rituals of contrition and expiation which Pound will defer until he leaves St. Elizabeths.

At the center of the passage, the "architectural" qualities of the giant *ling,* meaning both "sensibility" and "reverence," invite the reader to think of this character as a visual as well as a connotational counterpart to St. Mark's in Venice, especially as the two stone lions stand to the left of the facade of the cathedral as, in the line of verse, they stand to the left of the character.

as the lacquer in sunlight ἀλιπόρφυροϛ
& shall we say: russet-gold.
                            That this colour exists in the air
not flame, not carmine, orixalxo, les xaladines
lit by the torch-flare,

        & from the nature the sign,
as the small lions beside San Marco. Out of ling
the benevolence

        Kuanon, by the golden rail,
            Nile διὔπετέοϛ the flames gleam in the air.   [97/675]

These small stone lions over which, during the day, the children constantly clamber are associated by Pound in a general way with "benevolence" and, more specifically, with his own daughter as a child and hence with "the love of relatives," the subject of the Confucian quotation whose characters frame this passage. Just as St. Mark's itself overlooks the "shatter of sunlight" upon the waves of the Grand Canal, so the "architectural" *ling* is surrounded in the text by description of the play of sunlight on water. This Pound describes as a "colour [that] exists in the air" over the canals of Venice and as "flames [that] gleam in the air" above the waters of the Nile across which moves the sun boat of Ra-Set with its "golden rail," but now bearing Kuanon, the Chinese goddess of mercy and benevolence.

The characters with which the passage opens have a particularly heightened significance also.

New fronds,

novelle piante 新

        what ax for clearing?
親 ch'in¹ 旦 tan⁴ 親 ch'in¹

The theme of new beginnings is already clear from the English and is amplified by the inclusion of *tan⁴*, the dawn, with its suggestion for Pound of "making it new" day by day. The two *ch'in¹*s are excerpted from the six-character quotation with which the passage ends and which Pound has translated in his *Confucius* as "counting his manhood and the love of his relatives [*ch'in¹*] the true treasure" (75). The character following "novelle piante" is *hsin¹*, the "renew" of Pound's "Make it new" phrase. In *Jefferson and/or Mussolini,* Pound had glossed *hsin¹* with the note that the ideogram "shows the fascist axe for the clearing away of rubbish (left half) the tree, organic vegetable renewal. . . . The verb is used in phrases: to put away old habit, the daily increase of plants, improve the state of, restore" (*J/M*, 113*n*). Yet when he follows "New fronds" with "novelle piante" in this canto, it is not to allude to Italian fascism but to Italy's greatest poet and, more specifically, to the redemptive conclusion to the *Purgatorio,* in which Dante, having drunk from the waters of Eunoë, "came forth from the most holy waves, renovated even as new trees [piante novelle] renewed with new foliage [novella fionda], pure and ready to rise to the stars."

Here, as we have come to expect of Pound at this stage, when he focuses on the theme of redemption, he will skirt the issue of contrition. This allusion to the *Purgatorio* shows Dante's state of mind after the water of Lethe has erased all memory of sin and the water of Eunoë has "restore[d] the memory of every good deed" (28, 129). Now, when past sins are remembered, it is as the occasion of grace and forgiveness. It is not until after his release from St. Elizabeths that Pound will write ritual passages for his poem that are acts of contrition.

POUND'S RELEASE

Almost certainly, Pound's release need not have been delayed for as long as it was. His lawyer, Julian Cornell, felt that the prospects for obtaining a writ of habeas corpus were good if Pound were prepared to appeal the case to a higher court. A letter from Cornell to Arthur V. Moore, Dorothy Pound's London lawyer, makes clear the reason for requesting Pound's release from St. Elizabeths on the grounds of habeas corpus. The psychiatrists called by the government at Pound's sanity hearing on February 13, 1946, had testified that "he is now suffering from a paranoid state which renders him mentally unfit to advise properly with counsel or to participate intelligently and reasonably in his own defense" (Cornell, p. 37). Cornell explains that the doctors agree that it is unlikely that Pound's mental condition will improve sufficiently to make it possible for him to stand trial in the future and that this seems to raise "intricate and novel legal questions" because "Congress had failed to consider the possibility that a person might be unable to stand trial and yet not require permanent hospitalization." If Pound's paranoid state cannot be corrected by psychiatric treatment and if it can be shown that he would be neither a danger to himself nor to the public once released, then his constitutional rights would be violated by his continued imprisonment. "Although he would still be presumed innocent under the law, he would be incarcerated indefinitely, possibly for life, because the government had obtained an indictment against him" (Cornell, p. 49).

Thurman Arnold, who represented Pound in April 1958 when the case was finally brought for dismissal of the indictment against him, agreed with Cornell's reasoning. In a letter to the American Civil Liberties Union Arnold wrote that when he investigated the case, he was surprised to find that "Pound could have been rleased many years ago by habeas corpus, under decisions of the Ninth and Tenth Circuits and the *Greenwood* case [1956] in the Supreme Court of the United States, because (1) he was incurably insane and could never be brought to trial and (2) he was harmless to himself and society. The only justifications for the incarceration of an insane defendant in a criminal case are (1) that he may be cured and thus face trial, or (2) that if released he would be a danger to himself and others. Dr. Overholser's affidavit shows that neither one of these justifications exists in Pound's case. . . . Furthermore, Dr. Overholser believes he was insane at the time of the offense." He adds, "In this connection I have read Pound's broadcasts in Italy. They show insanity on their face." He concludes with the observation that Pound "has been confined for at least seven or eight years beyond the time that there was any legal justification for keeping him."[24]

The question then is why Pound remained in St. Elizabeths for twelve years and four months. The Pounds were initially in favor of Cornell's plan to try to obtain a writ of habeas corpus, but, in his words, "Mrs. Pound apparently got 'cold feet' about having her husband released and asked me to drop the appeal" (Cornell, p. 60). Possible difficulties that Cornell mentions in his letters to Mrs. Pound would almost certainly have influenced her decision to some extent. In a letter of December 15, 1947, he says that, although he considers the chances for her husband's release to be good, he warns her that, should the State Department decide to refuse Pound a passport, there would be no legal way of compelling them to issue one. He also advises her of the likelihood of a protracted legal battle and so urges her to be very precise about her ultimate plans in advance since, if her husband is released, her responsibilities will be much heavier and particularly so if she takes him to Italy. In a letter to her of March 4, 1948, Cornell is considerably more cautionary. Although he still says that he thinks "there is a good chance to obtain a reversal on appeal," he adds that "the appeal will be difficult, and . . . victory is by no means assured" and warns that the legal proceedings could take a long time (Cornell, p. 66). Nine days later Mrs. Pound writes: "Please withdraw the appeal at once. My husband is not fit to appear in court and must still be kept as quiet as possible; the least thing shakes his nerves up terribly" (Cornell, p. 67).

The prospect of being unable to return to Italy was obviously a considerable factor in the decision that the outcome of the appeal might not justify the trouble of making it. Cornell reports that Pound had told him that, "if he had to remain in the United States, St. Elizabeths was probably as good a place for him as any," and he also conjectures that Mrs. Pound "may have been fearful of the problem of shielding Pound both from his enemies and from his well-wishers if he should be released in her custody" (Cornell, p. 61). Unlike Olga Rudge, Dorothy Pound was not a very energetic person and would certainly have found it very taxing to have complete responsibility for Pound's care. Moreover, there was the problem of knowing how best to deal with his paranoid anxieties. Williams even mentions these as Pound's reason for wanting the appeal withdrawn: "Pound had refused to entertain the idea, stating that he knew he would be shot by an agent of the 'international crew' the moment he stood outside the hospital gates" (*Autobiography,* p. 340).

In his March 4, 1948, letter to Mrs. Pound, Cornell had written that, although Pound "obviously has the right to be released sooner or later if there is no medical reason for confining him . . . , [t]he case will not be an easy one . . . because of popular feeling against [his] position which will be reflected to some extent in the attitude of the courts. . . . Unfortunately, the courts are imperfect instruments and justice does not always prevail, particularly in cases which involve political emotions." In the matter of Pound's release, the most significant change that had occurred between March 1948 and April 1958, when the motion to dismiss the indictment was finally submitted, was in this area of political emotions. Another significant consideration was the length of his incarceration. A *Life* editorial of February 6, 1956, noting that General Sepp Dietrich of the SS, responsible for the Malmédy massacre of 1944, and also Tokyo Rose were along with many other war criminals now out of jail, called for a public consideration of the possibility of quashing the indictment against Pound.

By far the greatest part of the credit for the arrangements leading to Pound's release goes, without question, to Archibald MacLeish, even though at the time the credit went to Robert Frost, who was very emphatic in claiming it publicly as his due. MacLeish drafted the letter which, sent to Attorney General Herbert Brownell Jr. over the signatures of Frost, Hemingway, and Eliot early in 1957, initiated the process of review. Frost's biographer Lawrance Thompson claims that MacLeish "brought [Frost] reluctantly into 'The Pound Case,' and he conducted his backstage manipulations of RF with exceptional tact [so that] eventually and mistakenly, RF assumed he had played a truly decisive part in securing Pound's freedom."[25] On April 10 the Deputy Attorney General William P. Rogers wrote to Frost, but Frost did not reply. When MacLeish happened to meet Frost in London in May, he persuaded him to try to see someone in the attorney general's office and offered to go with him. They had an interview with Rogers on July 22, but it was judged best to do nothing until the segregationist John Kasper, who had attached himself to Pound at St. Elizabeths, was no longer in the public eye for his campaign of racist agitation in the South. On October 23, 1957, Frost called on Rogers again, and thereafter Rogers and Frost's friend Sherman Adams, White House chief-of-staff, made it clear that they would do what they could to facilitate a review of Pound's case. Gabriel Hauge, monetary adviser to Eisenhower, had been the first to suggest to Adams the possibility of a review, and Hauge personally undertook to make sure that the necessary paperwork was in order and forwarded expeditiously to the Justice Department.[26]

Frost, without consulting Mrs. Pound, asked Thurman Arnold if he would serve as Pound's lawyer and, when he agreed, the firm of Arnold, Fortas, and Porter said that they would take the case without fee. On April 18, 1958, Arnold submitted to Judge Bolitha J. Laws a motion for dismissal of the indictment against Pound. Robert Frost was not in court but had prepared a statement, which was read by Thurman Arnold, in which he expressed his admiration for the government's willingness, out of con-science, to consider this motion and called on the government to show its magnanimity. Appended to Frost's statement were brief statements of support for Pound from Dos Passos, Van Wyck Brooks, Marianne Moore, Hemingway, Sandburg, Auden, Eliot, Macleish, Robert Fitzgerald, Tate, and Dag Hammarskjöld, and a lengthy one by Richard Rovere, whose judicious article "The Question of Ezra Pound" in *Esquire* 48, of September 1957, had received a largely favorable response. Arnold's motion was supported by an affidavit by Dr. Overholser, which reiterated the position on Pound's mental state put forward at the sanity hearing and added that, during the intervening years, Pound's condition had proved "permanent and incurable, that it will not and has not responded to treatment, that further professional therapeutic attention under hospital conditions would be of no avail and produce no beneficial results and that he is permanently and incurably insane." Overholser also added, "There is a strong probability that the commission of the crime charged was the result of insanity, and I would seriously doubt that prosecution could show criminal responsibility even if it were hypothetically assumed that Ezra Pound could regain sufficient sanity to be tried" (Cornell, p. 129). Judge Laws considered "failure to oppose" the motion for dismissal by the government to be insufficient grounds for dismissal and required that the government give its consent to the motion. United States Attorney Oliver Gasch then consented and Pound was finally a free man.[27]

Events were to prove Dr. Overholser right. After little more than a year of predominantly good spirits during which he could continue to work on his poetry, Pound would be overcome by chronic depression. He would have to suffer mental distress which was much more painful and disabling than his state of mind had been at St. Elizabeths (once he was no longer in Howard Hall with the most violent patients) because now he was no longer evading and repressing his feelings of guilt. In the attempt to understand the reasons for Pound's depression one would expect that those close to him should want to consider the possibility that, had some decisions been made differently, his mental state might have been saved from its deterioration. Was it best for him to be with Mary in Brunnenburg, with Dorothy in Rapallo, with Olga in Venice, or away from family altogether, with friends in Rome? Would he have done better to have stayed in America or at least to have returned to America once, by 1960, he felt that he wanted to? Was his mental state essentially physiological in origin and could it have been significantly improved with better medical treatment? There are at least partial answers to most of these questions, but I would argue that, overall, these were largely secondary issues and much less decisive in determining his mental state than were those psychological strategies he had been relying on since 1935. The depression of the later years was the direct and inevitable consequence of having come to the point of confronting what had been repressed for so many years. That this confrontation was undertaken consciously is clear from *Drafts and Fragments,* and it is from this that the power and control of these final cantos come.

Pound's state of mind during the last years of his life would have been essentially the way it was no matter where he was living, or with whom. Surely no one could have been a better choice for a companion than Olga Rudge. She had the energy, dedication, and optimism necessary for keeping him active, even at his most depressive. She provided the reassurance of stability and regular routine, the diversion of activities that would interest him and acquaintances whom he found congenial, and even the stimulation and variety of periodic long trips, to Delphi, to London and Ireland, to Paris, to the United States. All of this made the circumstances of his day-to-day life as pleasant as it could be made, yet it was obvious that his most immediate and absorbing reality continued to be his troubled inner world. Just as, in the past, he had tended to be less responsive than most people to overtures from the people around him, so he remained. The resistance which before he had shown to attempts to restrain or question him, he now exercised against attempts to encourage, reassure, and exculpate him.

At the time of the dismissal of the indictment, Pound was seventy-two. He did not leave St. Elizabeths immediately and remained on the hospital rolls for two more weeks so that he could have some dental work completed and an eye examination. He was released on May 7, and it would be almost two months before the Pounds, with Marcella Spann, sailed for Italy. Their last visit before sailing was to the Williams's at Rutherford, and we see through the eyes of Williams's wife, Floss, how much of a strain both of the Pounds were under. She found Dorothy Pound "terribly nervous" and Ezra, whom she thought "definitely a mental case," to be "jittery as an eel."[28] Williams himself was more struck by the "fury of energy" that Pound displayed and called him a "tortured soul,"[29] but marveled that the long imprisonment showed no signs of having broken his spirit. Williams had noted after a visit to Pound in February 1951 that "his mind has not budged a hair's breadth from his basic position, he has even entrenched himself more securely in it" (*Autobiography,* p. 342), and this had continued to be the case, even during seven more years in the asylum.

This strategy of Pound's made possible an unimpeded flow of mental energy during the St. Elizabeths years. In this "controlled environment" his psychotic perceptions were simply not challenged. He refused to allow interviews by reporters; his visitors were handpicked and, in the unlikely event that a visitor who had been approved were to raise disturbing questions, that person would not be allowed further visits. His wife was not in the habit of questioning his views, and his regular visitors were the opposite of critical. The psychiatrists were concerned to note his views and try to analyze them but not to challenge them, and his interviews with them were anyway infrequent. With the likelihood of face-to-face challenge virtually eliminated, correspondence would offer the only other avenue of assault, and we have seen how adept Pound was at tuning out what he did not want to hear. This was the case even with those who had the strongest claims to his attention. On April 25, 1958, Olga Rudge was so distressed by Pound's persistent refusal to answer the pressing questions in her letters that she wrote to ask Dr. Overholser if her letters were being censored. She says that he writes to her several times a week but "if he gets my letters, his persistent refusal to face any facts which do not fit into how he would like things to be, seems to me deeply significant—I have known Mr. Pound for 25 years and have always found this tendency very strong, but besides this now seeming stronger. The quality of his character seems changing." Samuel Silk, the assistant superintendent, confirms her perceptions in his reply to her letter: "As you have noted, it is Mr. Pound's mental quirk not to face any facts which are not in conformity with his preconceived beliefs. Because of Mr. Pound's intelligence he is very cleverly able to distort reality to suit his own purpose."[30]

Yet this strategy of repression and denial provided Pound with a stability that, because it had no solid foundation, would ultimately prove very precarious when he tried to function outside the controlled environment of the hospital. The challenges to his peace of mind would be of two rather different kinds, one much more grievous than the other. The more manageable challenge would be in the area of personal relationships; the overwhelming one would be the onslaught of anxiety, guilt feelings, and depression that accompanied the surfacing of those misgivings about his past actions which he had been repressing so rigorously since 1935. In the cantos of *Drafts and Fragments* we see him confronting both these challenges, but the second would eventually involve such a tumultuous welling up from the unconscious of such devastating anxieties as to go beyond words altogether. His feelings of self-castigation would resist the shaping power of language, both of the formal verbal structures of poetry and even of the spontaneous overtures of private discussion and conversation.

The Return to Italy: "To Confess Wrong . . ."

6

Since 1948, Pound's daughter, Mary, had been living in Castle Brunnenburg in the mountains of the Italian Tirol. She writes that "since 1954, the castle had been [Pound's] house," and she had been told to bring there all his and his parents' belongings from Rapallo. When, discouraged on the occasion of her visit to St. Elizabeths that no one held out any hope of his release, she asked him what course of action they should try next, he replied, "All you can do is plant a little decency in Brunnenburg,"[1]

After Pound's return to Italy, the Confucian emphasis on the importance of order within the family assumed a more personal immediacy. "Thank God you have taken time to produce a family and lead a sane life," he said to his daughter when she visited him in St. Elizabeths, and it pleased him to be a grandfather, a *capostipite,* a head of a family of three generations. His thoughts about family figure prominently in Canto 114, which was written in the summer of 1959. In a nostalgic mood he recalls his great-great-uncle Joel, his great uncle Albert—whose conversation was "reputed"—and his paternal grandmother, Sarah, who was "quick on the uptake" and whose comment "Harve was like that" had led Pound in *Indiscretions* to credit her with an incisive "recognition of the demarcation and rights of personality" (12). In this canto he writes: "This is not vanity, to have good guys in the family / or feminine gaiety / . . . . / snobism— niente— / the *tribú.* / Armes et blasons! / me foot!!" and the best gloss on this is two passages from Eliot's *Notes Toward the Definition of Culture.*

Pound, when he read Eliot's contention that "the primary channel of transmission of culture is the family: no man wholly escapes from the kind, or wholly surpasses the degree, of culture which he acquired from his early environment," had endorsed it in the margin with "Yes Sir." He also wrote an emphatic "hear hear!" beside the lines "When I speak of the family, I have in mind . . . a piety towards the dead, however obscure, and a solicitude for the unborn, however remote. Unless this reverence for past and future is cultivated in the home, it can never be more than a verbal convention in the community. Such an interest in the past is different from the vanities and pretensions of genealogy; such a responsibility for the future is different from that of the builder of social programmes."[2]

Yet the consequences of family ties and strong personal attachments were by no means always positive, as Pound was particularly being made aware at this period. It was inevitable that there would be considerable tensions in the area of personal relationships. After leaving the hospital, Pound had to reconcile the claims of four women, all completely devoted to him but all inevitably bound to think of the other three as rivals to some extent for his affection. Dorothy Pound, after her years of self-denying attendance on him at St. Elizabeths, came to Brunnenburg bringing with her his young "disciple" and coeditor of the *Confucius to Cummings* anthology, Marcella Spann. Meanwhile, in Italy, Olga Rudge and Mary de Rachewiltz, who had been waiting out the long St. Elizabeths years, were eagerly anticipating his arrival. No one seems to have made much allowance for the fact that his problematic state of mind was not likely to be suddenly corrected by the simple fact of his release. Now that he was free, he was no longer able to rely on the reinforcement that came from the thought that he was innocent of the treasonable intent with which he had been charged and so was imprisoned unjustly. Now that the larger issue of guilt was no longer obscured by the immediate but much more limited issue of treasonable intent, it was likely that his temporarily repressed misgivings about mistakes that he *could* charge himself with having made would ride much nearer the surface.

He was, of course, very happy to be at Brunnenburg and at first full of energy, but, as out of touch as he was with his own motivations, he was hardly likely to be able to understand or react constructively to the emotional demands of those around him, no matter how reasonable the demands were, or to stand the tensions. "The family had been trained for a demigod, and as such he came," his daughter writes. "Yet something went wrong. The house no longer contained a family. We were turning into entities who should not have broken bread together" (*Discretions*, p. 305).

He was distressed by the painful moods which resulted from the jealousies which inevitably existed between the women around him. That he should have found the acrimonious feelings distressing is understandable enough, and he alludes to this distress briefly in most of the cantos of this sequence: "That love be the cause of hate, / something is twisted" (110/780); "the eyes holding trouble— / no light" (111/783); "Pride, jealousy and possessiveness / 3 pains of hell" (113/787); "When one's friends hate each other / how can there be peace in the world?" (115/794); "If love be not in the house there is nothing" (116/796); and "Under the Rupe Tarpeia / weep out your jealousies—" (117/801). In this last, speaking as the accused "traitor" who has managed to survive the ordeal that was his equivalent to the ancient sentence of the traitors of Rome, he reveals his impulse to distance himself from those around him who are suffering the pains of jealousy. The tone of his complaints suggests that there is something unreasonable in their behavior, and it is clear that his mental disorientation interfered with his ability to see their distress from their point of view. That he did eventually come to a full appreciation of the sacrifices they made for him and the suffering that he unintentionally caused them is eloquently testified to by his prayer in the previously designated Canto 120: "Let those I love try to forgive / what I have made."

Pound was able both to make peace with those he loved and to write about it in his poetry, but during that period when he was still able to write poetry, he was able only partially and provisionally to make peace with himself. In the area of self-confrontation, *Drafts and Fragments* sustains a redemptive vision, but it does also offer glimpses of the grim and darkened landscape of self-castigation and depression through which he would choose to wander during the years of his silence. The spirit of the court beauty Kakitsubata, from the Noh play of that name, is in many ways the presiding supernatural presence of *Drafts and Fragments,* but her redemptive message cannot entirely eclipse the ominous message of the Na-Khi suicide spirit: ²K'a-² mä-¹ gyu-³ mi-² gkyi. ²K'a appears on the first page of *Drafts and Fragments* immediately before the reference to Kakitsubata and is referred to again immediately after in the allusion to the oak tree on Mount Sumeru, where she hanged herself, and to her lover's words to her corpse: "Can'st 'ou see with the eyes of turquoise?"

While it may seem inconsistent with the importance of Kakitsubata in this sequence that her name is never given, this proves to be in keeping with the manner of her appearance in the play and also with the fact that her

name is represented in the play by the acrostic that Narihira, her lover, has
made upon it—a play on words that Pound provides a counterpart to in this
canto. Kakitsubata, now a spirit, first appears as a "simple young girl of the
locality" and only later assumes the brilliant court dress of the great lady
that she had been. Finally just her "shadowy apparition" remains, which in
turn also fades. Pound's first reference to her is the cryptic:

Yellow iris in that riverbed
$\qquad$ yueh$^{4.5}$
$\qquad$ ming^2
$\qquad$ mo$^{4.5}$
$\qquad$ hsien^1
$\qquad$ p'eng^2 $\qquad\qquad\qquad\qquad\qquad$ [110/778]

Here Pound has composed his own acrostic for his Narihira persona. In
the play, the Chorus tells how Narihira—poet, musician, lover, and
incarnation of a divinity—when wandering in exile saw the yellow irises
growing at the eight bridges of Yatsubashi and how the beauty of the flowers
recalled to his memory the beauty of the lady Kakitsubata, to whom he had
bound himself. Kakitsubata remembered in all her beauty is enacted by the
dancer who represents her spirit, and the Chorus presents Narihira's lament
for his lost youth and his lost glory at court. Since Pound does not give
characters, various readings of the Chinese words are possible. Pound's
grandson, apparently recording his grandfather's explanation of the passage,
had glossed it: "The brightness of the moon . . . there are no former
friends,"[3] and it seems very likely that the first four words are "moon,"
"bright, brightness," "not," and "former, of the past." "P'eng^2 can mean
"friend," "acquaintance," and "companion," and, since Narihira is lament-
ing his exile from the court and is reminded by the beauty of the irises of his
separation from Kakitsubata, it is entirely appropriate than he should be
saying, "there are no former friends."

P'eng^2, however, can also mean "luxuriant growth" and "to be strong
and handsome," and Pound may well have intended his readers to see his
Chinese "poem" as his own version of the poem of Narihira's, which the
Chorus sings right before the revelatory dance of Kakitsubata's that ends the
play. This dance, which reveals both the full extent of her former beauty and
her message of "enlightenment" about the immortality of the soul, is her
response to Narihira's "unenlightened" lament:

No moon!
$\qquad$ The spring
Is not the spring of the old days,

My body
Is not my body,
But only a body grown old.

Narihira, Narihira
My glory comes not again.[4]

The characters of the acrostic could, in fact, be rearranged and repeated to read "No moon . . . No luxuriant growth [spring] as in the past. No longer, as in the past, strong and handsome. No brightness [glory] as in former times."

Before we consider the importance elsewhere in *Drafts and Fragments* of other borrowings from this part of the play, it is worth noting an instance of highly idiosyncratic free composition with Chinese characters to which Pound, at least for a time, attached considerable importance and which could be seen as a precedent for the word play of the Narihira poem. On March 4, 1952, he sent to Angela Palandri a Chinese quatrain of sixteen ideograms which he himself had composed. He was aware of the highly idiosyncratic nature of his composition and admitted that the final line, "Hsien[2], hsien[3], hsien[1], hsien[1]," was a "trick line" of which he "did not expect a Chinese to approve." Palandri offers as a tentative and approximate prose translation:

> Respect for the kind of intelligence that enables the cherrystone to grow cherries and uphold the cutural florescence with utmost sincerity and perception.
> Based upon those aforesaid qualities the rulers of the Chou dynasty had cultivated and collected the fruit of their civilization (the odes?)
> Governmental and personal actions must progress to the ultimate goal and come to rest upon perfection;
> Only then can one enjoy the leisurely life (by watching the moon at one's door), and manifest and glorify the immortality of men (or *sennin* or sages?) of the past.[5]

Hugh Kenner says that when Pound showed him this poem, he explained that he had composed it of the sixteen ideograms that he found "most interesting" and that it was "for the last Canto."[6]

That Pound should have been forced to change his plan to use it for a conclusion seems inevitable when we consider how unrealistic its optimistic projections proved to be. From the protected environment of St. Elizabeths, it was possible for Pound to imagine a utopian "coming to perfection" of a plan of constructive social action and a subsequent retirement to a quiet old age of leisurely enjoyment of the beauties of nature and of the arts. Once out of St. Elizabeths, he would quickly discover how unrealistic his "sense of an ending" had been. Eventually, even the more realistic redemptive vision of *Kakitsubata* would be progressively darkened by the onslaughts of self-blame and despair.

In *Drafts and Fragments,* however, the light does manage to hold its own against the darkness, and the most memorable assertions of this are also allusions to Kakitsubata. In Canto 115, Pound writes: "A blown husk that is finished / but the light sings eternal / a pale flare over marshes," and in the play, Kakitsubata says of her apparition as it fades away after her dance: "It is only the cracked husk of the locust" and the Chorus explains, "The flower soul melts into Buddha" (*T,* 340). Although we think first of the "pale flare" of the poem as an effect of the light, when we read in the play, "the flowers Kakitsubata / That flare and flaunt in their marsh" (*T,* 338), we realize that the "pale flare over marshes" could also be the yellow flowers of the iris. Before her dance the Chorus says for Kakitsubata, "I who speak, an unsteady wraith, / A form impermanent, drifting after this fashion, / Am come to enlighten these people. / Whether they know me I know not"; then the dancer herself, as Kakitsubata's spirit, describes herself as "A light that does not lead on to darkness" (*T,* 338). The line which Pound had chosen for his translation over forty years before shines out again in the last complete canto in this sequence, both early in "a little light / in great darkness—" and in the closing lines: "A little light, like a rushlight / to lead back to splendour" (116/797). The "splendour" is the vision of ultimate and universal coherence λαμπρὰ συμβαίνει, which Pound had translated in his *Women of Trachis* as "what / SPLENDOUR, / IT ALL COHERES," and which he has just affirmed again with "it coheres all right / even if my notes do not cohere" (116/797). The rushlight is a "humble" image, the candle of the peasants and the poor, giving off the least light, at the farthest remove from splendor. It is also perhaps, metaphorically, the yellow iris itself, the flower of a rush, that appears as "a pale flare" in the marsh.

The moon figures prominently in the Noh plays that Pound has translated, and by the time that he comes to write *Drafts and Fragments,* the sun and the resolve "to build light" have been, to a considerable extent, "eclipsed" by the moon. Canto 110 contains two prominent references to the "Make it new" injunction and includes the characters hsin[1] and jih[4], but it also mentions Artemis and Endymion and ends, ". . . pray / There is power / Awoi or Komachi / the oval moon." In the two Noh plays about Ono no Komachi, *Sotoba Komachi* [Komachi at the Shrine] and *Kayoi Komachi* [Komachi Going], and also in *Awoi no Uye,* the moon is an important presence. In *Sotoba Komachi,* Ono in old age is described as "like a dull moon that fades in the dawn's grip," and she tells how her rejected lover, Shosho, came to wait for her ninety-nine nights in succession "in the moonlight and in the dark night and in the nights flooded with rain, and in the black face of the wind and in the wild swish of the snow," until his death (*T,* 224–25).

In *Kayoi Komachi,* Ono's spirit is converted to Buddhism by the prayers of the priest, and she says, "[m]y heart is clear as new moonlight" (228), but Shosho at first resists conversion: "Though she only asks me to drink a cup of moonlight, I will not take it. It is a trick to catch one for Buddha" (230). His mental distress before his conversion rhymes with the despair of the suicide-maiden that will sound an ominous undertone to this sequence of the poem. He says to Ono, "I've a sad heart to see you looking up to Buddha, you who left me alone, I diving in the black rivers of hell. Will soft prayers be a comfort to you in your quiet heaven, you who know that I'm alone in that wild, desolate place?" (227). "You in your quiet heaven" is echoed in "a nice quiet paradise / over the shambles" (116/796), and both comments are made with a certain amount of resigned fatalism, as we recall that the "source" of the latter is the radio speech about so-called experts on politics and economics, consulted by governments and fabricating nothing more substantial than "Imaginary futures for the land that never was and never will be . . . Alice in Wonderland . . . private worlds, in the gook house sense of these words. Over Hell's Kitchen."

Pound seems to have felt a particular fascination with *Awoi no Uye* when he translated it in 1916 if we judge from his lengthy introductory note to the play. Here he discusses the play as a study in obsession and explains how Awoi's jealous rage acquires such influence over her that it becomes a double, alternate false-self represented by two separate actors. Awoi's physical body is represented by a folded kimono; her mind clouded by jealous rage is represented by an actor whom Pound calls "Apparition" and the rage itself by the Hannya, or demon who appears first "in a disguised and beautiful form," and then in her true shape wearing "The terrible mask with golden eyes." Pound sums up by explaining that "the whole play is a dramatization, or externalization, of Awoi's jealousy. The passion makes her subject to the demon-possession" (*T,* 325).

The moon figures prominently in the play. When the Waki, or Priest, is called to perform the exorcism, he asks, "Do you call me to a fit place for prayer? To . . . a place full of holy waters, and where there is a clear moon?" When the Apparition of Awoi is drawn by the prayers of Miko, the wise woman, "to seek consolation," her reluctance is shown when she sings,

"Though I lie all night hid for shame in the secret carriage, looking at the moon for sorrow, yet I would not be seen by the moon" (*T*, 326). Awoi's obsession involves hatred as well as jealousy, and it seems likely that, in alluding to Awoi in these cantos, Pound is thinking less of jealousy as a problem in those he loves than of how his own obsession has drawn him to hatred. Awoi's hatred is certainly emphasized in the play. When Miko urges the Apparition to stop herself from striking "Awoi as kimono," she responds, "The woman is hateful: I cannot keep back my blows," and then "I cannot. However much you might pray." The Apparition rationalizes the hatred as "only repayment" and as "a just revenge." The Chorus, speaking for Awoi's "true self," tries to reassure her: "Hateful, heart full of hate, / Though you are full of tears / Because of others' dark hatred, / Your love for Genji / Will not be struck out / Like a fire-fly's flash in the dark" (*T*, 328), and then the Priest forces the demon to appear in its true form so that it can be exorcised.

Although in the play the exorcism is accomplished, there are suggestions in *Drafts and Fragments* that Pound is aware that, for him, the exorcism of hatred is not yet completed. When the Apparition first appears, she says, "Man's life is a wheel on the axle, there is no turn whereby to escape" and this is echoed both in "the mind as Ixion, unstill, ever turning," and in "The hells move in cycles, / No man can see his own end" (113/ 790, 787). We find an even stronger suggestion in Pound's question, "Fear, father of cruelty / are we to write a genealogy of the demons?" (114/793). Since this occurs in the "renunciation of hatred" canto, we see that Pound has chosen only to raise this question and not to pursue it at this point. The "genealogy of the demons" refers us to the climax of *Awoi no Uye*, where the exorcism takes the form of a "battle of invocation" with the Hannya conjuring the evil spirits by name and the Chorus, opposing, invoking the names of the "powerful good spirits" and with such authority that the Hannya is overcome: "O terrible names of the spirits. This is my last time. I cannot return here again." Finally, "pity has melted her heart" and Awoi can die in peace.

The exorcism of hatred requires contrition and purification, and in these cantos the most important ritual of contrition is the ^2muan ^1bpo ceremony of the Na-Khi people, whose culture Pound had studied in Joseph Rock's "The ^{2}Muan ^{1}Bpo Ceremony or the Sacrifice to Heaven as practiced by the ^{2}Na-^{1}Khi"[7] and *The Ancient Na-Khi Kingdom of Southwest China*. The latter contains 256 5 × 7 photographs of the remote, mountainous region and its people, and the Na-Khi passages in the St. Elizabeths cantos showed that these photographs had made an even stronger impression on Pound than Rock's text.

Pound had first written of the Na-Khi in the St. Elizabeths cantos. There the precipitous, rocky mountainsides and treacherous rivers were reminders of the precariousness of the lives of these people who, as the text tells us, were under constant threat from hunger, disease, violent weather, and "raiders." Pound's "Obit 1933, Tsung-kuan, for Honour. / Bears live on acorns / and come raiding our fields" (101/725) refers to a passage in which Rock writes of the raids, not just of bears but also of the Tibetan robber bands who drove off the livestock of the Na-Khi, burned their houses, turned loose their horses in the standing grain, and carried off their children into slavery. The local chief, or Tsung-kuan, called A Yun-shan had done his best to protect his people but, Rock writes: "Since the decease of that most active personality, who was like a father with a big heart for any one in trouble, the country has fallen on evil days. It is the beginning of the end of the native chiefs."[8]

There, in Canto 101, the linked allusions to the mountainous terrain and its vegetation, an idyllic lake setting, and the ceremonial rites of the Na-Khi had strong elegiac connotations for Pound. The image of the "rope bridge" across a torrential mountain river—a bridge that is little more than a "hemp rope? a reed rope?"—became a symbol of precariousness. The observation "here one man can hold the whole pass / over this mountain," followed by "Mont Ségur," with its associations for Pound of the massacre of the Albigensians, introduced the theme of embattled last stands.

The reference to the lake-island shrine of the mountain goddess "Sengper ga-mu," to whom "we burn pine with white smoke / morning and evening," referred us to plate 246, of the shrine, and to the six other plates of the idyllically beautiful and serene Yung-Ming Lake, which was to Rock something of what Lake Garda had been to Pound. Plate 244 shows a teahouse on a small promontory at the lakeshore, where, as Rock's caption tells us, he "spent many happy weeks translating Na-Khi literature." Rock's description is elegiac because this setting is now associated with his personal loss both at the death of his host, A Yun-shan, and at the larger loss of the whole tradition of the powerful Na-Khi chiefs and their once-flourishing culture (426–28).

This canto had concluded with references to several Na-Khi rites, but not to $^2muan\ ^1bpo$. Words were quoted from a rite for fertility and from a rite for courage in sons, but the final quotation was from the $^2Zhi\text{-}^3ma$ funeral ceremony and, as we shall see, the theme of suicide was introduced when Pound followed his description of a young Na-Khi woman who had "the sun and moon on her shoulders / the star-discs sewn on her coat" with, "at Li Chiang, the snow range, / a wide meadow / and the ^{2}dto-^{1}mba's face (exorcist's) / muy simpatico."

Pound had raised the issue of the ^{2}muan ^{1}bpo ceremony of contrition as early as Canto 98 with "Baller [editor of *The Sacred Edict*] thought one needed religion. / Without ^{2}muan ^{1}bpo . . . but I anticipate," yet he postponed a return to this theme for six cantos. The Canto 104 references show why his St. Elizabeths state of mind had made a ritual of contrition impossible. His calm opening, about the sounds of the Na-Khi language and the idea that they were intended to "fit in" with forest sounds and be "unperceived by the game," was disrupted by thoughts of political betrayals. He wrote: "semina. / Flames withered; the wind blew confusion" and followed it with the character *wu*, "ritual." This theme of ritual disrupted was carried forward by "and there is / no glow such as of pine-needles burning / Without ^{2}muan ^{1}bpo / no reality."

In Canto 90, referring to Hitler (and Eva Braun), Pound had written, "Evita, beer-halls, semina motuum, / . . . . / not arrogant from habit, / but furious from perception" (606). The disabling evasion of the truth signaled by these comments persists in Canto 104, as we see from "Adolf furious from perception" (741) and from "And Muss saved, rem salvavit, / in Spain / il salvabile [what was savable]" at the beginning of Canto 105.

In the Na-Khi passages in *Drafts and Fragments,* however, the ^{2}muan ^{1}bpo ceremony is "enacted" in the poetry. This painstaking and time-consuming rite is the chief of the Na-khi ceremonies and involves the exhaustive purification of everything with which the people come into contact and builds up to a communal confession of sin and the driving away of the scapegoat. Their initial confession of sin emphasizes how careful they have been in performing the rites precisely, but ends, "Wrong we did not, but perhaps we did wrong, so we come before Heaven to confess (our wrong). Faults we have not committed, but perhaps we have committed faults, so we come before Heaven to confess." The final confession is made three times, once to each of three saplings on the altar: the oaks that symbolize Heaven (^{2}muan) and Earth (^{2}Ndaw), and the central juniper (^{3}Khyu), which represents God.

Pound's uncompleted Canto 112, all of which is based upon Rock's "The ^{2}Muan ^{1}Bpo Ceremony," has a mythological and topological passage framed by references to the purification ritual itself. The opening lines ". . . owl, and wagtail / and huo^3-hu^2, the fire-fox [the lesser panda]" are taken from the "Impurities Smoke-Out" part of the ceremony and so follow on from "The purifications / are snow, rain, artemisia / also dew, oak and the juniper" in Canto 110. "The firm voice amid pine wood, / . . . . / the clear discourse" may have a personal referent for Pound, but its context here suggests that it is, at least in part, the voice of the ^{2}dto-mba, or priest who performs the ^{2}muan ^{1}bpo ceremony from memory in the sacred grove outside the village. Rock explains that the trees of the grove will be "either pines, oaks, or spruces, depending on the altitude" (9). "Artemisia," or ^{2}bbue, and "Arundinaria," or ^{1}mun, the small bamboo, are plants particularly associated with purification in these ceremonies. As one of the rites explains, "The ^{1}mun was born before all other trees, the leaves of the ^{1}mun close the road of the ^{2}nder (wrongs, sins, i.e., prevents sins from being committed); the ^{2}bbue was born before all other herbs, we use the ^{2}bbue to lead the ^{2}nder (sins) (away)" (144).

The word ^{1}mun is used also for the large winnowing tray made of the bamboo, and in the title of the "Pig Fate Offer" rite, the symbol of the tray stands for ^{2}mun, meaning a fate or a life. Here a pig is sacrificed to Heaven, the Earth, and the Juniper with a prayer for prosperity and freedom from discord: "Heaven, Earth and [the Juniper] to-day protect the family . . . let us have no quarrels with relatives, no litigations . . . let there be three generations under one roof" (70–71). Pound's

Winnowed in fate's tray

 neath luna

is a meditation of his own, concerned not with propitiation and the possibility of influencing one's fate favorably but with the contemplation of the workings of "fate" in general and, in a tentative way, the course that his own fate has taken. He chooses to end this canto as he has Canto 110, with the moon, and here, although he uses the Na-khi symbol for moon or night, this is to preserve the consistency of the canto and not because the moon is particularly emphasized in the Na-khi texts he is working with. This "luna," like the "oval moon" of Canto 110, has instead the Noh associations with spirits seeking redemption through expiation of old sins of hatred, jealousy, and pride and with the dark forces of unconscious obsession and fixation.

From "neath luna" the poem moves to the sun as, like the turning of Fortune's wheel, it moves through the signs of the zodiac: "Thru the 12 Houses of Heaven / seeing the just and the unjust / tasting the sweet and the sorry, / Pater Helios turning" (113/786). We see Pound in these cantos trying to balance the claims of the sun and the moon. The moon draws him toward introspection and confrontation of what is disturbing and painful to face, but the sun offers a respite from this. The lifting of the spirits which can come from seeing the play of sunlight on leaves and flowers is especially associated with the company of Marcella Spann: "Yet to walk with Mozart, Agassiz and Linnaeus / 'neath the overhanging air under sun-beat / Here take thy mind's space / And to this garden, Marcella, ever seeking by petal, by leaf-vein / out of dark and toward half-light" (113/786). In the sunlight he can occasionally experience "serenitas" but not sustain it. The canto ends: "Out of dark, thou, Father Helios leadest, / but the mind as Ixion, unstill, ever turning," and this unquiet "turning" is the dominant movement of the canto:

> and to know beauty and death and despair
> and to think that what has been shall be,
> flowing, ever unstill.
>
> Then a partridge-shaped cloud over dust storm.
> The hells move in cycles,
> No man can see his own end.
> The Gods have not returned. "They have never left us."
> They have not returned.
> Cloud's processional and the air moves with their living.   [113/787]

If we return to Canto 110, we can see how soon the theme of suicidal despair is introduced and how mesmerizingly it is presented before being "exorcised."

> Thy quiet house
> The crozier's curve runs in the wall,
> The harl, feather-white, as a dolphin on sea-brink
>
> I am all for Verkehr without tyranny
>   —wake exultant
>   in caracole
> Hast'ou seen boat's wake on sea-wall,
>   how crests it?
> What panache?
>   paw-flap, wave-tap,
>   that is gaiety,
> Toba Sojo,
>   toward limpidity,
>   that is exultance,
>   here the crest runs on wall
> che paion' si al vent'
> ^{2}Hăr-^{2}la-^{1}llü ^{3}k'ö
>   of the wind sway,
> The nine fates and the seven,
>   and the black tree was born dumb,

The water is blue and not turquoise
When the stag drinks at the salt spring
                    and sheep come down with the gentian sprout,
can you see with eyes of coral or turquoise
            or walk with the oak's root?

It is an abrupt descent from the mood of "panache," "gaiety," "limpidity," and "exultance" with which the canto opens to the story of suicide that follows, but the grim reality of the suicide is masked, both for the reader of the romance and for the reader of this canto—as it was in prospect for the young girl—by being described as a thing of beauty. The real emphasis of the story is the state of mind of a person contemplating suicide and alternating between being drawn by the seductive attraction of the prospect of "blissful release" and then repeatedly recoiling from taking the final step.

In the context of the romance, suicide is very much a deliberate and considered act rather than the consequence of mental derangement. In fact, had ^{2}K'a-^{2}mä-^{1}gyu-^{3}mi-^{2}gkyi been able to persuade her lover to continue with their plan of a double suicide, the suggestion is that she would have killed herself without much compunction. The sinister note that runs through the romance is the consequence less of the grimness of the idea of suicide than of the seductive way in which the prospect of suicide is presented. In his introduction, Rock explains that the frequent suicide pacts between young Na-khi lovers were the consequence of the imposition of Chinese customs of arranged marriages and premarital chastity upon this people who had traditionally practiced free love and made love matches. He blames the priests for effectively encouraging suicide pacts because "they paint a most beautiful picture of life after such a death [and] . . . lovers, high-strung and credulous, will take that fatal step in the belief that they will live forever young, in perfect happiness roaming with the wind and clouds, in the perpetual embrace of love, never to be reborn, never to be sent to an infernal region, but to live inseparably to the full in a state of eternal youth."[9]

Pound's "^{2}Hăr-^{2}la-^{1}llü-^{3}k'ö / of the wind sway" refers us to Rock's introductory account of this ceremony—translated "Wind sway perform"—which is intended to release from the control of the wind spirits the soul of a person who died unattended. The wind spirits "roam and liberate the dogs of the clouds and winds, bombard people's homes with hailstones, . . . close up the watercourses in field and village [and] . . . spread illness in the homes" (Rock, "Romance," p. 15). They are controlled by two demons who "entice people and especially lovers to commit suicide [and] . . . . . whisper to them that they will never grow old, will always be well dressed, and will be able to live a sensuous existence" (13). The souls of those for whom the ^{2}Har-^{2}la-^{1}llü-^{3}k'o ceremony is not performed are condemned to be driven for ever on the winds and so inevitably remind Pound of Dante's pairs of lovers, who are perpetually whirled around on the black wind of the "Circle of the Lustful" in Hell and remind him particularly of the spirits of Paolo and Francesca "che paion' si al vent" and whose sorrowful story makes Dante faint from pity.[10]

Pound's orientation toward his source changes as he moves forward with the canto. The information that "nine fates" refers to a man and "seven fates" to a woman is taken from a footnote to that part of Rock's plot summary which explains that ²K'a must make a suicide pact with her lover because, having been promised in marriage to a man she does not love, she is now pregnant by her lover. "[A]nd the black tree was born dumb" is taken from the romance itself, from the part which tells how, having taken her rope to a tree to hang herself, "the black crown of the tree waved, [her] heart was faint. . . . here, to commit suicide, here to decompose (the tree) did not invite her. . . . hence she did not commit suicide and again returned" (Rock, "Romance," p. 42). "The water is blue" refers to another recoiling from death: "[She] tied black rocks in her skirt, and went to the water to die . . . , the surface of the water was a deep blue, her eyes were also a deep blue, my heart is faint (she said), she did not (wish) to die . . . and again returned" (41). "When the stag drinks at the salt spring / and sheep come down with the gentian sprout" shows us ²K'a herself speaking. This is the message that she sends to her lover asking him how he could have forgotten their suicide pact, how, once having decided upon it, he could have failed to keep it "in his heart" permanently, as the stag, once having drunk from the salt spring and the lamb having eaten the 'yu grass, find the taste remaining in their mouths, so that they "hanker for it" (47).

Finally it is the lover, ²Ndzi-²bö-¹yü-¹ä-¹p'er, whose words are given. Having failed to respond to her messages or to meet her in the mountains to keep their pact, he comes upon her corpse by accident. She has been prevailed upon by the wind demons to hang herself on an oak on Mount Sumeru. He weeps and asks her corpse, "If I give you turquoise and coral eyes, will you again be able to see? If I attach the roots of the pine and the oak, will you again be able to walk?" (89). "Her body was dead but not her soul; her soul was still able to speak" (84), and so she answers him, "Even if you give me turquoise and coral eyes, I will not be able to see, there is no such precedent; if you add the roots of the pine and the oak, I will not again be able to walk" (92).

At this point Pound has inset the Kakitsubata reference and "acrostic," and "mo⁴⁵ / hsien¹ / p'eng²" does serve as a comment on ²K'a's fate whether we read the Chinese as "[there are] no former friends" or as "no longer, as in the past, strong and handsome" ("My body is not my body"). He returns to ²K'a's corpse with "Quercus on Mt Sumeru / can'st 'ou see with the eyes of turquoise?" and then in the canto itself enacts his own rite of purification, building an "altar" with words:

> heaven   earth
>   in the center
>   is
>   juniper
The purifications
>   are snow, rain, artemisia
>   also dew, oak and the juniper.   [113/778]

When we consider how soon after writing these cantos Pound himself would experience extreme, at times suicidal, depression we realize that his fascination with the mental anguish of ^{2}K'a was not simply coincidental. At Brunnenburg he was in an alpine setting where the "sheep came down with the gentian Sprout," very similar to the high alpine regions of the Li chiang snow range where the ^{1}yu-^{2}vu lovers go to hang themselves. "Come, let your eyes happily behold the lovely alpine meadows," the suicide demons tempt ^{2}K'a. "Let your happy feet tread on the grass of the ^{1}Yu-^{2}vu." "Let your house be of clouds, come where they rest on the high mountains, come drink the cold water on the mountain slopes." "Come milk the hind with the broad ears; weave the white clouds and white wind" (62, 63, 64). ^{2}K'a tells herself: "If I go and hang myself I will have peace, my troubles will be over, not to hang myself would leave me on the verge of misery or distress." The two demons distort her perceptions so that she sees "Three white clouds from heaven as if hanging there by the neck; three white streaks of rain on the land as if hanging by the neck" (66). "Three streaks of white wind on the mountain as if hanging there by the neck . . . three beautiful clumps of grass on the ground as if they were corpses hanging by the neck" (67).

In Canto 110, the suicidal state of mind of ^{2}K'a is exorcised with the words of the ^{2}Muan ^{2}Bpo rite and then by the invocation of memories of an idyllic mountain interlude—Pound's visit in the spring of 1959 with his wife and Marcella Spann to Lake Garda. Marcella Spann, associated in the poet's mind with both Artemis and Kuanon, appears as a beneficent presence and a counterforce to the "dark shade" of ^{2}K'a.

And in thy mind beauty, O Artemis,
>   as of mountain lakes in the dawn.
Foam and silk are thy fingers
>   Kuanon,
and the long suavity of her moving,
>   willow and olive reflected,

Brook-water idles
        topaz against pallor of under-leaf
The lake waves Canaletto'd
        under blue paler than heaven,
the rock-layers arc'd as with a compass
        this rock is magnesia.   [113/778]

Marcella Spann returned to the United States in October 1959, and almost immediately Pound had written to his daughter from Rapallo, "I want to come back to Brunnenburg, to die" (*Disc.*, 306). On December 1, 1959, James Laughlin wrote to Dr. Overholser: "I am so deeply concerned over his condition. During all the years in the hospital, when I used to come down to see him, he was always so wonderfully cheerful and optimistic. But now he is at the bottom of the pit of melancholy, and most of his talk was about dying and 'losing his mind.' "[11] It may have been in a response from Overholser to this letter that Laughlin received the information that he included in his reminiscence of Pound, "Ez as Waz," that very serious depression was the "natural follow-up to a paranoid state when [diminished] sexual vitality reduced the furor of the paranoia." On December 11, Omar Pound wrote to Overholser in a similar vein: "He is more than merely difficult, he seems to cause himself and others around him much anguish and sorrow. Getting out of St. Elizabeth's must have been too much for him. His years of waiting (and seeming, to him, martyrdom) for freedom buoyed up his spirits, but he seems to live from one 'crisis of the soul' to another, feeling that he has failed the world, and that his life's work has been purposeless."[12]

In January 1960, feeling that a complete change might raise his spirits, Pound went to Rome to stay with Ugo Dadone, but by the summer his mood and his health had deteriorated. For a while his spirits lifted somewhat and in March he was most eager to be interviewed by Donald Hall. This interview, finally published in the Summer/Fall 1962 number of the *Paris Review,* is reprinted in Hall's *Remembering Poets.*[13] It presents Pound as controlled, judicious, assured, and incisive in his responses. He reiterates his "Whitmanian" conviction, dating from his Imagist days, that "technique is the test of sincerity" (223) and suggests that the "greatest" qualities a poet can have are "a continuous curiosity" and "a persistent energy" (225). He explains in a calm and matter-of-fact way his wartime thinking: "I think the *New Age* office helped me to see the war not as a separate event but as part of a system, one war after another;" "I thought I was fighting for a constitutional point. I mean to say, I may have been completely nuts, but I certainly *felt* that it wasn't committing treason. . . . My method of opposing tyranny was wrong over a thirty-year period; it had nothing to do with the Second World War in particular" (235, 238, 239). He appears to have mellowed to the point of self-deprecation: "Eliot, having had the Christian patience of tolerance all his life and so forth, and working very hard, must have found me very trying. . . . Eliot says that [people] spend their time trying to imagine systems so perfect that nobody will have to be good. A lot of questions asked in [*After Strange Gods*] cannot be dodged. . . . People who have lost reverence have lost a great deal" (232, 237).

This interview is also the occasion for Pound's often-quoted comment on the rationale for his selection of heroes for *Thrones*: "I have made the division between people dominated by emotion, people struggling upwards, and those who have some part of the divine vision; . . . . *Thrones* concerns the states of mind of people responsible for something more than their personal conduct" (242). The main emphasis falls on the individual taking a stand against the onslaught of outside forces: "The whole fight is for the conservation of the individual soul . . . . against us is the bewildering propaganda and brainwash, luxury and violence" (238). Pound implies that this is primarily a challenge to him in his capacity as writer: "I must clarify obscurities; I must make clearer definite ideas or dissociations. I must find a verbal formula to combat the use of brutality—the principle of order versus the split atom." But, in fact, at this point he has not written a line of poetry for seven months (130), and he admits as much to the interviewer: "Okay, I am stuck. The question is, am I dead, as Messrs. A.B.C. might wish?"(241).

When Pound says of the challenge he faces in trying to continue his poem, "It's the fight for light versus subconsciousness", he is referring to the manipulation of the consumer by advertising and the possible use of similar techniques for political ends—the need to take a stand against "the propaganda of terror and the propaganda of luxury" (242). When we read Donald Hall's detailed account of interviewing Pound, however, it quickly becomes clear that the most immediate threat Pound faced came not from outside but from within; that there was now an urgent need that order be established, not in society but in his own mind.

As Hall explains in *Remembering Poets,* the control, assurance, and incisiveness of the poet's responses were not supplied by Pound at the time of the interview but created subsequently by the interviewer at Pound's request. Lying behind the published words, "neat and witty and energetic, with complete sentences and coherent paragraphs," was a three-day "interview" of roller-coaster alternations . . . triumph and despair . . . incomplete sentences, gaps, great leaps over chasms, great Icarian plunges from sun to ocean" (134–35). Hall's detailed, sensitive, and perceptive accounts of

Pound's behavior at this time provide us with invaluable clues to the course which his self-confrontation was taking. It is clear that Pound was at a transitional stage during which the process of his self-confrontation, now begun, took two forms, one conscious and verbally articulated and the other unconscious and expressed psychosomatically.

In the course of the interview, Hall says, "[Pound] let me know, gradually and reluctantly, that he doubted what he had done. . . . Now he said, 'I guess I was off base all along' " (148). Yet, because this conscious self-confrontation was only partial, it had pronounced physiological consequences. Pound was unhesitatingly self-critical on some points, as in deploring his former use of violent language, but on issues which went to the root of his self-deception—his misrepresentation to himself of the real nature of Mussolini—he still held back to some extent from full self-confrontation. He admitted "cryptically" that Bunting had been right to denounce Mussolini, that "Bunting knew a bit more in the thirties than E. P. did," but the "jaunty" tone in which he said this indicated to Hall that Pound was "[trying] out the notion that a man could admit his errors and even survive them" (132). In fact the "jauntiness" was an attempt to pretend to himself that he had "made a full confession," and what followed made clear that he had not: "He could not sustain the jauntiness. . . . Fatigue came over him like a sudden shower, and he lay back in his big chair with his eyes closed" (132).

This attack of fatigue was mild compared to others that overcame Pound in the course of the interview. Hall recalls one occasion when, as he watched Pound, "suddenly . . . horribly . . . I saw vigor and energy drain out of him. . . . the strong body visibly sagged into old age; he disintegrated in front of me, smashed into a thousand unconnected and disorderly pieces. . . . [H]is scarf slid to the floor; his stick . . . thudded to the carpet. His long body slid boneless down, until he lay prone, eyes closed . . . [as though] he had suffered a stroke or a heart attack" (156). In this instance, as in the case of a second attack shortly after, the collapse had been preceded by a very positive and optimistic mood in which he was encouraged about the quality of his drafts of new cantos and was projecting further work on them. To be feeling this way—energetic but not frenetic and driven—is essentially to be recreating his pre-1935 mood. But to sustain a pre-1935 mood is also something of a denial of his mood between 1935 and 1958—an oblique evasion of what he most needs to face. What he cannot bring himself to confront consciously he is unconsciously forced to face in the most inescapable way—by being physically incapacitated.

These onslaughts, even though they are much more intense in degree, seem to be similar in kind to the compulsions to lie down which had been noted by the staff at St. Elizabeths and which Pound had experienced even before this in Italy. They clearly show how, at the unconscious level, his sense of guilt had been preserved intact and had persisted until, the rationalizations for evading it having been removed, he must finally confront it.

One of the collapses that Hall witnessed, however, was different in kind from the bouts of incapacitating prostration. Hall records how Pound suddenly reacted after having told in company an inoffensive story about Bernard Berenson commenting on his own Jewishness: "I saw him crumple again. Now it was not fatigue. He passed his hand over his mouth and his eyes, his face abject: misery, shame, guilt. 'Oh,' he moaned, 'How did we get on the subject of race?' " (167). The less drastic and uncontrolled nature of Pound's reaction here is clearly connected to the voluntary and deliberate nature of the self-criticism and probably also shows, not just the sincerity of his criticism of his own antisemitic attitudes but also that his antisemitism was not the root cause of his rantings of the late 1930s but a symptom of the cause.

As this incident shows, some part of what Pound had to face could be faced and dealt with not only voluntarily and consciously but even verbally; yet this would not continue to be the case for long. For someone as sensitive and of such instinctive moral integrity as Pound, the full confrontation of such sustained self-delusion was bound to be overwhelmingly severe. As Hall's account reveals, Pound's response was remorse and self-accusation of such a thoroughgoing kind that they manifested themselves not just in the form of depression of mood but also, and in an extreme way, in psychosomatic states.

Even in March 1960, Pound could sense the implications of his bouts of catalepsy. After the one that followed his revived sense of the value of his *Drafts and Fragments,* he said, "The question is . . . whether to live or die," and then, after a long pause, "There can be such—communication—in silence" (160–61). This clearly shows that, at least to some extent, the descent into habitual silence which he would shortly make was chosen and not inadvertent. Pound was aware of this impending descent with the kind of prescience which belongs to people in whom access to their own unconscious—both its positive and negative drives—is particularly immediate. His most important "choices"—his creative decisions, aesthetic judgments, and exculpation of Mussolini—had been ones which relied heavily on unconscious impulses, and the choice of silence was also of this kind. Even when the symptoms of physical arrestation were not under his conscious control, the available evidence suggests that he still exercised the choice of accepting them.

Critics who want to insist that the rantings of the radio speeches are the voice of the essential Pound are also likely to insist that the expressions of self-accusation and remorse of the closing years of his life should not be taken seriously. The view that "the *Cantos* belong in those shops that sell swastikas and recordings of Mussolini's speeches, for they are, among other things, the sacred poem of the Nazi-Fascist millennium" leads naturally to the contention that Pound's late self-disparagements are "little but the expression of senile depression."[14] The attempt to dismiss the real anguish of a purgatorial state of mind as no more than mindless and so essentially painless senility shows not only the extent of presumptuousness and lack of sensibility that the desire to substantiate a preconceived notion can lead to but shows also a failure to review the available evidence.

From March 11 to April 16, 1966, Pound stayed at the Clinica Delle Malattie Nervose e Mentali of the University of Genoa, where he underwent thorough physical, neurological, and psychiatric examinations. The clinical report on his condition at that time and on the course of its development since 1959 is an invaluable aid toward gaining some insight into his state of mind during the time of his silence. The problems of most immediate concern between 1960 and 1963 had been a refusal to eat and urinary and prostate infections. In the summers of 1960 and 1961 Pound had spent some time in the clinic at Martinsbrunn outside Merano. In 1961 he was treated there for a urinary infection, but physically as well as psychologically he continued to be in distress and by late 1961 it was obvious that Olga Rudge knew best how to care for him. From then on he lived with her, either in Sant' Ambrogio (during the summers) or in Venice (from September to June.) In June 1962, his prostate problem was treated with partial surgery, a suprapubic cystostomy, and the following year a total prostatectomy was performed. This information is particularly relevant to an analysis of his mental confusion since one of the symptoms of the latter was a persistent hypochondriacal delusion. The clinical report notes that "he spoke of body impurity, and of closed and infected bowels" and would claim, "I am covered with microbes." The psychiatrist, basing his conclusion upon "the rigidity of the belief, the precision of the details, and the liveliness of the psychic representation," considered this state of mind to go beyond "phobic fear" and to constitute a "true delusion."[15]

In Pound's thinking on this issue we find a similar pattern to that of his thinking at the time of the radio speeches. In both instances we see an obsessive conviction, having some contact with actual circumstances but distorted into a genuine delusion because of the autistic characteristics of his personality. The psychiatrist notes how radical a change of attitude has occurred now that "quietness, withdrawal and detachment" have replaced his earlier state, in which the "unstable, aggressive and hypercompensated traits of his personality . . . converg[ed] to create a bold and confident mood [which was, however, only] feebly rooted in the actual reality of his inner experiences." Yet he also observes how, in both moods, the essential determinant is the poet's autistic habit of thought—the tendency "to follow particular inner associations, tending to meet internal needs, in disregard, of objective reality" (1161a).

The crucial issue now concerns the nature of the "inner line of thought" which had such a decisive influence upon Pound's deliberate and involuntary behavior at this time and even over his physical condition. The outward manifestations of its effects were very marked: the poet's silence since the summer of 1961, his frequent refusal to eat, and the increasing extent of his unwillingness or inability to move. Before October 1965, his immobility—albeit increasingly sustained, so that he would on occasion remain completely still for hours—seemed to be at least to some extent under his conscious control. After this time he began to experience "an involuntary difficulty in the initation of movements," even in the midst of an activity (1161c). The neurological report notes how "during an action, as washing or chewing, passing through a door etc., the patient shows sudden arrests with general muscular stiffening. Any attempt to help or force him to complete the action increased the motor arrest with presence of opposition and active negativism" (1161e). Before pursuing the implications of this latter type of behavior and of the fact that "an antiparkinsonian treatment improved only partially this situation," we need to be as precise as possible about the lucidity of Pound's thought at this time and the extent of his self-awareness.

The evidence available in this 1966 report shows that Pound, far from suffering from senile dementia, did not even exhibit the symptoms of a "full-blown depressive picture" other than in his expressions of self-accusation. Several times the report reiterates what a crucial determinant of mood, attitude, and behavior Pound's self-accusation was. "The contents of thought were pathological . . . and ideas of guilt, self accusation and financial preoccupations, as well as excessive fear of organic diseases, became apparent. . . . [t]hought was markedly dominated . . . by themes of self accusation and hypochondriacal delusions were always present . . . [and] could probably account for the refusal of food."

The report also reveals that the nature of Pound's delusion, far from freeing him from the mental anguish of self-confrontation, in fact aggravated this anguish. For the most part Pound seems to have continued to think lucidly behind the wall of his silence so that his line of thought was either rational or, to the extent that it involved self-accusation, consistent within the terms dictated by his delusion. The psychiatrist noted that Pound's memory was "lively; regarding both retention and recalling. Nor could there be observed troubles in space and time orientation or specific intellectual defects" (d). Pound was prepared to break his silence for the psychiatrist, but only minimally, usually "uttering only a few words when questioned, "so that "verbal expression was poor, inadequate and delayed, with frequent 'talking past the point'" (b, a). The doctor was well aware, however, that the "retardation of verbal expression was certainly not paralleled by an analogous slowing of thought" (c). When questioned, Pound often answered "very thoughtfully" (a), and although when addressed he initially looked "perplexed" and answered only after "a marked delay," his actual answers tended to be "correct and coherent" (c). On some occasions, "a sharp answer, a pertinent observation, a precise and competent recall [attested] to a certain degree of concealed liveliness of thought," and sometimes, "the precision and correctness of his answers were astonishing" (b, c).

At the same time, there were many hints that behind the silence and the brief answers was a turmoil of mental activity. Pound frequently "talked past the point" and seemed to be involved in an "inner elaboration . . . out of proportion to the questions," so that his thinking tended to the "hyperinclusive . . . following inner pathways without contact with . . . reality (a, c). The psychiatrist's intimations about the presence of inner mental" turmoil were strong enough to encourage him to venture: "It could not be ruled out that even when the patient was silent a scarcely coherent pressure of thinking was present overwhelming everything in an expansive disorder" (c, d). This hypothesis was supported by instances when Pound's speech became "pressing and continuous accompanied by a chaotic graphic activity represented by several disordered letters" (d).

The most crucial question concerns the extent and nature of the "expansive disorder." The persistent self-accusation recorded by the psychiatrist, together with comments that Pound made on other occasions, strongly suggest that he was not merely suffering from a numbling bewilderment and disorientation from being plunged into mental chaos. His state of mind seems to have been considerably more focused and more painful than that, not just bewildered or even frightened by mental confusion but frequently wracked by feelings of worthlessness and guilt. We have seen how Omar Pound wrote in December 1960 of Pound's feeling that he had "failed the world," and on October 1, 1961, we find Dorothy Pound writing to Dr. Overholser that "Ezra . . . has this 'complex' that he has done so many 'bad' things."[16] She goes on to dismiss this "complex" as "a most unnecessary worry," but of course it was not; it was exactly the reaction that Pound was bound to have once he ceased repressing his unconscious awareness of the intensity and extent of his previous self-delusion.

In Pound's state of mind after his return to Italy, we see operative the same mental forces that he had exercised at the time of the Rome Radio broadcasts, but now, just as intense as before, they were enlisted in the service of self-confrontation rather than self-delusion. Now the inventiveness of his imagination, the acuteness of his sensitivity, and the intensity of his moral earnestness which before had given such substance to his projections of a usurers' conspiracy, magnified and made hideous his conviction of his own guilt. When he called the *Cantos* a "botch"[17] and insisted to Allen Ginsberg that his writing was "stupidity and ignorance all the way through,"[18] this was less a comment about his poetry than about himself. He was not just saying that his poetry was worthless but that he himself was: "Everything that I touch, I spoil. I have blundered always," he said to Grazia Livi[19] and to Ginsberg, "anything I've done has been an accident. Any good has been spoiled by my intentions, the preoccupation with irrelevant and stupid things. But the worst mistake I made was that stupid, suburban prejudice of anti-Semitism. All along, that spoiled everything." His parting comment to Ginsberg was "I should have been able to do better."

Consciously, Pound was not able to analyze the exact reasons for his recourse to antisemitism—to see, for example, it was not itself his "worst mistake" but rather the symptom of this mistake. Yet unconsciously he seems to have intuited the most important things about his antisemitism. He understood the need to deplore it without qualification or extenuation. He registered the scope of its power to distort his perception with his realization that "it spoiled everything," and even his description of it as a "stupid, suburban prejudice" is exactly accurate. Far from minimizing its gravity, to call antisemitism a suburban prejudice is to recognize those very qualities which make it so potentially lethal: its ubiquity among "ordinary," "normal" and "respectable" people. To think of antisemitism in this way is to be reminded, for example, that, had it not first existed as a "suburban prejudice" in Germany, there would have been no death camps.

It was so disproportionately painful an experience for Pound at this time to have the unconscious riding so near the surface of consciousness that it is something of a relief to be reminded that he did have at least some access to positive unconscious convictions, even if they were most often eclipsed by his exaggerated feelings of guilt and worthlessness. As in Pisa and at St. Elizabeths, so still, memories of people, events, and achievements of his London and Paris years and before provided for him a body of evidence that there had in fact been more to his life than guilt and failure. In his last years, although he was no longer consciously able, as he had been at Pisa, to avail himself much of the reassurance that these memories could provide, their unconscious presence was enough to keep him from suicidal despair. His comments on other writers were often lucid and incisive, even though his sense of his own worthlessness made him inclined to deny or disparage the value of his own writing. The 1966 clinical report, for example, records that "Mr. Pound gave precise and competent judgement in the literary fields (for example about Dante and Eliot), even though he read his own poems almost automatically and showing lack of participation" (1161d). We see further evidence of his desire to distance himself from his own writing in his decision at the Spoleto Festival of 1965 to read poems by Marianne Moore and Robert Lowell but none of his own.

While Pound's expressions of doubt about the value of his work were sincere, his impulse to denigrate it was, nevertheless, secondary and was primarily the consequence of his impulse to denigrate himself. This meant that he was capable of being reassured, at least to some extent, when other great artists volunteered that they valued his work and had been helped by it. On August 31, 1959, Pound writes to Eliot from Rapallo:

This is the second time (once for 15 minutes) in 2 months have been able to write a whole page.
    sit up and
                        alzo got to files for 1933.
Favourable light on yr kerraKter and intelligence gleams from same.
        I fergit if YOUR letters, touching reality have been pubd/
        edited?   [EPA]

On September 3, Eliot writes back, unsure of the significance of Pound's comments, both about the letters and about Pound's own state: "When you say that you have only been able to sit up twice and write a whole page in two months, does it mean that you have been ill?" (EPA). Pound's reply immediately makes clear to Eliot that his friend needs, and is obliquely asking for, reassurance:

Sitting in my ruins, and heaven comes down like a net
                            and all my past follies.
BUT the quality of yr/ EPistolary style as from Cambridge, Mass.

in '33 wd/ revi[v]e even yr. benevolence toward yrself if to nowt
else.

 not as I am urging you to PRINT it.   [EPA, 9/15/59]

Eliot responds on October 31 with a cablegram, part of which, "decoded" from the strange hybrid part-German, part-Italian English into which the Tyrolean clerk has rendered it, reads: "Your letter received I never forget my own great debt to you to whom all living poets indebted stop your criticism has always been immensely helpful stop Your own achievement epoch-making . . . will write as soon as possible love/ Possum." This gesture of reassurance and affection greatly improved Pound's spirits. Similarly, when Donald Hall informed Pound that Henry Moore had "taken comfort" from Pound's insistence in *Gaudier-Brzeska* that carving direct in stone was superior to modeling, Pound was "moved almost to tears," and finally said, "There is no doubt—that I have been some use—to some people" (138). When Allen Ginsberg, visiting Pound in Venice in October 1967, reported to Pound how Williams had said to him in 1961, "Pound has a mystical ear," Ginsberg tells how Pound "looked away, smiling, pleased," even though, throughout the rest of their meeting, Pound responded either with silence or emphatic self-criticism.[20] It seems most likely that it was in this same spirit that Pound responded to Daniel Cory's reminder, after Pound had repeated "I botched it," that "a man's judgement of his own work did not necessarily coincide with the verdict of posterity." When Cory mentioned Keats "spitting blood all over the Piazza di Spagna and telling Severn to have graved on his headstone: *Here lies one whose name was writ in water,*" Pound "looked up and gave a sort of half-chuckle" (39).

 Contrary to the impression often given by critics who quote from Pound's late interviews, there continued to be more to his sense of himself than inert despair. The March 1963 interview by Grazia Livi is frequently quoted from to "prove" that Pound had succumbed to blank hopelessness and mental torpor. To this end, Heymann, for example, offers as a representative selection of Pound's comments on this occasion, the following:

I have lived all my life believing that I knew something. And then a strange day came and I realized that I knew nothing, that I knew nothing at all. And so words have become empty of meaning. . . . It is something I have come to through suffering. Yes, through an experience of suffering. . . . I have come too late to a state of total uncertainty, where I am conscious only of doubt. . . . I do not work any more. I do nothing. I fall into lethargy, and I contemplate. . . . Everything that I touch, I spoil. I have blundered always.[*Ezra Pound*, p. 276]

Accurate in recording Pound's self-doubt, this ceases to be accurate to the extent that it implies that, in this interview, Pound shows nothing more than self-doubt. As Donald Hall notes, Pound's responses show that he had not given up hope "if not for himself, then for others' minds and spirits engaged in the endeavors he had undertaken" (184). For here Pound had asserted: "I believe that there is something germinal in humanity which can survive mechanization. Finally, I believe that a part of human consciousness will remain, in spite of everything, and will be capable of struggling against the forces of subconsciousness" (222).

When Livi said she had hoped that old age could bring both a clarity of insight and also peace and beauty, Pound responded, "Yes, it can bring peace. The cosmos is so marvellous," and he repeated the point that he had made in Hall's *Paris Review* interview about the importance to a young poet of sustaining a sense of curiosity (223–24).

Pound was sincere in saying that he had arrived at the realization that he knew nothing, but he was moved, we should note, to add, "The greatest fools are those who believe that they know something. I, on the other hand, know that I know nothing" (223). When he says that he arrived "too late" at a state of doubt and Livi asks what different direction he would have taken in his life had he felt this doubt earlier, his answer suggests that the problem lay not with having chosen the wrong direction or goals but in having failed to understand the right way to pursue his goals. He answers, "I would have avoided many errors. I had good intentions which I did not know how to actualize. I was stupid . . . [I was looking through] the wrong end of the telescope. Awareness came too late" (223).

To read this whole interview is to be well aware that, as Hall points out, Pound has not been reduced to a condition of "senile dementia." He refers to himself, for example, as "a man who is capable of becoming [still] more aware of his errors" (223). He is frequently overwhelmed by lethargy and often finds it impossible to fit words to his thoughts, but the thoughts do not stand still. When Livi asks if the lethargy he has complained of is sadness or "simply detachment, absence of thought," although he first replies, "I do not think. I have only the certainty of my very great incertitude," he follows this with a response which makes it clear that he has neither stopped thinking nor become resigned to the progressive deterioration of his power to articulate his thoughts. He concludes the interview: "I have lost the power to get to the bottom of my thought with words. I would like to be able to explain: I . . . I . . . Ah, but everything is so difficult, everything is so useless" (224).

To be reminded of positive literary associations from the past was sometimes to be able to make contact with a source of energy within himself which could act as a counterforce to the despondency that drew him toward immobility and silence. Olga Rudge was well aware of this and was endlessly resourceful in finding ways to stimulate his interest and keep him physically active. Learning that Dorothy Pound had declined, on her husband's behalf, his invitation to attend the memorial service for Eliot in Westminster Abbey, Olga Rudge herself made the arrangements that would make it possible for Pound to attend. They traveled to England by plane and, accompanied by her brother Edward, who assumed the role of "attending physician" for the occasion, they were seated in the choir stalls among the distinguished guests. After a two-day stay in London, during which he visited Valerie Eliot, Pound went on to Dublin, where he visited Yeats's widow, and this was only the first of several trips which he made in 1965. In July he attended the Spoleto Festival; he also traveled to Paris, where he spent some time with Natalie Barney and then, because of an eightieth birthday present from a friend, was finally able to travel to Greece and visit Delphi.

Yet this year of fairly normal physical activity was followed by the period of increasingly incapacitating arrestation of movement that led to his stay in March and April at the clinic at Genoa, the results of which are summed up in the report's concluding sentence: "General somatic condition clearly improved; the psychic situation remained almost unmodified" (1161e). The following year, after Ginsberg's visit in late October, Pound traveled to Zurich, where he visited Joyce's grave. In 1968 he referred to this visit in an interview filmed for Italian television—the last interview he gave. Here Pound recalled: "I visited the tomb of Joyce in Zurich last winter: A tomb without flowers, among others decorated with Christmas trees and wreaths with little candles, as is the custom there; the names of Joyce and Nora nearly illegible on a stone hidden in the grass." Like the *Paris Review* piece, this interview, as David Anderson explains, arrived at its final form only as the result of a good deal of prearrangement.[21] Pound not only had copies of the questions several days in advance but also prepared his answers, translated them into Italian, and had Olga Rudge write them onto large cards from which he could read them off from a distance during the interview.

Carefully set up by arrangement with his interviewer Vanni Ronsis-valle to eliminate any need for extemporaneous commentary by Pound, the interview, on the last day of filming, departed from its format after all. Stepping in at the last minute for Ronsisvalle—Olga Rudge suspected by prearrangement—Pasolini added to the official list questions of his own for which Pound had no prepared answers. Pound's spontaneous responses to these are among the most interesting parts of the interview and, in addition, show how, even at this late stage, he was capable of thinking lucidly, judiciously, and even wittily. At one point, Pasolini is examining the effect of the industrialization of Italian culture on the nature of avant-garde writing in Italy. He states, "[T]he elements that make up *The Cantos* . . . are innumerable, but . . . can be reduced to a small space at the bottom of a well, where you work over your life—one of these elements is Italy." In the course of working up to his question he observes, "At this moment, Italy is one of the regions that are industrialized, and therefore culturally advanced, and that express a . . . literature . . . typical of highly bourgeois, industrialized nations." Before attempting a reply, Pound calls him on this: "You say 'nations that are industrialized and *therefore* culturally advanced.' It is your 'therefore' that I can not agree with." When Pasolini asks if he is pleased to find his name invoked by some of the current Italian avant-garde writers, and if there is a basis for connecting Pound's work with theirs, Pound rejoins, with dry wit, "If your thesis that Old Ez is at the bottom a dark well ruminating on his years gone by is correct—I don't think so, but it may be that you are right—I would not be in a position that would allow me to see clearly into what happens outside, in the light of the world of the neo-avantgardistes, who, I hope, will understand and forgive Old Ez, *che non li può vedere*." The response is doubly witty in that the punch line—literally, "who cannot see them"—means idiomatically, "who cannot stand them."[22]

The most telling of Pound's comments occurs in a discussion of the problem of unity in *The Cantos*. When Pasolini reads out, "Under white clouds, cielo di Pisa / out of all this beauty something must come," Pound's immediate response is "Those are good lines," but he is quick to insist also that the good lines in his work are only "pebbles" which he has not been able to unify into a "cosmos." He continues, doggedly, to insist upon this point, overriding Pasolini's rather fulsome commentary and next two questions, but he has been following Pasolini's argument also, as he shows when he loops back to respond to a point raised earlier. Pasolini had said, "You say that your poetry is made of things intelligent people say to one another. Surely [these] things . . . follow a rather casual curve. In fact, they come at random." After Pound interrupts him to pursue his contention that he has failed to make the good passages cohere, Pasolini resumes, "Do you think this randomness allows beauty to be born from other beauty, almost spontaneously?" Pound cuts in twice more with comments about his failure to impose a unity but finally picks up the interviewer's earlier point with

"Chosen at random." Pasolini, now on another topic, has forgotten his suggestions about the acceptability of randomness—"Chosen at random? What? The critics or the quotations." Pound's response is unequivocal: "They say they are chosen at random, but that's not the way it is. It's music. Musical themes that [find each other out]."

At his most despondent, however, Pound's self-accusation could be devastating. His conviction that he had been guilty of grave errors could give him a sense of worthlessness that made him feel very vulnerable. He was entirely sincere when he wrote, "Let those I love try to forgive / what I have made," and he added to his other grounds for guilt the idea that, in his incapacitated state, he was burdening those who were taking care of him. One of the saddest glimpses we have of him is provided by James Laughlin in his reminiscence of an incident that occurred when he and his wife were driving Pound back to Connecticut from Hamilton College, where Pound had been a guest at the conferring of Laughlin's honorary degree. They had stopped at a Howard Johnson's restaurant, where Ann Laughlin had managed to persuade Pound to get some apple pie and milk. Laughlin explains how resistant to eating Pound continued to be and how, when he would eat, he made a point of always ordering the least expensive thing on the menu. As they were leaving the restaurant, Pound was suddenly missing. They spotted him walking off, in the dark, into a wood and when Laughlin caught up with him and asked him where he was going, Pound replied, "Why don't you discard me here and then I won't be any more trouble to people."[23]

In the last year of Pound's life, on February 5, 1972, Marianne Moore died. When her literary executor telephoned Pound in Venice to inform him of her death, Pound immediately contacted Father Stanley, pastor of Saint George's, the Protestant church at San Vio, to arrange a memorial service and the English language newspaper in Venice to have it carry an announcement of the service. Pound had been responsible for the publication, in 1921, by the Egoist Limited, of Moore's first book, *Poems*. He had suggested to Harriet Weaver that these poems were more worthy of being published by her than his own articles on early translators of Homer and Aeschylus, for which Weaver's projected booklet had been intended (*Life*, 219). Although Pound and Moore corresponded with each other over the years, they did not actually meet until his visit to New York in May 1939. Up until then, Moore had existed for him "through the written word"— mediated by her poetry and her letters.

The timing of Moore's first visit to Pound in St. Elizabeths in July 1947 amounted to a profound tribute to him. She had written to him shortly after his arrival there but had been unable to visit him because her mother's final illness required her constant attention. Her mother died on July 9 and Moore drove to Gettysburg with her brother to carry the ashes to the Evergreen Cemetery. From Gettysburg they drove immediately to St. Elizabeths to see Pound. After the visit she wrote to thank Pound, on her own and her brother's behalf, for the comfort that he had given them in their mourning—for "the anomaly of bounty despite captivity," which, she wrote, "did them a great deal of good."[24] In his note of acknowledgment on July 21, Pound praises her own courage, pronouncing her worthy of a "Special award of valor."[25]

On the morning of Tuesday, February 8, Marianne Moore's funeral service was conducted in Brooklyn. That same morning, but several hours earlier—because in Venice—her death had been commemorated in Saint George's Church, San Vio, where Pound had read her poem "What Are Years?" Intended by Pound as a tribute both to Moore's poetic gift and to her own courage, this poem and Pound's decision to read it on this occasion remind us of several other things. We think of the circumstances of the publication of Moore's first book of poems, of Pound's disinterested encouragement of other poets and artists at the time when they were still unknown, of his lack of egotism, and of the mental astuteness that persisted alongside the self-excoriation until the very end of his life. In a note on "What Are Years?" Moore had explained: "The desperation attendant on moral fallibility is mitigated for me by admitting that the most willed and resolute vigilance may lapse, as with the Apostle Peter's denial that he could be capable of denial; but that failure, disgrace, and even death have now and again been redeemed into inviolateness by a sufficiently transfigured courage."[26]

As Pound's last years show, he had taken to heart Elektra's admonition—"Shall we to all our ills add cowardice?"—and had shown "whence / is courage." Pound died in his sleep on November 1, 1972, and his funeral service, on November 3, was conducted in the Benedictine Abbey on the island of San Giorgio Maggiore by the abbot, the Reverend P. Egidio Zaramella and the Reverend Canon V. Stanley. On the day between his death and his funeral, Lotte Frumi, an artist, had sat with the body and made a sketch of Pound's head. Eight years after his death she spoke emphatically of her admiration of him and her devotion to him. After she had left, Olga Rudge mentioned to me that Lotte Frumi was Jewish and that her parents had been murdered by the Nazis during the Holocaust. For Frumi it was the courage and not the antisemitism which characterized the real Pound.

Afterword

This study of Pound's wartime behavior appears at a time of new resolve to explore long-neglected evidence of the extent and nature of all kinds of collaborationist activity during World War II. Any thorough consideration of collaboration must take into account not only entirely voluntary participation but also the complicity of military personnel acting under orders, civilians engaged in criminal activity under military auspices, those who expressed their support for nazism and Fascist oppression, and even all those collaborators-by-default whose silence and failure to act facilitated Nazi murder and genocide. It is no coincidence that this reexamination of the case of Pound should be appearing at this time, since the same impediments to the close examination of the ramifications of collaborationism which have kept them from being discussed in the United States, Germany, Austria, France, and the iron curtain countries (for somewhat different reasons in different countries) have been a deterrent to any full-scale investigation of the case of Pound. Recently the issue of the accountability of the Nazi functionary has been impressed upon the public consciousness by the case of Kurt Waldheim. Similarly, the academic community has been confronted with the issue of the collaborationist-intellectual as a consequence of closer examination of Heidegger's unrecanted nazism and of the revelation of Paul de Man's journalism for Fascist periodicals in his youth. Yet these are only the more sensationalist evidence of a growing concern that the issues of collaborationist accountability that have been largely evaded for so many years now be addressed and their implications examined.

To establish the factual evidence of collaboration is a straightforward even if time-consuming process, but systematic examination of the psychological and moral implications of collaboration is a far more complex and uncertain task, one for which postwar philosophy and psychoanalytic theory have generally provided little help. Investigation of collaborationist behavior can be primarily concerned with passing judgment (assessing accountability in individual cases) or with arriving at a general, theoretical understanding of those psychological strategies which either encourage normal individuals to become complicit, at no matter how many removes, in acts that are clearly criminal, or allow them to rationalize or repress knowledge of their complicity. As the summary nature of the response of most people to Pound's wartime activities shows, we are not yet very practiced in making the kind of close and systematic analysis of the particular case that will consider the exact nature of the individual's intentions, the moral choices made and their consequences. A common alternate recourse is to settle for a priori judgments or polemical denunciations. Even Sartre in his *Anti-Semite and Jew* fundamentally misrepresents the nature of antisemitism by implying throughout that the antisemite is a very different kind of creature from the author and his like-minded readers—that antisemites are always "them" and never "us." He is even prepared to deny the facts for the sake of making a Marxist point with his completely unfounded claim that among workers we find "scarcely any anti-Semitism."

For a long time after the war there was great ambivalence about examining the facts of collaboration and their implications. The immediate postwar period saw charges brought against the more obvious war criminals, yet even by the time of the 1948 Nuremberg Subsequent Proceedings Trials, public interest was minimal and there would be little subsequent enthusiasm for searching investigations of collaborationist guilt or for demands of reparations for surviving victims. Many considerations contributed to this: a desire to be done with the war and return to normal life; considerable antisemitism now aggravated by a tendency to "blame the victim"; the diplomatic, cold war consideration of the United States' need to keep Germany as an ally; the interests of the international business community, which made any thoroughgoing investigation of the involvements of German business in crimes against humanity financially "inexpedient."

In his *Quiet Neighbors*, Allan Ryan shows, for example, how the Displaced Persons Act of 1948 was specifically designed by the United States Congress to exclude as many Jewish concentration camp survivors as possible and to give preferential status to groups known to include many

Nazi war criminals, more than 8,000 of whom he estimates were admitted under this act. Only the most nominal attempt was made at the time to screen out such people and it was not until 1979, with the Justice Department's establishment of the Office of Special Investigations, that the government made any commitment to bring these Nazi functionaries to trial.

Not until the late-1970s would we see—signaled by the concerted efforts of historians, archivists, and the compilers of oral testimonies—a widespread resolve to discover and preserve as many details as possible of all aspects of Nazi genocide. Part of the delay was attributable to the time that was necessary to collect detailed evidence of the historical record. By 1985, for example, we would have Raul Hilberg's masterly, three-volume edition of *The Destruction of the European Jews*. Now also, important lacunae in the very incomplete record of collaborationist activity began to be filled in. The culpability of German businessmen who profited from slave labor was examined in such works as Joseph Borkin's *The Crime and Punishment of I. G. Farben* and Benjamin Ferencz's *Less Than Slaves;* that of German scientists in Robert Lifton's *The Nazi Doctors* and Tom Bower's *The Paperclip Conspiracy*. The collaboration of the French was investigated in *Vichy France and the Jews* by Michael Marrus and Robert Paxton. Works such as Walter Laqueur's *The Terrible Secret* and David Wyman's *The Abandonment of the Jews* have encouraged serious discussion of the implications of the failure of the politicians and religious leaders of the Allied countries to take action upon the information they were receiving about the Final Solution.

One reason for a proliferation of such studies at this time is the arrival at scholarly and artistic maturity of the war's-end generation—those who were children during the war or born shortly afterward. It was likely that this generation would examine the wartime record with a sense of immediacy, even of intense fascination, and yet from a vantage point which made possible a more overarching view of the war as a whole than that available to their parents. For members of this generation the war could seem paradoxically both close and distanced. In particular, they were free, in a way in which their parents were not, to conceive of the Nazi era as a discrete period of history. For their parents' generation the war years were, most immediately, "these years as they had lived them"—a gradual unfolding or an incremental accumulation of day-by-day experience. For the children of these parents, this period could be very immediate to the imagination because of their parents' involvement, yet with an objectivity not complicated by the fact of responsible participation.

My own experience also suggests that, for some children at least of this war's-end generation, what they knew of nazism and the Holocaust could well be the most dominant influence upon their imaginative life, providing the almost obsessively recurring context for all their thinking about human nature and the nature of evil. Images from documentary films of the concentration camps became part of the indelible iconography of one's childhood fears of death. That Sylvia Plath, for example, experienced this reaction is testified to eloquently by her poem "The Thin People." For the reflective adolescent, all revelations about the Nazi ascendancy tended to lead to a kind of speculation about moral choice and moral accountability that could become habitual.

Confrontation with documentary evidence of the Holocaust was likely to be a less problematic and troubling experience for a member of the war's-end generation in Britain or the United States than for a contemporary in Germany, France, or an iron curtain country. For a Gentile in Britain or the United States, the most important "message" of the war was that nazism had been defeated. America's wartime role overseas and Britain's role both at home and abroad could be seen as validating optimism, stoicism, and the appropriateness of resistance and interventionism and as an argument against defeatism, capitulation, and nihilism. Intellectuals of the war's-end generation in these countries might well be less disposed to adopt a deterministic or fatalistic world view or, because the whole topic of the Holocaust was so painful, to avoid a systematic analysis of it. That a country's wartime role would influence in a general way the postwar attitudes of its people and that these general attitudes would consequently vary dramatically from country to country was obvious enough. Yet surprisingly little attention has been given to the full extent of the ramifications of these attitudes, especially upon intellectual trends and predispositions.

Claude Lanzmann's film *Shoah* is unequaled in the power with which it evokes the horror and the particularity of what the Holocaust had been to its victims. It is also an exemplary and groundbreaking text in the compelling way in which, pointing beyond the need to complete the historical record, it insists also upon the need to address as fully as possible the issues of moral choice and moral accountability raised by the Holocaust. During the postwar period such fundamental moral issues have far more often been addressed in the arts than in philosophical or psychological writings. Psychoanalytic theory as a science of human behavior has essentially limited itself to description of behavior in the context of cause and effect rather than focusing upon the phenomenon of moral choice and moral accountability. A succinct general review of this tendency can be found in E. Mansell

Pattison's "The Holocaust as Sin" in *Psychoanalytic Reflections on the Holocaust* (ed. Steven Luell and Paul Marcus).

The more committed psychological or philosophical inquiry is to a scientific, programmatic, and hence generalizing approach, the more bound it is by the need to be faithful to the system which it has erected or inherited, and consequently the less adapted it is to the investigation of issues of moral choice. This is inevitably so since particulars must always take precedence over generalizations when the focus of inquiry is the unique configuration of the details of the individual case. For both philosophers and psychologists in the Freudian tradition, the primary direction of attention is likely to be away from the moment of individual moral choice in the present. The Freudian psychoanalyst is constantly looking backward toward the patient's childhood complexes and circumstances, and then even further back to Freud's own theoretical formulations. The philosopher's observations are made with constant reference to the tradition of Western philosophical thought, either building upon, modifying, or dismantling previous philosophical positions and hypotheses.

In this context, it is instructive to consider the way in which, in postwar French intellectual circles, the strong antihumanist orientation of structuralist and poststructuralist theorizing has problematized and even, in some cases, proscribed the discussion of issues of moral choice and moral accountability. In philosophical, psychological, and literary critical contexts equally, the concepts of the integrity of the self and of individual identity and the belief in the efficacy, even of the possibility of self-awareness, suffer constant attrition. We see this in the fatalism of the Heideggerean preoccupation with "being-toward-death"; the Saussurean diminishing of the authority or authoritativeness of the subject—its disempowering as originator of or locus of meaning; the "death of the author" at the hands of Michel Foucault and Roland Barthes; Lacan's affinity for the Heideggerean notion of consciousness as self-extirpating and his view of recourse to the symbol as the "murder" of the thing. Significantly, disempowerment is presented here not as the consequence of outside threat but as an inherent condition. It is as though the threat from outside has become internalized and is conceptualized not as something inflicted but as a property of the self.

Structuralists and poststructuralists do not invite the reader to consider the extent to which an antihumanist position may be a response, either intentional or inadvert, to revelations of Nazi brutality and depravity. Yet as the Holocaust increasingly becomes the subject of more unconstrained and searching reflection, it seems likely that at least some postwar intellectual trends will be reconsidered in this light. Lacan's decision, for example, to place his work "in direct opposition to the ideological bias toward life, toward being, toward the flowing of an essential humanity"[1] invites this kind of speculation. That the horrifying spectacle of nazism in its ascendancy might appear to some to validate fatalism and invite an impatient rejection of humanistic "pieties" is understandable enough. We note, however, that the antihumanist response is not necessarily the inevitable one or the one that comes from having confronted the enormity of the Holocaust most directly. In *Shoah,* for example, Filip Müller, a Jew who worked in the crematoria of Auschwitz for three years, says, "Every day we saw thousands and thousands of innocent people disappear up the chimney. With our own eyes, we could truly fathom what it means to be a human being. There they came, men, women, children, all innocent. . . . But the situation taught us fully what the possibility of survival meant. For we could gauge the infinite value of human life."[2]

In the writings of postwar theorists, such matters as the problematization of the concept of the self, delegitimization of the concept of essence, and privileging of the principle of difference over the principle of identity are addressed only as textual issues, within the context of philosophical, psychological, and literary critical inquiry. When Derrida, for example, privileges difference (and *différance*) over identity, his conscious intention is to employ an exploratory and expansive strategy, a way of breaking free from traditional, constricting, predetermined ways of conceptualizing and of experimentally opening up new perspectives. Yet it is possible also to see the ways of conceptualizing he has chosen as an instinctive response to the fate of the Jews under nazism—as an unspoken protest, a gesture of resistance, even as an attempt at recuperation.

On the one hand we have Derrida's rejection of attempts to designate a self and his determined commitment to a way of thinking which insists upon a proliferation of differences so fertile as to exceed the power of the intellect to adequately identify, enumerate, or name, and so to control. On the other hand we have the Nazi commitment to a crudely reductive definition of difference which becomes, for the European Jew, a de facto obliteration of difference in the sense of "the particularity of unique individuality." According to the Nazis' lethal system of classification, all possible kinds of differentiation were subsumed by the two mutually exclusive identifications: "Gentile—potentially worthy of life," "non-Gentile—not worthy of life." For the Jew, the self was erased as an authentic and unique identity and was replaced beyond possibility of appeal by the generic and lethal designation: "non-Gentile," a classification intended to erase all other characteristics, all individualizing traits, theoretically the humanness, and in actuality the existence of every individual within that group.

When, as here, the self as locus of identification has been seen to be the ultimate threat, the will to remove the self from the realm of labeling and identification altogether is an understandable response. Something of this impulse would seem to lie behind the endlessly inventive and sophisticated maneuverings of Derrida, for whom, it appears, the sine qua non is to be able always to slip through the net of definition. His Protean strategy of argumentation and "definition" constantly acts to subvert the possibility of adequate or reliable identification, to offer the greatest possible protection against being categorized or characterized. Eschewing both idealism and fatalism, he is always in the course of moving toward or away from provisional positions of his own. He is constantly modifying, qualifying, multiplying his views; always challenging, contesting, looking for blindspots in the views of others; always swerving away from the "center" and from the concept of self as center; always in flight from the locus of identification.

In *Shoah,* what we see most of all is a return to the center, a call for the imaginative reconstituting of the lost subject, of the essence—the essential humanity of each individual—whose denial was the prerequisite for and facilitator of the annihilation of each individual body. *Shoah* offers an invitation to repeople the absence, and not with the victims as unimaginable statistics, but with the multiplication of individual victims—and individual collaborators and persecutors. The viewer responding to *Shoah* can, by an emotional and imaginative act, reverse the process of the progressive attentuation of the fact of the self, take a stand against the violation of the concept of selfhood, and attempt to reclaim individual selves from the most devastating and determined attempt to deny their selfhood to them. The whole approach of *Shoah*—the nature of the emotional and imaginative participation it requires from the viewer, the presentation of material by means of the accumulation of individual testimonies and scenes of specific locales—continually acts to block the impulse to be drawn to generalization and insists upon attention to the particular, the individual participant—the victim, the perpetrator, the collaborator, the person who made no protest— as individual.

We must turn to the self and the center, also, if we are to take advantage of the greater particularity and specificity of understanding that follows when these issues are examined with reference to the concept of moral choice. To see how rationalization or repression instantly takes over when one acts against or fails to act in accordance with one's conscience and to understand how unerring this rationalization is likely to be, and how tenacious this repression, is to be forewarned and hence potentially safeguarded against them. One is even further safeguarded by understanding that high intelligence and intellectual sophistication offer no guarantee that the individual will be protected against the impulse to rationalize or repress. The highly intelligent may well be less inclined to suspect themselves of self-delusion, and the rationalizations of the intellectually sophisticated are often even more tenacious because more inventive and apparently plausible. To examine immoral or inhumane behavior in the light of an understanding of the dynamics of these psychological strategies is to be able to think about it far more analytically than when it is seen as the consequence of some impulse as general—and hence unanalyzable and uncontrollable—as fear of death.

To pass summary judgment upon Pound is a largely self-indulgent and certainly unproductive gesture. By analyzing and discussing a case such as his, simultaneously paying full attention to its uniqueness and discerning in it general principles, we will go far toward understanding the psychological dynamic of rationalization which was most directly responsible for his wartime behavior. That readers should agree with the conclusions about Pound arrived at in this study is far less important than that they should have considered the evidence presented and reflected upon the issues raised. Above all, there must be discussion, even of those cases that seem most problematic and most unpromising. These will sometimes prove to offer the most valuable insights into those strategies of rationalization and tendencies toward self-delusion which, whether they are relied upon or resisted, are an inescapable fact of the human condition.

Notes

INTRODUCTION

1 Hilton Kramer, "Pound as Critic: More than a Footnote," *New York Times,* Thursday, Jan. 22, 1981.

2 Sacvan Bercovitch, *The American Jeremiad* (Madison: University of Wisconsin Press, 1987), 176, hereafter *AJ.*

3 Walt Whitman, *Democratic Vistas: The Collected Writings of Walt Whitman, Prose Works 1892* (New York: New York University Press, 1963), vol. 2.

4 T. S. Eliot, "A Prediction in Regard to Three Authors," *Vanity Fair,* 21. 6 (Feb. 1924): 29.

5 T. S. Eliot, "A Sceptical Patrician" [review of *The Education of Henry Adams*], *Vanity Fair* (February 1924): 29, 98.

6 C. David Heymann, *Ezra Pound: The Last Rower* (New York: Viking, 1976), 325.

7 *Cantos 14 & 15 of The Cantos.*

8 Nathaniel Hawthorne, "Earth's Holocaust," *The Complete Works of Nathaniel Hawthorne: Mosses From an Old Manse* (Boston: Houghton, Mifflin, 1883), 2: 455.

9 T. S. Eliot, *After Strange Gods* (London: Faber & Faber, 1934), 42.

CHAPTER 1   AN AMERICAN CHILDHOOD

1 Medical Files of Ezra Pound, St. Elizabeths Hospital, item 1381.

2 I, 7.

3 Hilda Doolittle, *End to Torment* (New York: New Directions, 1979), 22.

4 Hilda Doolittle, *Hermione* (New York: New Directions, 1981), 103.

5 *Chippewa County, Wisconsin: Past and Present* (Chicago: S. J. Clarke, 1913 [1914]), 1:421–22.

6 *Ibid.,* p. 422.

7 *Ibid.,* p. 426.

8 Homer Pound Scrapbook, p. 33.
9 *Chippewa County Wisconsin,* p. 412.
10 Ambrose Shotwell, *Annals of Our Colonial Ancestors & their Descendants* (Lansing, Mich.: Robert Smith, 1895–97), 6–8.
11 Gatter Collection, vol. 2, Van Pelt Library, University of Pennsylvania.
12 Letter *EPA,* November 1904.
13 Noel Stock, *Ezra Pound's Pennsylvania* (Toledo, Ohio: Friends of the University of Toledo Libraries, 1976), 14.
14 Gatter Collection, vol. 14.
15 *Ibid.*
16 *Ibid.*
17 Ezra Pound's letters to Mary Moore. Ms. file, Van Pelt Library, University of Pennsylvania; date: "Crawfordsville, 1907."
18 In "Letters to Viola Baxter Jordan," ed. with commentary by Donald Gallup, in *Paideuma* 1. 1 (Spring and Summer 1972): 108 (letter of Oct. 12, 1907).
19 Included in C. David Heymann, *Ezra Pound: The Last Rower* (New York: Viking, 1976), 321.
20 These quotations from newspaper articles by and about Thaddeus Pound are on p. 31 of the Homer Pound Scrapbook.
21 Gorham Munson, *Aladdin's Lamp: The Wealth of the American People* (New York: Creative Age Press, 1945), 129.
22 Munson, p. 132. See also Munson, p. 347: "Kitson never finally embraced any one scheme, and he fell behind in the progress of English monetary thought. In his old age, he was uncritical in accepting the Jewish International Banker myth and gullible about Hitler's promises of financial reform." [Kitson died in 1937.]
23 Ezra Pound, *Impact: Essays on Ignorance and the Decline of American Civilization* (Chicago: Henry Regnery, 1960), 184.

CHAPTER 2   VISIONARY ECONOMICS

1 Philip Mairet, *A. R. Orage: A Memoir* (New York: University Books, 1966), 119.
2 Letter from Orage to Pound, May 14, 1934, *EPA.*
3 *New English Weekly,* Nov. 15, 1934, p. 119; Hereafter *NEW* followed by date of article, as *NEW,* 11/15/34.
4 T. S. Eliot, "A Commentary," *Criterion,* 14 (January 1935): 261, 262, 264.
5 Quoted in Mairet, p. 40.
6 See my *Ezra Pound and* The Cantos: *A Record of Struggle* (New Haven: Yale University Press, 1980), 102–06.
7 *Ibid.,* pp. 62–83.
8 *New Age* 18 (Jan. 27, 1915): 307; hereafter *NA* followed by date of article, as *NA,* 1/27/15.
9 St. Elizabeths Medical File on Ezra Pound, file no. 1381g.
10 See *Ezra Pound and* The Cantos, pp. 11–12.
11 Wallace Martin, *The New Age Under Orage: Chapters in English Cultural History* (Manchester: Manchester University Press, 1967), 128.

12 G. D. H. Cole, *The Second International, 1889–1914* (London: Macmillan, 1956), 244.

13 A. R. Orage, "The Fear of Leisure," in a pamphlet reprint, *"Social Credit" and "The Fear of Leisure"* (Vancouver, B.C.: Institute of Economic Democracy, (1977), 20.

14 *Ibid.*, p. 14.

15 *Commonweal* 3 (Feb. 24, 1926): 435.

16 *Ibid.*, p. 434.

17 For a detailed explanation of the different rates of flow of purchasing power distributed and of prices, see Munson, pp. 144–50.

18 Quoted in James Sterngold, "On Wall Street, A Greedy New Breed," *New York Times*, 7/27/86, p. D24.

19 Ezra Pound, *Impact: Essays on Ignorance and the Decline of American Civilization* (Chicago: Henry Regnery, 1960), 116.

20 See Munson, pp. 76–77.

21 Thomas Jefferson, letter to John W. Eppes, Nov. 6, 1813, in *The Writings of Thomas Jefferson*, ed. H. A. Washington (New York: Derby & Jackson, 1859), 239–40.

22 Thomas Jefferson, letter to William Crawford, June 20, 1816, in *ibid.*, p. 8.

23 Andrew Jackson, Farewell Address of March 4, 1837, quoted in Munson, p. 118.

24 Abraham Lincoln, letter to Colonel E. D. Taylor, Dec. [16?], 1864.

25 Quoted in Munson, p. 123.

26 Abraham Lincoln, letter to William P. Elkin, Nov. 21, 1864.

27 Munson, p. 173.

28 C. H. Douglas, *Social Credit* (New York: Norton, ca. 1933), 207–08.

29 *New York Times Book Review*, Apr. 24, 1983, p. 18.

30 Orage, "Social Credit," p. 11.

31 Orage, "The Fear of Leisure," pp. 25–26.

32 *Ibid.*, pp. 15–16.

33 Jeffrey Mark, *Where is the Money to Come From?* (London: C. W. Daniel, 1938), 25–27.

34 *EPA*, 1936, no day or month given.

35 Munson, pp. 205, 207.

36 Quoted in Munson, pp. 208, 209.

37 James Generoso, "Social Credit, 1918–1945: An Essay and Select Bibliography," UCLA master's thesis, 1981. I am greatly indebted to James Generoso for information on the theory and history of Social Credit.

38 See Lloyd G. Reynolds, "Economics in History: The Poetic Vision of Ezra Pound," *Yale Review*, 3 (Spring 1986): 289.

39 Letter from Douglas to Father Coughlin, Jan. 3, 1936, *EPA*.

40 Paul Mariani, *William Carlos Williams: A New World Naked* (New York: McGraw-Hill, 1981), 298.

41 *Ibid.*, pp. 395–96.

42 Quoted in Munson, p. 374.

43 "The Fear of Leisure," pp. 14–15.

CHAPTER 3   POUND AND MUSSOLINI

1　*New English Weekly,* July 25, 1935, pp. 287–88.

2　Unpublished letter, EPA.

3　*Selected Letters of William Carlos Williams,* ed. John C. Thirlwall (New York: New Directions, 1984), 6: letter from Williams to his mother, Mar. 30, 1904.

4　Benito Mussolini, *The Doctrine of Fascism,* English trans. (Florence: Vallecci Editore, 1936), 45.

5　Denis Mack-Smith, *Mussolini* (New York: Alfred A. Knopf, 1982), 232.

6　*Ibid.,* p. 234.

7　*Ibid.,* p. 238.

8　A. James Gregor, *Italian Fascism and Developmental Dictatorship* (Princeton: Princeton University Press, 1979), 96.

9　Bruno Caizzi, *Storia dell' industria Italiana* (Turin: Unione Tipografico–Editrice Torinese, 1965), 457ff.

10　Rosario Romeo, *Breve storia della grande industria in Italia,* 3d ed. (Rocco San Casciano: Cappelli, 1967).

11　Pound's footnote to p. 136 of *Italy's Policy of Social Economics* (Pound's translation of Odon Por's book), quoted in Noel Stock, *The Life of Ezra Pound* (New York: Random House, 1970), p. 390.

12　Letter from Williams to Pound, May 18, 1938, Williams Collection, Beinecke Library.

13　Letter reproduced, in translation, in C. David Heymann, *Ezra Pound: The Last Rower* (New York: Viking, 1976), 335.

14　Gregor, pp. 237–38.

15　Giovanni Bechelloni, "Fascismo visto da Londra," *Gazetta del Popolo,* 12/15/79."

16　*Ibid.*

17　Unpublished letter from Pellizzi to Pound.

18　Felice Chilanti, "Ezra Pound Among the Seditious in the 1940's," trans. David Anderson, *Paideuma* 6.2 (Fall 1977): 242.

19　*The Ciano Diaries, 1939–1943,* ed. Hugh Gibson (Garden City, N.Y.: Garden City Publishing, 1947), 463.

20　Felice Chilanti, *La paura entusiasmante* (Verona: Mondadori, 1971), 184.

21　Heymann, p. 334.

22　Unpublished letter from Pound to Pellizzi.

23　John P. Diggins, *Mussolini and Fascism: The View from America* (Princeton: Princeton University Press, 1972), p. 59, note.

24　Letter from James Laughlin to the author, Apr. 14, 1983.

25　*Franklin D. Roosevelt: His Personal Letters, 1928–1945,* ed. Elliot Roosevelt (New York: Duell, Sloan & Pearce, 1950), 1:352.

26　Reverend Charles E. Coughlin, *A Series of Lectures on Social Justice* (Royal Oak, Mich.: Radio League of the Little Flower, 1935), 42.

27　Letter to John Buchan, reproduced in *Paideuma* 8.3 (Winter 1979): 477.

28　*Paideuma* 8.3 (Winter 1979): 474.

29　*P/L,* 183.

30　Wyndham Lewis, *Hitler* (London: Chatto & Windus, 1931), 19.

31 *P/L*, 206, 208. Although in this edition the signature to the letter of March 12, on p. 208, is printed "Ez.P," Pound has signed the original 十² P.

32 All the letters of Pound, Eliot, and Williams which follow are in the Beinecke Archive.

33 Romano Bilenchi, "Rapallo, 1941," trans. David Anderson, *Paideuma* 8.3 (Winter 1979): 436–37.

34 *Ibid.*, p. 439.

35 Chilanti, "Ezra Pound Among the Seditious" pp. 235–50.

CHAPTER 4   THE ANTISEMITISM OF THE ROME
RADIO BROADCASTS

1 See "Should Ezra Pound be Shot," *New Masses*, 57 (Dec. 25, 1945): 4–6. Lion Feuchtwanger wrote: "He who regards the aim of justice to be . . . to deter . . . can with the clearest conscience imprison or hang the wrecker-poet." Albert Maltz wrote that "it is *because* Pound is a poet that he should be hanged, not once but twice—for treason, as a citizen, and for his poet's betrayal of all that is decent in human civilization." Norman Rosten wrote: "Because he was a traitor, he should be shot." In "Ludlum Wise, Pound Foolish" (*Village Voice*, 11/17/87:109–10), a review of Carey Perloff's November 1987 production of Pound's translated version of Sophocles' *Elektra*, Michael Feingold wrote, "How wonderful it would have been for civilization if Ezra Pound had been executed for treason in 1945, instead of copping a dubious plea of insanity and moldering in St. Elizabeth's for the next 13 years. We'd have been spared all the silly Pound-adulation . . . his huge final version of the intolerable Cantos and . . . this *Elektra*. . . . You might say [Pound's version of *Elektra*] does for Sophocles what Hitler tried to do for the Jews."

2 "The Psychology of Antisemitism: Conscience-Proof Rationalization and the Deferring of Moral Choice," in *Antisemitism in the Contemporary World*, ed. Michael Curtis (Boulder and London: Westview Press, 1986), 238–50.

3 Hannah Arendt, *Eichmann in Jerusalem* (New York: Viking, 1963), 93, 253.

4 *Ibid.*, pp. 100–01.

5 Heymann, p. 320.

6 Camillo Pellizzi, "Ezra Pound, uomo difficile," *Il Tempo*, 10 (March 20, 1953): 3; translation mine.

7 See my "The Pound Problem," in *Ezra Pound & William Carlos Williams: The University of Pennsylvania Conference Papers*, ed. Daniel Hoffman (Philadelphia: University of Pennsylvania Press, 1983), 107–30.

8 Gatter Collection, Van Pelt Library, University of Pennsylvania.

9 Stock, *Ezra Pound's Pennsylvania* (Toledo, Ohio: Friends of the University of Toledo Libraries, 1976), 33.

10 Ezra Pound, *Patria Mia*, in *Ezra Pound: Selected Prose, 1909–1965* (New York: New Directions, 1973), 104.

11 E. Digby Baltzell, *The Protestant Establishment: Aristocracy and Caste in America* (New York: Random House, 1964), 203.

12 Baltzell, p. 248.

13 George Wolfskill, *The Revolt of the Conservative: A History of the American Liberty League, 1934–1940* (Boston: Houghton Mifflin, 1962), 102.

14 Meir Michaelis, *Mussolini and the Jews: German-Italian Relations and the Jewish Question in Italy, 1922–1945* (Oxford: Clarendon, 1978), 55.

15 Romano Bilenchi, *Amici: Vittorini, Rosai, e altri incontri* (Turin; Einaudi, 1976), 15–25.

16 Translation mine. This section of *Amici* ("Rapallo, 1941") has been translated with notes and an introduction by David Anderson in *Paideuma* 8.3 (Winter 1979): 431–42.

17 James Laughlin, "Ez as Waz," keynote address, Ezra Pound Centennial Colloquium, San Jose State University, Nov. 7, 1985. I am quoting from the tape of the address. A version of this talk has been published as "Ez As Wuz" in *San Jose Studies* 12.3 (1985): 6–28, and in *Pound as Wuz* (Saint Paul, Minn.: Graywolf Press, 1987).

18 William Carlos Williams, *The Autobiography* (New York: New Directions, 1967), 337.

19 Quoted in Mariani, p. 456. Pound did not receive this letter, as it was intercepted and returned to Williams by a postal inspector.

20 Albert Londres, author of *Le Juif Errant Est Arrivé* (Paris: A. Michel, 1930).

21 "Ezra Pound: Letters to John Buchan, 1934–1935," ed. S. Namjoshi, *Paideuma* 8.3 (Winter 1979): 466.

22 Letter to W. E. Woodward, July 5, 1934 (New York Public Library).

CHAPTER 5   ST. ELIZABETHS

1 Admission note on EP, prepared Dec. 22, 1945; St. Elizabeths Medical File on EP, file no. 1368a.

2 E. Fuller Torrey's *The Roots of Treason: Ezra Pound and the Secret of St. Elizabeths* (New York: McGraw-Hill, 1984) offers a sensationalist account of Pound in St. Elizabeths, which purports to be an "exposé" of what the jacket blurb alleges to be "the collaboration of psychiatrists and poets in maintaining the charade of Pound's insanity." Although the avowed purpose of the book is to demonstrate that Pound was sane and thoroughly enjoying his hospital stay as head of his own salon, the book has its own "secret agenda": the discrediting by one psychiatrist, the author, of another, the superintendent of St. Elizabeths, Dr. Winfred Overholser. Showing only minimal familiarity with Pound's poetry and other writings, Dr. Torrey relies on the opinions of other critics and biographers of Pound and includes only "evidence" that seems to support his a priori conviction of the guilt of both Overholser and Pound. Stanley I. Kutler, in "This Notorious Patient: The Asylum of Ezra Pound," *The American Inquisition: Justice and Injustice in the Cold War* (New York: Hill and Wang, 1982), who is most concerned with the legal implications of Pound's insanity plea, also alleges that Pound was sane and that "Overholser's cover-up of Pound's true condition was the real conspiracy in the case" (p. 87). Torrey and Kutler were in consultation with each other as they worked on their projects. Their arguments are virtually identical.

3 *Diagnostic and Statistical Manual of Mental Disorders,* 3d. ed. (American Psychiatric Association, 1980).

4 File no. 1381j, Jan. 24, 1946.

5 File no. 1398a, Oct. 17, 1947.

6 See interview of Mar. 18, 1949, file no. 1399e.

7 Julian Cornell, *The Trial of Ezra Pound* (New York: John Day, 1966), 37.

8 Interview of Dec. 31, 1945, file no. 1397b.

9 "The Fall of Hyperion: A Dream," 148–49, in *The Poems of John Keats,* ed. Jack Stillinger (Cambridge, Mass.: Harvard University Press, 1978), 481.

10 "Recommendations for Diagnosis," July 20, 1953, file nos. 1411d, 1411c.

11 See reminiscences of EP by Charles Olson, Angela Palandri, Deba Patnaik, Bill MacNaughton, William Fleming, Marcella Booth, David Gordon, and Carroll Terrell in *Paideuma* 3.3 (Winter 1974.) See also Catherine Seelye, *Charles Olson and Ezra Pound* (New York: New Directions, 1975); Eustace Mullins, *This Difficult Individual: Ezra Pound* (New York: Fleet, 1961); Harry M. Meacham, *The Caged Panther: EP at St. Elizabeths* (New York: Twayne, 1967); and David Rattray, "A Weekend with EP," *Nation,* Nov. 16, 1957.

12 *Paideuma,* 3.3 (1979): 329–34.

13 See David Gordon, "Meeting EP and then . . .," *Paideuma,* 3.3 (1979): 366–67.

14 Carroll F. Terrell, "St. Elizabeths," *Paideuma* 3.3 (1979): 366–67.

15 *Pound/Theobald Letters,* ed. Donald Pearce and Herbert Schneidau (Redding Ridge, Ct.: Black Swan Books, 1984).

16 Ezra Pound, *Confucius: The Great Digest, The Unwobbling Pivot, The Analects* (New York: New Directions, 1969), 81. Also, see *Paideuma* 3.3 (1974): 358.

17 Ezra Pound, *Women of Trachis* (New York: New Directions, 1957), 50.

18 Ezra Pound, *Elektra,* from typescript in the Princeton University Library manuscript collection.

19 "[U]nscrewing the inscrutable" is a catch phrase for metaphysical inquiry which Pound was delighted to borrow from Warren G. Peabody, a fellow inmate, who is twice credited as the originator of the phrase, in 98/688 and 101/724.

20 The Chinese characters for this phrase are given on 97/676.

21 Kuan Chung, *Economic Dialogues in Ancient China: Selections from the KUAN TZU,* ed. and publ. Lewis Maverick, 1954.

22 James Legge, ed. and trans., *The Chinese Classics,* vol. 4, *The She King,* 2d ed. (Hong Kong: Hong Kong University Press, 1960), 646.

23 See *Ezra Pound and The Cantos,* pp. 39–41.

24 *Selections from the Letters and Legal Papers of Thurman Arnold* (Washington, D.C.: Merkle Press, 1961), 39–41.

25 *Selected Letters of Robert Frost,* ed. Lawrance Thompson (New York: Holt, Rinehart & Winston, 1964), 563.

26 Laughlin, "Ez as Waz."

27 For further details see Thurman Arnold, "The Criminal Trial as a Symbol of Public Morality," in *Fair Fights and Foul* (New York: Harcourt, Brace & World, 1965). See also Robert Anthony Corrigan, "What Thou Lovest Well

Remains: Ezra Pound and America, 1940–1958," Ph.D. diss., University of Pennsylvania, 1967, 226–373.

28 Letter to Charles Abbott, July 17, 1958, Library of the State University of New York at Buffalo, quoted in Mariani, p. 741.

29 Letter to Cid Corman, July 30, 1958, University of Texas Library, quoted in Mariani, p. 742.

30 Letter from Olga Rudge of April 25, 1948; reply from Samuel A. Silk, assistant superintendent of St. Elizabeths, file no. 2012.

CHAPTER 6   THE RETURN TO ITALY

1 Mary de Rachewiltz, *Discretions* (New York: New Directions, 1971), 302–03.

2 Eliot, *Notes Toward the Definition of Culture* (London: Faber & Faber, 1948), 43, 44.

3 Hugh Kenner, "A Note on CX/778," *Paideuma* 8.1 (Spring 1979): 51–52.

4 Ezra Pound, *Translations* (New York: New Directions, 1963), 338–39; hereafter, *T.*

5 "Homage to a Confucian Poet," *Paideuma* 3.3 (Winter 1974): 303.

6 Hugh Kenner, *The Pound Era* (Berkeley: University of California Press, 1971), 535.

7 The ²Muan ¹Bpo Ceremony or the Sacrifice to Heaven as Practiced by the ²Na-¹Khi," *Monumenta Serica* (Peiping: Catholic University Press, 1948), 13:100.

8 Joseph Rock, *The Ancient Na-Khi Kingdom of Southwest China*, 2 vols. (Cambridge: Harvard University Press, 1947), 422.

9 "The Romance of ²K'a-²Mä-¹Gyu-³Mi-²Gkyi," translated, transcribed, and annotated by J. F. Rock, 3.

10 *Inferno*, Canto V.

11 Letter from James Laughlin to Winfred Overholser, Dec. 1, 1959, file no. 1126a.

12 File no. 1126b.

13 Donald Hall, *Remembering Poets* (New York: Harper & Row, 1978), 130.

14 Massimo Bacigalupo, *The Forméd Trace: The Later Poetry of Ezra Pound* (New York: Columbia University Press, 1980, x, 459.

15 File no. 1161b. A copy of this clinical report is included in Pound's St. Elizabeths file, document numbers 1161a–e (to which parenthetical letters in text refer).

16 Letter from Dorothy Pound to Winfred Overholser, Oct. 1, 1961.

17 Daniel Cory, "Ezra Pound: A Memoir," *Encounter* 30 (May 1966): 38.

18 Allen Ginsberg, "Encounters with Ezra Pound," *City Lights Anthology*, ed. Lawrence Ferlinghetti (San Francisco, 1974), 13–15.

19 Interview with Grazia Livi, *Epoca*, March 24, 1963, reprinted in *Ezra Pound*, vol. 2, *Les Cahiers de L'Herne* (Paris, 1965), 223.

20 Ginsberg, "Encounters with Ezra Pound," p. 14.

21 "Breaking the Silence: The Interview of Vanni Ronsisvalle and Pier Paolo Pasolini with Ezra Pound in 1968," ed. and trans. David Anderson, *Paideuma* 10.2, (Fall 1981): 331–45.

22 Pointed out to me by David Anderson.
23 "Ez as Waz." *Pound as Wuz* gives "ice cream" rather than "milk."
24 Letter from Marianne Moore to Ezra and Dorothy Pound, July 21, 1947, Rosenbach Library.
25 Letter from Ezra Pound to Marianne Moore, undated, Rosenbach Library.
26 *The Complete Prose of Marianne Moore,* ed. Patricia C. Willis (New York: Viking, 1968), 645. I am indebted to Patricia Willis for alerting me to Moore's visit to Pound.

AFTERWORD

1 Stuart Schneiderman, *Jacques Lacan: The Death of an Intellectual Hero* (Cambridge: Harvard University Press, 1983), p. 181.
2 Quoted in Claude Lanzmann, *Shoah: An Oral History of the Holocaust* (New York: Pantheon, 1985), pp. 145–46.

Index

244 Index

Ocellus, 178, 179
Odysseus, 176
Office of Special Investigations, 223
Orage, A. R., chap. 2 passim; effect of death on Pound, 42–43; as editor, 44; interest in mysticism and social reform, 45–47; as E. P.'s teacher, 48; optimistic view of human nature, 49; critical of Mussolini, 104–05; on Pound as propagandist, 105
Osservatore Romano, 124
Overholser, Winfred, 157, 161, 167, 185, 187, 206, 213
Owen, Robert L., 108–09

Paige, D. D.: edition of letters of E. P., 84–85
Palandri, Angela, 195
Paolo and Francesca, 204
Paperclip Conspiracy, The, 223
Pasolini, Pier Paolo, 217–19
Paterson, William, 121
Patria Mia, 29, 136
Pattison, E. Mansell, 224–25
paura entusiasmante, La, 101
Paxton, Robert, 223
Pellizzi, Camillo, 97–99, 101, 135; catalogues anti-Fascist library, 99
Penty, A. J., 45
Perloff, Carey, 233n
Picasso, Pablo, 100
Pisan Cantos, 179
Plath, Sylvia, 224
Plato, 47
Platonism, 50; Orage's interest in, 46
Popolo di Italia, 98
Por, Odon, 99–100
Pound, Albert, 19
Pound, Daniel, 21
Pound, Dorothy, 185, 186, 187, 188, 192, 205, 213
Pound, Elijah, 21
Pound, Ezra: caricatured views of, 2; compared to Eichmann, 3, 131, 133–34; war criminals and, 3, 221–23; lack of introspection, 8–9, 10; attitude toward religion, 9; lack of deviousness, 12, 139, 157; tendency to self-deception, 12, 189–90; relationship with father, 22–23; relationship with mother, 23–24; religious views, 26–28; and Mary Moore, 29–31; engagement to H. D., 30–31; use of slang, 33–34, 175;

effect of Orage's death on, 43–44; as student of Orage, 48–49; as aesthete, 48, 50; discovers Social Credit, 49; mysticism, 50; Confucianism, 50, 173, 176–79; faith in education, 55, 142–43; on stamp scrip, 71–73; response to invasion of Abyssinia, 82–83; evasion of truth about Mussolini, 86–87; overreliance on intuition, 87, 89; changing attitude toward FDR, 88, 109–12, 137, 141; in Paris, 90–91; move to Rapallo, 91; on Fascist militarism, 91–92; photographs of Abyssinian atrocities, 102; rationalizes Mussolini's war mongering, 102–03, 161–64; on Coughlin, 106, 108, 109; letter to FDR, 109; on Mosley, 112–13; on Spanish Civil War, 115–16; psychotic view of World War II, 113–15, 126; on Hitler, 116–22, 165; loss of mental control, 126–28; suspected of spying, 135; and Jewish refugee, 138–39; on war dead, 144–45; on race, 145–55; admitted to St. Elizabeths, 156; paranoid delusions, 157, 162, 186; diagnosis of, 157–62, 165, 168; fatigue attacks of, 159, 168–70; psychosis of, 161, 163; self-destructiveness of, 164; attitude toward psychiatry, 172; Pythagoreanism of, 178; on love of relatives, 178, 191–92; and rites, 181; at Brunnenburg, 191–93; interviewed by Hall, 206–09, by Livi, 216, by Pasolini, 217–19; cataleptic attacks, 208, 209, 211, 217; on his antisemitism, 209, 213; mental condition in 1966, 210–13; self-accusation, 213–19; reassured by T. S. Eliot, 214–15; at T. S. Eliot's memorial service, 217; visits Joyce's grave, 217; death, 220
Pound, Homer, 14, 17, 22–27, 148
Pound, Isabel, 16, 23–27
Pound, Omar, 206, 213
Pound, Thaddeus C., 13–22, 36–39, 62, 148
Preziosi, Giovanni, 138
"Princess, The," 28
Protocols of Zion, 127, 171
Psychoanalytic Reflections on the Holocaust, 225
Purgatorio, 184
Putnam, H. C., 17
Pythagoreanism, 178